GODS OF LOVE AND ECSTASY

THE TRADITIONS OF SHIVA AND DIONYSUS

ALAIN DANIÉLOU

INNER TRADITIONS
ROCHESTER, VERMONT

Inner Traditions International, Ltd.
One Park Street
Rochester, Vermont 05767

First U. S. edition published in 1984 under the title *Shiva and Dionysus* by Inner Traditions International

Reprinted under the title *Gods of Love and Ecstasy* by Inner Traditions International in 1992

First published in French under the title *Shiva et Dionysos* by Fayard in 1979

Copyright © 1979 by Librairie Artheme Fayard

Translation copyright © 1982 East-West Publications

LIBRARY OF CONGRESS CATALOGING-IN-PUBLICATION DATA

Daniélou, Alain.
    [Shiva et Dionysos. English]
    Gods of love and ecstasy : the traditions of Shiva and Dionysus / Alain Daniélou.
        p.   cm.
    Translation of: Shiva et Dionysos.
    Previously published: Shiva and Dionysus. New York : Inner Traditions, 1984.
    Includes bibliographical references.
    ISBN 0-89281-374-1
    1. Siva (Hindu deity)   2. Dionysus (Greek deity)   3. Sivaism—History. I. Title.
    [BL1218.D3313 1992]
    294.5'513—dc20   92-1042
                                                                                    CIP

Printed and bound in the United States

10 9 8 7 6 5 4 3 2 1

Distributed to the book trade in the United States by American International Distribution Corporation (AIDC)

Distributed to the book trade in Canada by Book Center, Inc., Montreal, Quebec

GODS OF
LOVE AND
ECSTASY

Shiva in yoga posture, Temple of Vaital Deul, Bhuvaneshwar, Orissa, 9th century. (In the author's collection).

CONTENTS

FOREWORD

This book is not an essay on the history of religions. It reflects my personal experience of discovering the most fundamental of religions in that veritable museum of world history which is India. Prior to Vedic Hinduism, Greek religion, Zoroastrianism and even Abraham, this early religion is the outcome of man's efforts since his remotest origins to understand the nature of creation in its balanced beauty and cruelty, as well as the manner in which he can identify himself in the Creator's work and cooperate with him. This religion is naturistic, not moralistic, ecstatic and not ritualistic. It strives to find the points of contact between the various states of being and to seek their harmonious relationship which allows every man to achieve his self-realization on a physical, intellectual and spiritual level and to play his role more fully in the universal symphony.

It gradually dawned on me that all those things which seemed of value in later religions were only partial and deformed survivals, often perverted or skilfully disguised, of that ancient wisdom found in the cults of Shiva or of Dionysus This religion, so often persecuted but always reborn, appeared to me to still correspond to the deepest needs of man today. What is usually called "Primordial tradition" can, ultimately, only be linked to this stream of knowledge the origins of which go back to the first ages of the world.

Throughout its long history, humanity has inevitably produced men of exceptional intelligence and it is from their experience and accumulated intuition that all cultures and civilizations derive. Humanity begins by using language forms as an instrument, so that symbols and myths express the relationship between man and the invisible world of spirits and gods.

Shivaite concepts concerning the nature of the material and subtle world, as well as the Shivaite methods, such as Yoga, Sânkhya (cosmology) and Tantrism, constitute an unparalleled knowledge of the nature of human beings and of the cosmos. A rediscovery of Shivaism-Dionysism would allow an effective return to the source and the re-establishment of that almost-broken link with a multi-millenarian knowledge of which we are the unwitting and ungrateful heirs.

This does not involve any exotic innovation for the Western World. European religious sources are the same as those of India, and their traces have only been lost in the relatively recent past. The legend according to which Dionysus sojourned in India is an allusion to the identification of his cult with Indian religion. The rediscovery at the beginning of this century of the joyful and peaceable Cretan civilization and religion, which is so similar to Shivaism and which appears to be the deepest root of Western civilization, may thus be considered a premonition, a return to what Arnold Toynbee calls "a right religion".

I spent more than twenty years in the traditional Hindu world, as far removed from the modern world as though I had been miraculously transported back to the Egypt of the Pharaohs. On returning to Europe, I was amazed at the childishness of theological concepts, and of the barrenness of what is called religion. I found a rudderless humanity, clutching the dying tree of Christianity, without even understanding why it was dying. Those people, feeling this vacuum, were searching for their equilibrium in a visibly threatened world, but could find no help. They have to content themselves with having "their own religion", or else they become the easy victims of countless false prophets, market-place gurus, or of false initiations, "drawing-room Yoga" or "transcendental meditation". Sometimes they seek to escape by entering communities of "hippies" or ecologists, which can only isolate them and lead to nothing, because their approach is too restricted, negative and improvised. The return to Christianity or Islam in countries suffering from excessive materialism, as in Poland, Iran and elsewhere, are also expressions of the same need. Unfortunately, these dogmatic and tyrannical religions cannot supply man with what he is seeking.

The dark forces which seem to rule the modern world have shown great ability in diverting, deforming and annihilating all man's instinctive urges toward basic realities and the divine order of the world. As soon as a spark of light is glimpsed, it is taken over by those whose mission it is to pervert and exploit it, thus transforming what is beneficial into something maleficent.

It is difficult for man to attain true knowledge and wisdom. Men, say the Upanishads, are part of the gods' cattle, and it displeases the gods to lose heads of cattle. This is why the gods place obstacles in the way of knowledge which would otherwise allow man to free himself, to escape from slavery and from the ties (*pâsha*) of the natural world. During their training, yogis acquire magical powers which become more and more astonishing. These are temptations which, if allowed to take hold, will turn them aside from their goal. In the same way, when humanity as a whole becomes a peril for other species and for the balance of nature, the gods inspire men with the madness which leads them to destruction. A way is always open, however, for man to return to his proper role of cooperating with the divine plan. This way, as taught by Shivaism, has nothing to do with false virtues, or with artificial moral or social problems in which modern religion and society take such delight, and whose precise aim is to deceive the soul, keep man from seeking true values, and thus lead him to suicide. The way of Shiva-Dionysus is the only way by which humanity can be saved.

I have written this book, insufficient though it may be, for men of goodwill lost in a world of false values, so that it may remind some that a "way of wisdom" did exist, and still exists. This "way" consists simply in seeking to comprehend the nature of the world and in cooperating in the divine work. Whoever honestly seeks this way will find it, but it is necessary to question almost all established values and to ignore all senseless words, all those slogans which nowadays pass for ideas or doctrines. "The present adherents of the Judaic monotheistic religions and of [their] post-Christian substitutes... are, all of them, ex-pantheists. This historical fact suggests that there might be some hope of their reverting to the pantheistic attitude, now that they have become aware of the badness of the consequences of the monotheistic lack of respect for nature." (Arnold Toynbee, *Choose Life*, p. 298.)

I do not claim to present a solution. On the basis of my personal experience, I have made a small effort to clear the ground which seems to be encumbered with ignorance and error, and to remind those who believe that "Religion" and "Christianity" are synonymous that the way of the divine is found outside the prison of dogmatism.

This essay is not an instruction manual. The ritual elements indicated herein serve only as a starting point for reflecting on the nature of man, of the world and of the divine as taught by the most ancient, and at the same time, most modern of religions.

It is evident that certain rites and practices of ancient Shivaism or Dionysism, such as human sacrifices, could not be contemplated nowadays. Perhaps I should have avoided mentioning them, as they could easily be used as a pretext for rejecting the whole of Shivaite concepts, but, in my opinion, it was necessary to do so because they reflect tendencies of the human being and aspects of the nature of the world, which it would be imprudent to ignore. They form part of our collective unconscious and risk being manifested in perverse ways if we are afraid to face up to them. We regard with horror the "crimes" of certain fanatical sects, without seeing their relationship to war, genocide, and the destruction of some animal species, all of which we too easily accept. We live in a world in which we must come to terms with the gods without cherishing illusions. We should always be conscious of our responsibilities and share them with the gods who conceived the world as it is, not as we like to believe it should be. This is the profound message of Shivaism, the only message which can help us face the divine reality of the world and cooperate with the work of the gods. There is no other true religion.

INTRODUCTION

The universe is a wonderful work of harmony, beauty and balance. There may be other universes, founded on other formulae. Man's universe is the result of a choice made in the mind of the immense, unknowable, indefinable Prime Cause, out of whom came the gods, matter and life.

Nothing exists which is not involved in its own cause. If thought exists in individuals, then thought must perforce be part of the cosmic principle from which they themselves came. There exists therefore a universal thought, a universal self-consciousness, and thus creation is not simply a chance matter, but the choice of a transcendant will which caused it to be as it is. All the elements which constitute the world are interdependent, and form part of the whole. There is no break or discontinuity in the Creator's work. The mineral, vegetable, animal and human worlds, as well as the subtle world of spirits and gods exist through and for each other. No true approach to, or seeking after, the divine, no knowledge, religion or mystery, can possibly exist which does not take into account this basic unity of the created world.

From the beginning of time itself, we can see the appearance of this search, this thirst for knowledge, for an understanding of the nature of the world and the purpose of life, and thus the desire to draw closer to the Creator and to take refuge in him. In order to have any value, this search can accept no barriers or preconceptions and cannot ignore any aspect of beings or things. It traverses the most diverse civilizations, religions and ways of thinking, and inevitably puts them in question. The idea of the profound oneness of the creative thought and of all the aspects of creation is always present in man's consciousness, if only at a latent level. It only needs a messenger from the gods to awaken this consciousness and to remind us that the only way to happiness and self-realization is to cooperate wholeheartedly in the Creator's work, in the love and friendship which should unite plants, animals, men and the subtle world. It is not a question of sentimentalism, of loving one's garden and one's dog or painting everything in rosy colours, but rather of man's humble search for his proper place in this savage, wonderful and cruel world which the gods have created.

It is the principle of Shivaism that nothing exists in the whole universe which is not a part of the divine body and which cannot be a way of reaching the divine. All objects, all natural phenomena, plants and animals, as well as all aspects of man himself, may be starting points to bring us nearer to the divine. Thus there is neither high nor low, inferior or superior function, sacred or profane. If we recognize the divine order in all our tendencies, all our physical functions, and in all our actions or potential, we become masters of ourselves, companions (*kaula*) of the god, and participants (*bhaktas* or bacchants). If, on the other hand, we ignore or refuse to see the universal order in all those things which constitute our physical and mental being, and the bonds which unite us at all levels to the natural and cosmic world, we shall bring upon ourselves that destructive madness which is the manifestation of the wrath of the gods.

Chapter 1

ORIGINS

The Two Sources of Religion

Since the beginning of urban civilization, religious phenomena among sedentary peoples have been manifested and established in two opposed and contradictory forms. The first is tied to the world of nature, the second to the organization of communal city life. Primordial religion represents the sum of man's efforts to understand creation, to live in harmony with it and penetrate its secrets, to cooperate in the Creator's work, drawing nearer to Him and becoming identified with Him. This approach does not separate the physical from the intellectual and spiritual domain, which are all indissolubly linked together. The body is the instrument of all human accomplishment and, as taught by Yoga, should be treated as such.

The entirety of Creation in its beauty, cruelty and harmony, is the expression of Divine thought and is the materialization, or body of God. Only those who understand this, identifying themselves with the natural world and taking their proper place amongst the trees, flowers and animals, may truly draw near to the world of spirits and gods, and have an understanding of the Creator's plan and perceive His divine joy. For the man who is conscious of creation not only as the work of God, but as the form of God himself, all being, all life, every act takes on a sacred character and becomes a rite, a means of communication with the celestial world.

"To conform to what one is, is *dharma.*" (*Svalakshana-dhâranâd dharmah*".) *Dharma* is a word which means "natural law". To conform to it is the only virtue. There is no other religion than that of conforming to what one is by birth, by nature, by one's natural disposition. Each must play, as best he can, his assigned rôle in the great theatre of creation. Man's happiness and survival depend on his conforming to the position he occupies as a species amongst living creatures and as an individual amongst men. Should he seek to take on a rôle which is anti-social, he becomes an enemy of humanity. If he is a predator – an enemy of other species – he becomes the enemy of the gods, the enemy of creation.

The other form of religion is the religion of the city, the society of mankind, which claims to impose divine sanctions on social conventions. It exalts human laws as sacred enactments. It serves as an excuse for the ambitions of men who seek dominion over the natural world and make use of it, claiming for themselves a unique position to the detriment of other species, whether vegetable, animal or supernatural. Due to a strange and evil perversion of values in the modern civilizations and religions which characterize the Kali Yuga – the Age of Conflicts in which we are now living – man has renounced his rôle in the universal order embracing all forms of being or life. Taking no interest except in himself, he has become the destroyer of the harmony of creation, the blind, vain and brutal instrument of his own decline.

Under the influence of the rudimentary religious concepts of the nomadic conquerors, the religions of the city took on an anthropocentric character. Nomadic peoples have no true contact with the world of nature. They do not live together in communion with places, trees and animals, except those they have subjugated or domesticated. They take their gods and legends with them and are inclined toward monotheistic simplification. Nature is seen as an anonymous pasture to exploit and destroy, and the gods as guides in the service of mankind. Anti-Dionysiac beliefs are always at the basis of nomadic religions, whether Aryan, Hebrew or Arab. Such characteristics are retained even when the nomads become sedentary. Any religion which considers its faithful a chosen race – claiming to have received from a god the right and duty to propagate their beliefs and customs, and to destroy or enslave "unbelievers" – can only be an impostor! Crusades, missions and holy wars are the masks of hegemony and colonialism.

The number one is the symbol of illusion", say the Tantras and the religion of the city finds its justification in monotheistic illusion. The philosophic concept of causal unity is a speculation which cannot be transferred to the plane of life or action. It is evident that the Prime Cause, or origin of that first explosion which gave birth to matter and antimatter, space and time, galaxies, stars and the principles of life, is by no means comparable to a sort of village guardian-angel who troubles about whether we have kept the Sabbath or tasted so-called forbidden fruit, giving instructions to prophets, all in the interest of civic law and order. The danger of monotheism is that it succeeds in reducing the divine to the image of man, an appropriation of God to the service of a "chosen" race. This is contrary to true religion, since it serves as an excuse for subjecting the divine work to man's ambition.

According to Toynbee: "The belief that what I have called the spiritual presence in and behind the universe was concentrated in a single transcendent humanlike god, involved the further belief that nothing else in the universe is divine... God placed the whole of his nonhuman creation at the disposal of his human creatures to exploit in any way that they might choose... The salutary respect and awe with which man had originally regarded his environment was thus dispelled by Judaic monotheism in the versions of its Israelite originators, and of Christians and Muslims... Communism is an outcome of Christianity... I diagnose Communism as a religion, and specifically as a new representative of the Judaic species, in which the Judaic mythology has been preserved under the disguise of a montheistic vocabulary." (Arnold Toynbee and Daisaku Ikeda, *Choose Life*, pp. 39 and 179, Oxford, 1978.) We shall speak again of the origins and role of monotheism in connection with the religions of the Kali Yuga.

Shivaism is essentially a nature religion. Shiva, like Dionysus, represents but one of the aspects of the divine hierarchy, that which concerns terrestrial life generally. By establishing a realistic co-ordination between subtle beings and living creatures, Shivaism has always opposed the anthropocentricity of urban society. Its western form, Dionysism, similarly represents the stage where man is in communion with savage life, with the beasts of the mountain and forest. Dionysus, like Shiva, is a god of vegetation, of trees and of the vine. He is also an animal god, a bull-god. The god teaches man to disregard human laws in order to rediscover divine laws. His cult, which unleashes the powers of soul and body, has encountered a lively resistance from city religions, which have always considered it antisocial. Shiva, like Dionysus, is represented by city religions as the protector of those who do not belong to conventional society and thus symbolizes everything which is chaotic, dangerous and unexpected, everything which escapes human reason and which can only be attributed to the unforeseeable action of the gods. The *Rig Veda* (VII, 21, 5), which is the sacred book of the Aryan invaders, prays that the god Indra will not allow the followers of the cult of Shiva – whom they call *Shishna-devas* or worshippers of the phallus – to approach their ritual sacrifices. However, the power of the god's mysterious magic can never be ignored with impunity, and a place had to be left for the cult of Shiva-Dionysus, despite the hostility of the masters of the city.

"With the growth of Neo-Brahmanism the non-Aryan phallic rite came to be associated with the Aryan belief, as an essential element of historic Shivaism." (P. Banerjee, *Early Indian Religions*, p. 41.) Even the greatest Hellenic sanctuaries, doubtless unwillingly, were forced to give him considerable importance. God of the young, of the humble (*shudras*) and of ecology, the protector of animals and trees, Shiva is accused of teaching the secrets of wisdom to the humble, and of being accompanied by bands of youthful delinquents who mock the institutions of society and the rule of old men. "In Shivaism, transcendence, in relation to the standards of ordinary life, is interpreted on a popular level by the fact that Shiva, among others, is represented as the god or 'patron' of those who do not lead a normal life and even of outlaws." (Julius Evola, *Le Yoga tantrique*, p. 92.) The faithful of Shiva or Dionysus seek contact with those forces which animate both the infrahuman and suprahuman and lead to a refusal of the politics, ambitions and limitations of ordinary social life. This does not involve simply a recognition of world harmony, but also an active participation in an experience which surpasses and upsets the order of material life. "It is not through (passive) contemplation of divine order, but through the frenzied impulse preceding and preparing the intimate union with the god – by a total self-abandonment to his all-powerfulness and the abasement of reason before this power, – that Dionysism seeks the way of salvation." (H. Jeanmaire, *Dionysos*, p. 423.) The god's followers are called *bacchoi* (bacchants) in Greece and *bhaktas* (participants) in India. It is in their intoxication of love and ecstasy that true wisdom lies. Communion with nature and with the gods thus becomes possible, whilst the calculations and frustrations imposed by city religions isolate the world of men from the rest of creation. According to Euripides, the message of Dionysus is a call to joy in communion with nature and simplicity of heart. Those who pretend to assert the superiority of reason and refuse to heed his call will be confounded. The god inspires in them the madness with which they destroy themselves.

Throughout the course of history, urban and industrial societies – those exploiters and destroyers of the natural world – have been opposed to any ecological or mystical approach to the liberation of man and his happiness. Wars, genocide, and the destruction of entire civilizations have always had as a basis the religions of the city. Abel "looked after the beasts," but Cain, who "cultivated the soil," became a "builder of cities." (Gen. 4, 7 and 17.) "The first murder is thus accomplished by a man who in some way is the incarnate symbol of technology and of urban society." (Miréa Eliade, *Histoire des croyances et des idées religieuses*, pp. 180–181.)

Whenever it has reappeared, the cult of Shiva or of Dionysus has been banished from the city, where only those cults in which man is given paramount importance are acknowledged, allowing and excusing his depredations and condemning all forms of ecstasy which permit direct contact with the mysterious world of the spirits.

Throughout the history of India, we find diatribes against the various Shivaite sects, their practices, bloody sacrifices and rites. Such diatribes recall Livy's malicious and perfidious descriptions of the Dionysiac rites, made in order to justify the persecution of their followers. The political persecution of bacchants was also known in Greece. Throughout Brahmanism, official Greek or Roman religion, Zoroastrianism, Buddhism, Christianity or Islam, we always find the same opposition to the survival of the ancient religions of Shivaism, Dionysism, Sufism and mystic sects in general founded on the love of nature and the pusuit of ecstasy. One of the weapons of city religion is moral tyranny, based on dogmas which allow it to discipline man and to oppose his self-realization. Puritanism is totally unknown in the primitive or natural world. Christianity in its later forms – which must be distinguished from the teaching of Christ – represents a characteristic deviation of the religious concept, which no longer envisages the overall picture of the Creator's work, but solely the indoctrination of man in the interest of power. The colonial expansion of the Christian world is a clear illustration of this. "Especially in things of the flesh, the Christian religion imposes an extremely strict moral code. It condemns love in itself, the pride of life. It therefore goes against the most powerful instincts of the human animal... Having introduced for moral transgressions the theological notion of sin, which is to say a direct attack on God, this religion weighs down man's entire existence with an unbearable load of guilt, and with the expectation of judgement and eternal punishment, which threatens to hamper every action and kills all joy. There is nothing of all this in ancient religions." (A. J. Festugière, *Etudes de religion grecque et hellénistique*, p. 240.) The persecution of sexuality – the essential element of happiness – is a characteristic technique of all patriarchal, political or religious tyrannies.

India, where Shivaism has remained an essential component of religious life, has been partly preserved from the moral fetishism which has unfortunately overrun the West. It has attributed no absolute value or categorical character to standards of behaviour. In the present-day practice of Indian Shivaism we find a great number of elements which are identical to those mentioned in the most ancient Hindu and Greek texts. Shivaism, Yoga and Tantrism constitute a profoundly realistic approach to the natural and supernatural world, and tend to re-establish their influence in those periods when men come to realize that urban religion has diverted them from the observance of the natural law. They try to return to those practices and rites which they feel are more in accordance with the *raison d'être* of creation.

In India, the deep influence of Shivaism on the country's whole philosophy, including the Hindu's attitude toward animals, men and gods has largely safeguarded a respect for the Creator's work, as well as providing a rare spirit of tolerance. After the attacks suffered from Vedism and Buddhism, and later on from Christian and Islamic puritanism, Shivaism has tended to withdraw into esotericism.

The modernized classes of India pretend to ignore it, a fact which, however, does not affect its deep vitality. Shivaism remains essentially a religion of the people, but at the same time it is also the religion with the highest degree of initiation in the Hindu world. Indeed, there exists no other true initiation except the Shivaitic one. All mystery cults have a Shivaite or Dionysian character.

The heritage of Shivaism remains the basis of Hindu spiritual experience, although often in a form which has been degraded and dulled by puritanism and "sexual avarice", the endemic disease of Vedic Brahmanism and of all other State religions. Certain Dionysiac currents have survived in Islam. In the Christian world, on the other hand, repeated persecutions have little by little almost wiped out the tradition. Temporal power, riches and authoritarian hierarchy of the Church are incompatible with the freedom required for any research, whether for mystical experience or scientific discovery. The Church has sought to eliminate both mystics and scientists. Her sacraments have become mere social rites and are no longer the transmission of sacred power. Her moral teaching is reduced to a persecution of the sexual element, making those who submit to this tyranny frustrated, aggressive and dangerous people.

ORIGINS

Historical elements

Due to the Indian social system, the various races of that subcontinent have been able to coexist and survive without intermixing or being destroyed, and thus retain a large part of their own institutions and culture. Religious rites, symbols and beliefs are still found in a living form, the existence of which elsewhere is only known through archaeological remains and literary allusions. In India it is still possible to relive and understand the rites and beliefs of the Mediterranean world and the Middle East in ancient times. Apart from their physical characteristics, the ethnic groups of India are also linguistically recognizable, the main ones corresponding approximately to the three great epochs in the development of civilization: palaeolithic, neolithic and modern. In India, these linguistic families are represented by the *Munda*, Dravidian and Aryan languages. Sino-Mongolian languages play only a secondary rôle.

Each group, with its particular ethnic, linguistic, religious and social elements, represents the various stages of evolution peculiar to the human race. These stages are not necessarily synonymous with progress and their traces can be discovered all over the world, sometimes only in prehistoric remains. The great racial and linguistic families of India may be a key to the understanding of civilizations which elsewhere have disappeared.

The much-decried caste system has allowed the survival of the most diversified peoples, especially those who are least aggressive and least suited to an industrial civilization. In so-called democratic societies, the weakest are inevitably dispossessed, destroyed, or culturally annihilated. We have examples today of the genocide of Pygmies and Australian Aborigines. Over several centuries the ethnic peoples of the Americas have lost their culture, their religion and their language and have been left without even a memory of their own history.

Devastating invasions and cultural revolutions which are the tragedies of history, are always backed up by new cults. Communism is effectively a cult in this sense like Christianity or Islam. The most barbarous and least advanced ethnic groups are those who massacre the possessors of knowledge, burn libraries and destroy monuments in the name of often rudimentary ideologies. Nothing remains of the stupendous City of Mexico which the first Spanish conquistadors describe as the most beautiful in the world. Whether it is a question of outside invaders or of internal revolution, the results are the same. It can take centuries to recover vestiges of a lost heritage.

The Proto-Australoids

The Proto-Australoids, in India called *adivâsi* (first inhabitants), speak *Munda* or *Mom-Khmer* languages. They form one of the great racial and linguistic groups, the other two being the Dravidians and the Aryans. According to S. S. Sarkar (*Aboriginal Races of India*), the Proto-Australoids are "the most archaic race which has survived". They show affinities with Neanderthal man (according to Huxley, Sollas, Von Luschon and Howells), a more ancient race than the Negroids. To this group belong the Veddas of Ceylon and the Khonds of Central India, the Khasis of Assan and the Shom Pen of Great Nicobar. Outside India, the Sakai of Malaysia, the Moi of Indochina, the Orang batin, Lubu and Ulu of Sumatra, the Toula of the Celebes, certain populations in Southern Arabia and the Dhofar, as well as the Aborigines of Australia, may all be included in the same anthropological group. Their relationship with the African Pygmies and Bushmen of the Kalahari appears probable. They seem to have been the most ancient inhabitants of Europe, India and Africa. Skeletons of this type have also been discovered in predynastic Egyptian tombs, as well as at Mohenjo Daro in present-day Pakistan.

"The hunting tribes of whom the Bushmen and Pygmies are the last remnants, once covered all Africa. Even the Caspian art of the late Palaeolithic period, found in areas around the western Mediterranean has affinities with Bushman painting... The Bushmen represent an early group of humans ancestral to the larger and darker skinned peoples who lived around the fringes of the Indian Ocean before they in turn spread to all parts of Africa, except for the far south." (Cottie Burland, "Africa, South of the Sahara," in *Primitive Erotic Art*, p. 198.) It was this race of small, gracile men who peopled Europe at the beginning of the Neolithic Age and who were eliminated by the stronger Cro-Magnon-type men.

The Dravidians

During the Neolithic Age a new race appeared amongst the *Mundas* in India. They had brown skin, straight hair and spoke an agglutinative language. The origin of these people, who are called Dravidian (from the Prakrit *damila*: Tamil), is obscure, but they and their religion,

20

Shivaism, played a basic role in the history of humanity. According to tradition, they came from a continent situated to the southwest of India which was engulfed by the sea. This myth recalls that of Atlantis. The possibility cannot be excluded that other branches of the same people may have reached Africa and the Mediterranean – hence the difficulty of attributing with any certainty a place of origin to Shivaite or Dionysiac revelation. "The people who created and developed the first Greco-oriental civilization, of which the Isle of Minos was the principal centre – despite their relations with Mesopotamia and Egypt – confirm that they were neither 'Greek', nor Semitic, nor Indo-European... It is possible to suppose... that the people involved spread throughout the whole of Greece... There was in the Greek language a substratum of words of foreign origin... which must have survived from long before, despite the occupation of the country by various invaders... Their Anatolian, Pelasgian, and even Proto-Indo-European origin is still being debated....... The language thus formed was spoken throughout the Aegean, the whole of Greece and southwest Anatolia." (Charles Picard, *Les Religions préhelléniques*, pp. 53–54.)

The Dravidian language and culture, which even today are those of the population of Southern India, seem to have spread their influence from India to the Mediterranean before the Aryan invasions. It was this civilization, some of whose linguistic vestiges – such as Georgian, Basque, Peuhl, Guanche and the dialects of Baluchistan – survive still in outlying areas, which served as a vehicle for ancient Shivaism. It appears that Sumerian, Pelasgian, Etruscan and Lydian, as well as Eteocretan, also belonged to the same linguistic family: the relationship between Sumerian, Georgian and Tamil leaves no doubt as to their origins. Moreover, the Basque language (Eskuara) and Georgian both have the same structure and, even today, have more than three hundred and sixty words in common. Again, Basque songs and dances are related to those of the Caucasian Iberians.

Herodotus (*Histories*, I, 57) speaks of the barbarian language used by the Pelasgians who in his time were living in Southern Italy and at the Hellespont. He considered that the Pelasgian language was closely related to Etruscan and Lydian. Saint Paul, who was shipwrecked at Malta in 69 A.D., mentions the "barbarian" (non-Aryan) language which was still spoken there. "The main provenance of the Pelasgians was... from the far side of the Black Sea. There is some possibility that they did not arrive in Crete before the beginning of the second millennium B.C. . . . [*The name of the place where they lived, Larisa, proves it*]." (R. F. Willetts, *Cretan Cults and Festivals*, pp. 135 and 136.)

According to Jacques Heurgon (*La Vie Quotidienne chez les Etrusques*, pp. 14–15), "The Etruscans were not newcomers to Italy, but the first inhabitants of a land whose sovereignty was taken from them by the Indo-European invasions, without eliminating them entirely... They were the indomitable descendants of the Bronze Age... The relationship between Etruscan, Caucasian, Lycian and the speech of Lemnos points to the existence of an Etruscan-Asiatic language, at first in current use in Italy, the Balkan Peninsula, the Aegean and Asia Minor and then thrust aside by the linguistic pressure of the invaders."

"The Eteocretan language spoken by the inhabitants of Praisos in Crete, up to the third century B.C., was thus the remnant of the common non-Greek language which was once spoken in Greece, Crete and the other islands as well as in the south-west of Asia Minor. Inscriptions at Praisos in Greek characters have not yet been deciphered." (R. F. Willetts, *Cretan Cults and Festivals*, p. 133.) This was apparently a Dravidian language. It appears that modern linguists have never dreamt of using the agglutinative Dravidian languages, which are still widely spoken in the south of India, as a basis for their research into the ancient languages of the Mediterranean world.

The myth concerning the Aryan origin of civilization, which René Guénon termed "the classic illusion", is still far from being forgotten. Dravidian languages have a common origin with Finnish-Hungarian languages (Balto-Finnish, Hungarian, Volgaic, Uralian, Samoyedic) and Altaic languages (Turkish, Mongolian and Eskimo), but it seems that the division between this great linguistic family and the Dravido-Mediterranean group during the Palaeolithic Age took place long before the formulation of Shivaism as we know it.

In the Middle East and the Mediterranean world, there was an important civilization of Asian origin, or which was at least linguistically related to Asia before the Aryan invasions. The megalithic monuments, myths and religious traditions common to India and the Mediterranean indicate moreover that this civilization was indeed the vehicle of Shivaism.

Even before the sixth millennium, "the myth of Anat may be classified as belonging to the common elements of the old agricultural civilization which stretched from the Eastern Mediterranean to the

Ganges plain". (M. Eliade, *Histoire des croyances et des idées religieuses*, p. 169.)

After the last Ice Age, the great migrations from India to Portugal began in a climate which finally became more temperate during the fifth millenium. However, it is only starting from the third millenium, that we find remains of an advanced level of civilization. These cultures bear the undeniable stamp of Shivaite thought, myths and symbols, and all of them are more or less contemporary in the cities of the Indus, Sumer, Crete or Malta. The megalithic sanctuaries which are found everywhere from India to the British Isles and America, belong to the same culture, but are often the only vestiges of this stupendous civilization to have survived. The fact that the principal archaeological remains are all of the same period, but at apparently different technological levels, does not exclude the possibility of an advanced civilization. Their preservation depends entirely on the materials used and on prevailing climatic conditions, or sometimes on the total destruction of sites by invaders or by natural catastrophes, such as the eruptions of Santorini or Vesuvius.

The civilizations of the Indus

On the Indian continent the centres of pre-Aryan Dravidian culture which have left important archaeological remains are mainly found in the Indus valley in present-day Pakistan, especially at Mohenjo Daro and Harappa. The siting of these important cities in a region which has become almost a desert has preserved certain elements. This civilization spread over a large part of India and towards the West.

"The contacts [of the cities of the Indus] with the ancient proto-historic and historic civilizations of Mesopotamia, Anatolia, Egypt and the Aegean, are important... There exists proof of contacts with Sargon of Akkad (about 2370–2284 B.C.), and with King Urnammu (about 2100 B.C.), although Mohenjo Daro was in existence long before. Objects coming from Mohenjo Daro have been found at Tel Asmar and at Troy (about 2300 B.C.), as well as in a royal tomb at Ur. Bronze objects from Luristan and Mesopotamian weapons have been discovered at Mohenjo Daro... Identical painted steatite necklaces have been found at Harappa and at Knossos... A great number of steatite seals bearing inscriptions in characters of the Indus were discovered at Bahrein (Dilmun), as well as at Ur (about 2350 B.C.) and Lagash (Larsa period)." (Mortimer Wheeler, *The Indus Civilizations*, pp. 111–115.)

The towns of the Indus were founded before 3800 B.C. and lasted until their destruction in 1800 B.C. by the Aryan invaders. The principal religion of the Indus civilization was without doubt Shivaism. Extant seals represent an ithyphallic and horned Shiva seated in a Yoga position, or dancing triumphantly as Natarâja. Numerous Shivaite symbols are also found there, such as stone phalli, swastikas, and the images of the bull, the serpent and the Goddess of the Mountains.

"The likelihood that both Shiva and *linga* (phallus) – worship have been inherited by the Hindus from the Harappans is perhaps reinforced by the prevalence of the bull... [and also] in less degree, to the tiger, elephant... and 'Minotaurs'... as well as man-faced animals." (Wheeler, *ibid.*, p. 109.)

Given the importance of the contacts mentioned above, it is not at all surprising that the same religion and symbols are found extending from India to the Mediterranean. The problems posed by the Aryan invasions are the same and the survivals of this ancient religion and its periodic reappearance are similar in India, the Middle East and the West.

The Aryans (Indo-Europeans)

The migration of the nomadic Aryan peoples – erroneously called Indo-Europeans – played a considerable role in the history of mankind. They left the regions which today compose the Soviet Union, probably for climatic reasons, and successively invaded India, the Middle East and Europe.

"The irruption of the Indo-Europeans into history is marked by terrible devastation. Between 2300 and 1900 B.C., numerous cities in Greece, Asia Minor and Mesopotamia were sacked and burned, such as Troy about 2300 B.C., Beycesultan, Tarsus, and some three hundred towns and settlements in Anatolia... The dispersal of the Indo-European peoples had begun a few centuries before, and was to last through two millennia... The Dorians from Thessaly descended on Southern Greece towards the end of the second millennium B.C. By about 1200, the Aryans had penetrated into the Indus-Ganges plain, the Iranians were firmly installed, Greece and the islands were Indo-Europeanized... This process only ceased in the last century. It is not possible to find another such example of linguistic and cultural expansion." (M. Eliade, *Histoire des croyances et des idées religieuses*, p. 199.)

The Aryan tribes who occupied Latium around 1000 B.C. and founded Rome in about 753, were one of the principal agents of Aryan linguistic expansion. Aryan colonization under the form of Hindi in India, and French, English, Portuguese and Spanish in the rest of the world, still continues today especially in the African and American continents. We do not hesitate to speak of French- or English-speaking Africa and of Latin America, as though we were speaking of something clearly beneficial.

The Vedic texts evoke the struggles against the *dâsa* or *dasya* and the *pani*, the continuators or survivors of the Indus civilization who rejected the Vedic cult. They are described as being dark-skinned and having small noses. They spoke a barbarian language and venerated the phallus (*shishna deva*). They owned large herds and lived in fortified towns (*pur*). According to the Purâna genealogies, it is calculated that the *Mahâbhârata* war, which completed the Aryan conquest of India, took place about 1400 B.C. in the Madhyadesha, near Delhi. Other Hindu sources, however, seem to indicate an earlier date.

Primaeval religions

The four religions

We know almost nothing of the religious and philisophical thought of mankind since his appearance nearly two million years ago. Since the beginning of that very recent period which we can consider historical, traces of highly developed civilizations are everywhere to be found, together with languages which, whatever the level of material life, whether primitive or refined, are all equally suitable for expressing the most abstract notions and bear witness to an extremely long evolution of thought.

In India, four main religions correspond to the different approaches to the problem of the supernatural. These have often influenced or opposed each other throughout the course of their long history. They demonstrate mankind's attainment of religious thought since remote prehistory. All later religions can only be considered as adaptations of elements deriving from this marvellous heritage. Really new elements are never found, whatever their claims. The four religions of ancient India correspond to four distinct concepts of the world and of the gods, whose extension well beyond the frontiers of India seems to have been universal. The first of these concepts could be termed animistic.

In the natural order of the world living beings know what they require in order to ensure survival. Side by side with a perceptive mechanism of a practical order all beings are conscious that there is a limit to their senses. They feel more or less confusedly the presence of "something inexplicable", of more subtle powers with which they eventually try to communicate. These powers, which mankind respects and worships, are called spirits or gods. The man who finds his proper place in the natural world becomes conscious of spirits, or aspects of the divine to be found in mountains, springs, rivers and forests. "For all people who live in harmony with the consensus of the powers which surround them... many animals are sacred, and therefore, in this sense, *everything* is sacred: sky, earth, fire, air... The whole life of 'primitive' man is a succession of magical operations aimed at creating an 'affective tie' between himself and the world around him, 'to bind', 'to put a spell on', 'to conjure up' the powers of nature." (Paolo Santarcangeli, *Le Livre des Labyrinthes*, p. 108.)

Animals too are conscious of invisible presences and have a foreboding of the wrath of the gods, which is made manifest in what we call natural catastrophes. The sudden and absolute silence of the forest during the moments preceding an earthquake is a startling phenomenon. Never do so called savage animals kill for pleasure. They always avoid disturbing the balance of nature. Animistic man behaves in the same way and thus acquires a very acute sense. He asks pardon of the spirit of the tree from which he has to cut a branch. He tries to conciliate the divinities whom he believes protect the world. His life is a perpetual ritual. Respect for the spirit which dwells in all things, in all beings, is thus the basis of all morality and religion, and allows man to reach a level of intuitive knowledge which the logical mind can never grasp. Animistic concepts have been perpetuated amongst the "primitive" tribes of India. Animism is opposed to the appropriation of land, to property, and to agriculture which destroys natural order and to anything which subjects nature to man. It is against the development of urban and industrial civilization. Such a concept, however, appears to be one of the most fundamental approaches to the religious problem. The animistic attitude is not sentimental or "naturist". Hunting is the basis for survival, and the cruelty of the gods and spirits requires sacrifice. It is in this climate that the cult of Murugan or Kûmara (the youth) developed, corresponding to the Kouros (the youth) in Crete. He is an infant or adolescent god, a god of Beauty and War, avid for the blood of the animals sacrificed to him. Indeed, his cult originated amongst the *adivasi* (the first inhabitants), of which such tribes still existing today speak *Munda* languages. The symbols associated with this cult are the hunting-spear, the cock and the ram. The *Munda* legends which Rudyard Kipling has transcribed in the *Jungle Book* give an interesting insight into the poetic level of Indian Animism.

During the Neolithic Age and early part of the Old Bronze Age, the cult of Pashupati, the Lord of the Animals, and of Pârvatî, the Lady of the Mountains, became established amongst the Dravidian invaders. It involved a great philosphical and religious movement which under the name of Shivaism was superimposed on Animism, and became the principal source from which later religions have been drawn. The Lord of the Animals and the Lady of the Mountains, who are found in Crete under the names of Zagreus and Cybele, are also found in all the civilizations which are linguistically or culturally related to the Dravidian world. The salient features of this religion are the cult of the phallus, the bull and the snake and, to a lesser extent, of the tiger and lion, the mounts of the goddess. Historical Shivaism was codified towards the end of the sixth millennium B.C. as the result of a fusion between the religions of Pashupati and Murugan, and was designed to satisfy the world's religious needs up to the end of the present cycle. Murugan becomes the son of Shiva. He is called Kumâra (the youth), or Skanda (the jet of sperm). The two cults are closely intermingled in their later forms. Murugan, born in a reedy marsh and nourished by nymphs, is elsewhere called Dionysus. Pashupati corresponds to the Cretan god, husband of the Lady of the Mountains. He is called Zan, then Zagreus, and later, Cretan Zeus (Kretagenes). His legend, as in the case of Shiva and Skanda, gradually becomes merged with that of Dionysus.

Another religion which can claim a very long history is Jainism, a puritan religion which believes in transmigration, in the development of the human being through many lives, both in human and animal form. Without being precisely atheistic, Jainism does not envisage the possibility of contacts between man and the supernatural. According to Jainism man can never know with certainty whether or not there exists a creative principle, a god, or prime cause, and there is therefore no reason to be concerned with it. This religion which is more moralistic than ritualistic, insists upon the protection of life, on strict vegetarianism, and total nakedness amongst its followers. Original Buddhism is an adaptation of it.

Mahâvira, the last Jaina prophet, was the contemporary and rival of Gautama Buddha. Like the Buddhists, the Jainas sent missionaries to all parts of the world. The influence of these naked ascetics was very important in Greece, as can be perceived in certain of the philosophical schools and in Orphism. Later Hinduism took from Jainism the theory of transmigration and vegetarianism which originally existed neither in Shivaism nor in Vedism.

With the Aryan invasions, the great religion of the nomadic peoples of Central Asia was imposed on India and the whole of the Western world. The gods of this religion are in fact natural phenomena and personified human virtues. Indra is the god of the Thunderbolt, Varuna the god of the Waters, Agni the god of Fire, Vayu god of the Wind, Surya god of the Sun, Dyaus the god of Space, while Mitra represents Solidarity, Aryaman Honour, Bhaga the Sharing of goods. Rudra is the Destroyer, Time, the principle of death. He is subsequently identified with Shiva. Although seeking to propitiate the powers of nature by means of sacrifice, the Aryan religion is not a nature religion. It is a religion centred on man which only seeks the aid of the gods in order to ensure his safety and dominion.

From the second millennium, Shivaism was gradually absorbed into the Aryan Vedic religion, forming on the one hand later Hinduism, and on the other, Mycenaean and Greek religion. However, Shivaism has resisted this merger and periodically reappears in its ancient form in India as well as in Hellenic Dionysism, and in many later mystic or esoteric sects up to modern times.

Orphism is derived from the influence of Jainism, which was very important in the ancient world for its impact on Shivaism-Dionysism. Mithraism, on the other hand, is the attempt of a soldier community to rediscover part of the ritual and initiatory aspects of original Shivaism.

These four great currents of religious thought spread throughout the world combining with local divinities, legends and cults, as did Christianity at a later period. They remain the basis of almost all existing forms of religion, including the Semitic religions, Judaism, Christianity and Islam, which derived from ancient Hebrew polytheism. The great Semitic civilization of Egypt absorbed numerous Shivaite elements, in particular the cult of Osiris, and was able to avoid the danger of monotheism, despite the attempt of Akhnaton in the fourteenth century. Monotheism was later to isolate the Semitic religions from ancient cosmological and religious thought.

ORIGINS

The religions of the Far East will not be included in the scope of this book, although Shivaite influence on Taoism is evident and Jaina rationalism had a great influence on Confucianism. Later, through Buddhism, Jaina and Shivaite influences again made themselves felt in China, Southeast Asia and Tibet, by means of Mahâyâna Tantrism, which was largely a fusion of the two religions. Indian Tantric texts moreover, often mention the existence of "Chinese rites" (Cinâchara).

Mythology

Whether dealing with heroes, divine incarnations or gods, all mythology is founded on the personification of certain cosmological principles or particular virtues. "Together with the gods, I will tell of the birth of the elements which they personify," says Hesiod. What counts in mythology are the inherent principles and not the legends with which they are surrounded in order to make them more readily understood. It is of no importance that these legends are legion, differing from one region to another, from one visionary poet to another. We should not lose sight of the fact that such myths or legends are only there to make abstract ideas and universal realities more comprehensible.

The wicked fairy remains the wicked fairy even if we invent new fairy-tales. Heroes are attributed with certain acts which surpass reality, but which are designed to emphasize their virtues and the teachings which they personify. To attribute to Jesus of Nazareth the miracles and legends of Dionysus or Krishna does not detract from his message, but serves to make his divine nature more easily understood. To try to see only strictly historical facts is to deny his divinity and his value as an eternal symbol.

The legends surrounding a particular divine aspect in the various civilizations only differ in the indigenous names given to the heroes and gods. These wonderful tales illustrate universal cosmological or philosophic concepts by incorporating them in a local pantheon to make them more accessible and, occasionally, to mask their meaning from the uninitiated who take these legends literally. The same process is found everywhere, whether in the myths of Dionysus, Bacchus, Zagreus or the Minotaur, of Egyptian Osiris or Roman Liber. In the same way, the legends were adapted so as to include Shiva and his cult amongst the Vedic gods or in Tibetan Buddhism. Thus saints are substituted for gods in the Christian world: the life of Buddha appears in the lives of the saints under the name of Saint Joshaphat.

GODS OF LOVE AND ECSTASY

We are so used to connecting the idea of civilization with a certain level of technological development that we lose sight of the level of human knowledge and culture in those times which we term prehistoric. Only through a few archaeological accidents have the extremely evolved art forms and culture of the Neolithic and even Palaeolithic periods been brought to light – periods during which we imagine the Earth to have been peopled with bearded savages armed with clubs! It is evident that some of the artists invited to decorate the subterranean sanctuaries of Lascaux or Altamira, between the fifteenth and sixth millennia B.C., possessed an excellent technique and a masterly hand. They did not live below ground and their usual occupation must therefore have been the decoration of relatively luxurious dwellings. Similar forms of art exist even today in Indian villages built of daub and wood which, once destroyed, leave no trace.

The first Egyptian dynasties date from the end of the fourth millennium. In the same period the Sumerians, speaking an agglutinative (Dravidian) language, migrated from the Indus to Mesopotamia which was already highly civilized. More than a thousand years later the builders of the megaliths brought a similar civilization to Northern Europe.

From the beginning of the sixth millennium, the marks of Shivaism are to be found everywhere: the cult of the bull, the snake and the phallus, the royal symbol of the horns, Yoga positions, funeral chambers, both in those places where urban remains have survived and where only cliff-face engravings still exist.

It is very often the case that in order to explain ancient rites and symbols, we have only much later attempts to rediscover knowledge almost lost as a consequence of cataclysms, barbarian invasions, or religious upheavals. This is true of the Greeks in relation to the Minoans or of the Celts in relation to the megalithic civilization. Behind Hesiod's *Theogony*, the most ancient Greek text on mythology, a more precise and less superficial text may be glimpsed, the deeper meaning of which Hesiod does not always comprehend.

The first great period of Minoan art in Crete dates from about 2600 B.C. Knossos and Phaistos were destroyed for the first time by a sudden catastrophe, probably the explosion of the volcano of Santorini in about 1700 B.C. The first Achaeans seem to have appeared around 1600 B.C. As "a prize of war", they brought back to Peloponnese the Minoan religion, which was the basis of what is termed Mycenaean culture. The Achaeans gradually installed themselves in Crete and must have destroyed Knossos for the first time around 1400 B.C. Its final destruction by the Dorians took place in about 1100 B.C. In Malta, the monumental temples of Ggantija were built between about 2800 and 2400 B.C. There appear the cults of the bull, the phallus and the goddess. The dolychocephalic-type Mediterranean population was totally annihilated in about 2400 B.C. and after a vacant period was replaced by a round-headed (brachycephalic) population who created the Tarxien civilization, similar to the Mycenaean, which was also destroyed about 2000 B.C. Such was the destruction that no survivor remained.

"The disappearance of the Minoan civilization, the most ancient to have flourished in Europe, is one of the most appalling dramas in the history of Europe, which has always been particularly dramatic... Until the flowering of the new Greek civilization, the continent fell back into an agricultural life without a history." (Paolo Santarcangeli, *Le Livre des labyrinthes*, pp. 96 and 187.) "The Achaean conquerors were not capable of making their own, any more than they were capable of promoting, the artistic efforts and organization of those whom they had conquered and subjected... The Minoans, after two thousand years in which they had built up the first Western civilization, disappeared from the scene of European history." (Gaetano De Sanctis, *Storia dei Greci*, p. 138.) We must understand that the same distance which separates the end of the original Minoan civilization from the Greece of Pericles, separates us from the Roman Empire. It is therfore quite logical that only popular traditions concerning the Yogic and philosophical bases of rites and symbols were able to be transmitted through the still barbarous conquerors. The seriousness with which mythological accounts are taken nowadays sometimes appears highly comical. It is imagined that ancient peoples took symbolic accounts for realities, even though today the Hindu *kīrtana* poets still invent daily new episodes in the legend of the gods. Christians take as historical fact the symbolic accounts of the Bible and the Gospel. They go and dig on the top of Mount Ararat to find the remains of Noah's Ark even though the flood myth is universal, known to the Hindus as to the Babylonians and the American peoples, and each tradition makes the Ark ground on a different mountain.

Modern interpretations, although giving proof of considerable erudition and certain intuition, are often founded on a lack of appreciation of the intellectual level and knowledge of man in relatively distant times. At this level, we are not yet entirely free from the dogma of the creation of the world in the year 4963 B.C., still held as an article of faith by certain Christian theologians at the beginning of this century.

The origins of Shivaism

According to Indian sources and as confirmed by numerous archaeological data, it was during the sixth millennium B.C. – a period which more or less corresponds to what we call the Neolithic Age – that Shivaism was revealed or codified. This great religion was derived from animistic concepts and from the long religious experience of prehistoric man, of which there remain only a few rare archaeological indications and allusions to mythical sages in later writings. Starting from this period, Shivaite rites and symbols begin to appear both in India and in Europe: the cult of the bull, the phallus, the ram, the snake, the Lady of the Mountains, as well as ecstatic dances, the swastika, the labyrinth, sacrifices, etc. Thus it is difficult to determine where Shivaism was born. Its origins stretch far back into the history of man. The megalithic monuments and symbolic representations testifying to its presence are so widespread: the traditions, legends, rites and festivities deriving from it are found in so many regions, that it appears everywhere as one of the main sources of later religions. There is nothing to prove that India was the place where it originated, since Shivaite rites and symbols appear almost simultaneously in different parts of the world. However, only in India have these traditions and what are known as Dionysiac rites been maintained without interruption from prehistoric times until today. Greek texts speak of Dionysus' mission to India, and Indian texts of the expansion of Shivaism towards the West. According to Diodorus, the epitaph of Osiris (identified with Dionysus) mentioned Osiris' expeditions to India and the countries of the North. Innumerable similarities in mythological accounts and iconographic survivals leave no doubt as to the original unity of Shivaism and the wide extent of its influence.

A great cultural movement extending from India to Portugal took place during the sixth millennium B.C. This movement is apparently related to the diffusion of Shivaism, and is characterized by a naturalistic art giving great importance to animals. We only possess vague legendary allusions to the period and only the chance discovery of "prehistoric" sites has been able to supply some points of reference.

It was, in fact, the era during which civilization used wood, and it appears almost strange to call such a period the "Stone Age". 'Wood' civilizations still exist in India and Southeast Asia, and it is well known that, whatever their degree of refinement, they leave practically no trace behind them. All the symbols associated with the cult of Shiva – the erect phallus, the horned god, the bull, the snake, the ram, the Lady of the Mountains – are found in this cultural and agricultural complex which, starting from 6000 B.C., spread westward to Europe and Africa and eastward to southern Asia. "The young naked ithyphallic god seated on a throne is present at all stages in Ancient Europe, from Proto-Sesklo and Starčevo (sixth millennium) to Dimini and the Vinča period. He wears a horned mask. He is also represented standing, holding his sexual organ with both hands... However, the principal manifestation of the male god seems to have been in the form of a bull, sometimes a bull with a human face or a man with a bull's head." (Valcamonica Symposium, *Les Religions de la Préhistoire*, p. 135.) During the Vinča period in Rumania (from the seventh to the fifth millennium), archaeological research has given evidence of the bull cult, the bull with human face, the ithyphallic and horned god, the phallus cult, and the phallus with a face. The dead are buried in a Yoga position, as at Lepenski Vir, near the Iron Gates of the Danube.

The first true Shivaite images are found at Çatal Höyük in Anatolia, dating from about 6000 B.C. The cults of Osiris, the bull and the ram, appear just after the dawn of Egyptian civilization. In Egypt, the cults of bull-Osiris and ram-Osiris are found in a fused form, although originally separate, as in the case of the fusion of the cults of bull-Shiva and ram-Skanda. There also exists a colossal statue of the ithyphallic god Min, coming from predynastic Egypt and dating from the middle of the fifth millennium B.C. It was during this period that the Minoan peoples arrived in Crete (about 4500), as well as in Anatolia, Cyprus, Malta and Santorini. Concepts such as the *Yin* and *Yang* – a Chinese transcription of the words *Yoni* (vulva) and *Linga* (phallus) –, representing the closely entwined female and male principles, are in no way different from the *Linga* inserted into the *arghia* (receptacle) as used in the Shivaite cult, and indicate the influence of Shivaite symbolism at the very source of Chinese thought.

Images of the bull-god or horned god, the Lord of the Animals, similar to those at Mohenjo Daro, are found in pre-Celtic and Minoan tradition. In southeast Asia (Cambodia, Java, Bali), Shivaism is closely linked with the very beginnings of civilization. In Bali, it is even now the predominant aspect of religion. The temples of Angkor, like the ancient temples of Java, are for the most part Shivaite.

During the fourth millennium, a Shivaite civilization arose in the Indus plain. The Sumerians, who probably came from the Indus, arrived in Mesopotamia by sea. The religion which they practised spread all over the Middle East, to Crete and continental Greece. From the beginning of the third millennium up to the Aryan invasions, the three great sister-civilizations of Mohenjo Daro, Sumer and Knossos developed along parallel lines, extending over the whole European continent on the one side, and central and east India and southeast Asia on the other.

The end of the third millennium appears as an important date. It was in fact in about 3000 B.C. that the (historical) flood took place, dividing the Sumerian dynasties into antediluvian and postdiluvian. According to Hindu chronology, the beginning of the Kali Yuga, the Age of Conflicts, or Modern Age, also dates from this period.

During the same period, a new people of Atlanto-Mediterranean race appeared in Malta, and subsequently in Armorica, coming from the Mediterranean probably by way of the Iberian Peninsula. "They introduced a new religion and new burial customs. The megalithic civilization belongs to them: during the course of two thousand years, the soil of the peninsula was covered with their monuments. The tumulus of Saint-Michel at Carnac was built about the year 3000 B.C., the lines of the stones dating from around 2000. The builders of the megaliths... certainly preserved contacts with Iberia and, further afield, with their origins in Crete or in the Middle East... or, at least were not ignorant of their existence... nor of the rites practised there by the bull-worshippers." (Gwenc'hlan Le Scouëzec, *Guide de la Bretagne mystérieuse*, pp. 72 and 99.) "The palace [of Knossos], the temple of the solar bull, has a subtle but close link with the stone circles to be found in our countryside." (R. A. Macalister, *Ireland in Preceltic Times*.) "The menhir statues of upper Adige and Liguria... (as well as) Stonhenge and other megalithic monuments... seem to derive from a prototype which appeared at Mycenae around the sixteenth to the fourteenth century B.C." (Paolo Santarcangeli, *Le Livre des Labyrinthes*, p. 139.) The designs of the labyrinths at Valcamonica date from 1800 to 1300 B.C. Those of Malta are several centuries older.

The birth of Dionysus

The beginnings of Minoan civilization seem to stretch back to the middle of the fifth millennium and are therefore contemporary with predynastic Egypt. The greatest Minoan period, however, as shown by its incredible artistic development, (which may well be a period of spiritual decadence and does not necessarily correspond to a parallel progress on an intellectual and religious level), stretches from about 2800 to about 1800 B.C. The monumental temples in Malta were built between 2800 and 2000. This Mediterranean civilization is thus contemporary with the postdiluvian Sumerian civilization and also with the greatest period of Mohenjo Daro and the cities of the Indus, with which there is an evident relationship. Whatever the importance of the most ancient archaeological data emerging from all over the Mediterranean world – Anatolia and the Middle East, as well as of Sumerian or Babylonian literary references – it is only with the Minoan civilization and its Greek heritage that Shivaite rites and myths, in their Dionysian version, make their real debut into what we know as the religious history of the Western world.

Cretan civilization developed due to a considerable contribution from Asian civilizations. "Neolithic Crete may be considered as the most important extension of the Anatolian province as a whole." (Evans, *The Palace of Minos*, chap. 1, p. 14.) Relations with Egypt, Greece and the Middle East were constantly maintained throughout Cretan history. "Trained... architects and painters... were invited... from Asia (possibly from Alalakh...) to build and decorate the palaces of the Cretan rulers... The technique of fresco painting... and methods of construction... employed in Yarim-Lim's palace, [on the Syrian coast] are the same as those... of Knossos... Moreover, Yarim-Lim's palace antedates by more than a century the Cretan examples in the same style." (R. F. Willetts, *Cretan Cults and Festivals*, p. 17.)

According to Homer (*Odyssey* XIX, 178), Minos governed Crete and the isles of the Aegean three generations before the Trojan War, which took place during the thirteenth century B.C. He is therefore referring to the second Cretan civilization, which was influenced by the Achaeans. As in the Mesopotamian civilizations, many elements characteristic of Shivaism are found in Minoan Crete: the young god, the Goddess of the Mountain, the bull and the Minotaur, the snake, the horns, the lion, the he-goat, the sacred tree and the phallic pillar, the bull sacrifice and the ecstatic dance of the Korybantes and

Kouretes, who are in all aspects identical to the Ganas, the young companions of Shiva and his followers. The symbols of the swastika, the double axe and the labyrinth derive, as we shall see later, from Indian ideas related to Yogic experience and to the Earth cult. The same symbols are found at Malta, where extremely important monumental remains have survived.

The Minoans sought harmony between man and nature. Their paintings show us a peaceful and idyllic life in fairy-like, enchanted surroundings, recalling the earthly paradise of Shiva-Pashupati, the Lord of the Animals. We do not know what name was given to the god at the time of the first King Minos, but it was probably Zan, Hellenized into Zagreus and later identified with Zeus. The name Zeus is Indo-European. "The Achaeans who came into Crete gave the name of their sky-god to a Minoan deity... Zagreus... was an Oriental name... [from] Phoenicia... [and is probably an] ethnic from Mount Zagron, between Assyria and Media... This Idaian Zeus, also honoured by the Kouretes... is the old Cretan god who is so like Dionysus elsewhere that it is natural for the initiated mystic to describe himself as Bakkhos... [This god] who dies and is born again... causes the renewal of life in the worshipper who enters into his mysteries, culminating in the eating of the raw flesh of the animal which is the god himself made manifest – the bull, whose blood also sanctified his shrines." (R. F. Willetts, *Cretan Cults and Festivals*, pp. 200–203, 240.) Euripides mentions Zagreus in *The Cretans*: "I have sounded the thunder of Zagreus who wanders by night, accomplished the raw-flesh feasts and held high the torches to the Mountain-mother, torches of the Kouretes, Hallowed and named as a Bakkhos. All-white are the clothes I wear and I shun human birth, touch no urn of the dead and their tombs, have been on guard to all taste of meat".

The myths concerning the young god and the Cretan goddess are similar to those of Shiva and Pârvatî. An echo is found in the myths of Ishtar and Tammuz, Isis and Osiris, and Venus and Adonis. Rhea, the Goddess of the Mountain, is the Indian Pârvatî (she of the mountain). The names of Diktynna and Artemis also evoke the idea of a mountain-mother. The name Diktynna comes from the name of a mountain, Mount Dikte. Pârvatî is the daughter of Himâvat (the Himalayas).

Dionysus in the Aryanized world

The enemies who burnt the principal centres of the Minoan

civilization in about 1400 B.C. may be identified as the Homeric Achaeans who also destroyed Ugarit and Troy during the thirteenth century. It was during this second Minoan period, influenced by the Achaeans, that the Cretan god took the name of Dionysus, the god of Nysa. The religious ideas which he embodies were formerly attributed to Zagreus, also called Cretan Zeus (Kretagenes). A renewal of the Orphic cults during the sixth century B.C. led to a strengthening of the indigenous mystery cults under a new name. This is confirmed by Euripides and Fimicus who refer to this ancient Cretan Dionysus, who is none other than Zeus-Zagreus and whose mystic followers communicated with him by eating the raw flesh of a bull. The spread of the Cretan religion was considerable, as well as its influence on Greek thought and religion. Diodorus says that, according to the Cretans, "the gods went from Crete to most of the regions of the inhabited world... Thus, the goddess Demeter arrived in Attica, and then in Sicily and Egypt". The Mycenaean tablets from Pylos (about 1500) already mention the name of Dionysus together with those of the Aryan gods. In the *Bibliotheke*, a summary of mythological fables attributed to Apollodorus, the latter emphasizes the affinities of the Dionysian cult with other mystery cults and with the wisdom of ancient peoples. He also insists on those legends which speak of *mania* (ecstatic madness) and which show how the god punishes those who resist him. The reappearance of Shivaism or Dionysism represents a return to an archaic and fundamental religion, kept alive underground despite invasions and persecutions. The ancient god of Crete, Anatolia, Sumer and pre-Hellenic continental Greece could appear a stranger only to the Achaean and Dorian invaders, who thought he came from Asia through Thrace and pretended that his cult had been introduced into Greece by his missionaries and votaries. "The cult of Dionysus was all the more easily acclimatized... as Dionysus was capable of being easily assimilated to the indigenous divinities, and since the rites of the Greek god offered many points of contact with the practices of ancient Thracian religion, apparently including female orgiastic rites." (H. Jeanmaire, *Dionysos*. pp. 77 and 431.) Dionysism was, in fact, none other than the ancient Shivaism of the Indo-Mediterranean world, little by little re-establishing its place in an Aryanized world. This cult, which overturned and renewed the Greeks' religious experience, had extremely deep roots in Hellenic soil.

The same assimilation process had taken place in India. Shivaism had been slowly integrated into Vedic Brahmanism, which it had profoundly changed. Vedic religion absorbed, incorporated and preserved the rites of other cults. Far from destroying them, it adapted them to its own needs. It borrowed so much from the institutions of the Dravidians and the other peoples of India that it is extremely difficult to separate the original Aryan elements from the others. In innumerable legends included in the Purânas on the one hand and in Dionysiac and Orphic accounts on the other, Shiva-Dionysus already appears as one of the gods of the Aryan pantheon in which he is often given a predominant place. Dionysus is evoked in the Homeric hymns. "It is of Dionysus, son of the most glorious Semele (the Earth), that I speak, and I shall tell how he appeared on the shore of the untiring sea, on an outmost promontory, with the aspect of a young man in his first adolescence." (*Hymn to Dionysus*, I, 1–4.) "I am the boisterous Dionysus, of whom the mother who bore him was Semele the Cadmean after being united in love with Zeus." (*Hymn to Dionysus*, I, 55.)

Euripides admits the universality of the religion of Dionysus, which the god himself, escorted by his Maenads, had propagated all over the East before returning to implant it in the place of his birth. The Greeks explained the similarities in the cults of Shiva and Dionysus by a journey of Dionysus to India. Dionysus' mission to the Orient to propagate his cult there became a fabulous conquest of India by him and his army of Maenads and Satyrs. The expedition lasted two years and the god returned through Boeotia after three years. He celebrated his victory riding on an elephant. According to Diodorus, it is due to the memory of his expedition to India that the Boeotians, the other Greeks and the Thracians instituted trieteric sacrifices to Dionysus. The ancient Hebrews had also been greatly influenced by the Dravidian and Shivaite world. Abraham came from Sumerian Ur, and despite Moses, the Hebrews also continued to take part in ecstatic rites up to David's time. In Egypt, it is Osiris whose myths and legends are connected with Shivaite myths. Osiris represents the powers of generation and growth. He is also the god of trees and plants. Herodotus and Diodorus identify Osiris with Dionysus. Osiris had originally come from India riding on a bull. He took into his army the Satyrs (the Indian *Ganas*) as dancers and singers, prone to all sorts of mischief. Later, he returned to India where he founded many cities. The direct contacts between Egypt and India are extremely ancient, and are independent of India's relations with Sumer, Anatolia and

Crete. Highly important commercial exchanges were normally routed through the Indian Ocean and the Red Sea. At the time of the development of the Cretan civilization, the parallels between the cults of Osiris and Dionysus became evident. The first portrayals of Cretans in Egyptian paintings are found in the tombs of Sonmut and Useramon at Thebes, and date from between 1490 and 1480 B.C. The unity of Shivaite and Dionysiac concepts was recognised in the Hellenic world as a fact. "Dionysus was already considered by the ancients as a god who was analogous to Shiva under one of his main aspects, as evidenced by the practices of left-hand Tantrism." (Julius Evola, *Le Yoga tantrique*, note p. 15.) Megasthenes, a Greek who lived in India in the fourth century B.C., identifies Dionysus with Shiva, whose cult, according to him, was particularly widespread in the mountains where the vine is cultivated. He refers to the similarity between the expeditions of the king (Chandragupta) and the processions of Dionysus. When the soldiers of Alexander rushed to the Shivaite sanctuary of Nysa (near modern Peshawar, in the north of present-day Pakistan) to embrace their brothers in Dionysus, it did not enter their minds that this may have been another divinity, or a different cult.

"According to the Cretan myth, Lampros was the son of Pandion. This name... connects with the sun and moon... The bisexual offspring of Lampros and Galatea... were like the bisexual creatures that Plato identifies with the sun and moon. The Attic festival of the Pandia seems to have been celebrated at the time of the full moon. The festival... derived its name from... Pandion, the eponymn of the tribe Pandionis, being held in honour of Zeus." (R. F. Willetts, *Cretan Cults and Festivals*, p. 178.)

It should be noted that Pandia is the name of a Dravidian dynasty descended from the Moon, which reigned since time immemorial in India and which is mentioned, amongst others, in the great Tamil epic poem, the *Shilappadikaram*. The Pandavas, sons of Pandu (the White), were members of the dynasty who fought the Aryans in the Mahâbhârata war.

About the year 700 B.C., the Celts arrived in the West. As in the case of the Greeks or the Vedic Indians, it is through them that the remains of the great megalithic civilization which preceded them have been preserved. An ithyphallic god, dating from the eighth or seventh century B.C., is figured on a rock at Skäne in Sweden. In Denmark, too, there exists a series of wooden phallic figures dating from the Bronze Age or from the beginning of the Iron Age. We find "*Ana mater deorum Hibernensium*" in the Irish *Sanas Cormaic*. The Great Goddess Anna, mother of the gods of Ireland, later became Saint Anne; also the Ganas or Korybantes, who are "the facetious Korrigans... capable of great gentleness and terrible vengeance... They certainly originate in the beliefs of the dolmen people, and perhaps even earlier... Tarw, the sacred bull, is clearly connected with the megaliths and his cult reaches back to prehistory... The reality of the Celts' human sacrifices is undeniable. Caesar... accuses the Druids of particularly cruel rites". (Gwenc'hlan Le Scouëzec, *La Bretagne mystérieuse*, pp. 74–78.)

"There are two distinct types of Celtic deity depicted in the iconography and described in the literature... The first of these is one of the most basic of the Celtic god-types, with an ancestry in Europe which takes us right back to the imagery of the Swedish and the Spanish rock-carvings, and beyond into an indefinable past. This is the horned, phallic god of the Celtic tribes – aggressive, fertile, bull – or ram-horned; or antlered and non-phallic... The second type of horned god is likewise associated with pastoral pursuits, with the rearing of stock, with war... He is naked, strongly ithyphallic, holding shield and spear... It is in this guise that he appears, for example, at Maryport (Roman Alauna), at Brough-by-Sands, and elsewhere. The earliest Celtic portrayal of the antlered god occurs in the ancient sanctuary at Valcamonica in northern Italy, where for centuries the evolving peoples of Europe gave expression to their religious ideas on the rock faces of this sacred place. The Celtic drawings must date from the time of the Celtic conquest of Etruria... The antlered god is known from one inscription as Cernunnos, 'The Horned One'; this may well not have been his name throughout the Celtic world because the Celts had few divine types but many divine names. The great god... has over his right, bent arm the sacred neck-ring – the torc – worn by gods and heroes alike. Over his bent left arm are traces of the horned serpent, his most consistent cult animal... His worshipper... is markedly ithyphallic." (Anne Ross, in *Primitive Erotic Art*, pp. 83–84.) In India, Shiva is also called Shringin, the horned one, and wears a serpent necklace.

The Romans identified the Celtic god as Apollo. Stonehenge, then more than two thousand years old, was still a place of cult at the time of the Roman conquest (57 B.C.). Diodorus of Sicily, quoting Hecataeus on the Isle of Britain, tells us that "the inhabitants honour

Apollo more than anywhere else . . . A sacred precinct is dedicated to him on the island, as well as a magnificent circular temple adorned with rich offerings".

Erect stone phalli, sometimes decorated with a face or entwined with a serpent, are found in England, Sweden, Italy, Brittany, Corsica, Greece, Arabia and India, as also the bull-cult and sacrifice, the snake-cult and its legends, springtime carnivals or libidinous festivities, ecstatic dances, and sacred places bearing the more or less deformed name of Nysa. We also find legends connected with the cult of the infant-Skanda, the *bambino*, born in a reedy marsh and nourished by the seven Pleiades which later turned into stars. There are numerous accounts relating the universal message of the god born in a cave. Near him is the ox or bull, the sacred animal, although he is also associated with the ass, an unclean animal, on which he rides during his festivals. He is the god of life, who dies and rises again, who unites the inseparable mysteries of procreation and death.

Thus it appears that all religious movements have been inspired by the Shivaite message, even though they seek to deny it, or have distorted their heritage. Shivaite philosophy is so little known largely because we are not willing to recognize its primacy, nor to see its myths and rites showing through in those of later religions.

Texts and documents

No Indian text of the pre-Aryan period seems to have survived in its original form, except for a few inscriptions in the Mohenjo Daro writings, which have not yet been deciphered. The Aryans, however, were very soon influenced by the philosophy, practices and rites of Shivaism. The ancient Dravidian sages were accepted side by side with the Vedic prophets and many texts were gradually translated or adapted into Sanskrit, the great literary tongue derived from Vedic. There is a similar relationship between the Etruscan language and Latin.

The fourth Veda, the *Atharva Veda*, is almost exclusively based on pre-Aryan traditions concerning rites, magic formulae and ceremonies. It was joined to the three original Vedas, the *Rik*, the *Yajuh* and the *Sâma*. "The *Atharva Veda* represents the real religion of the people." (P. Banerjee). The teachings it contains are attributed to the non-Aryan sage Angirasa. Fifty-one of the philosophical treatises, the Shivaite Upanishads, such as the *Shvetâshvatara Upanishad*, the

Mundaka Upanishad, etc., are also attributed to him. Amongst the Brâhamanas, the rituals attached to the *Atharva Veda*, the most important is the *Gopatha Brâhamana* (the way of the bull). According to tradition, the poems in archaic Tamil, the poems of the "club of poets," or *sangham*, are also pre-Aryan.

The *Atharva Veda* is the part of the ancient religion which was adopted by the Aryans, and thus corresponds to the Mycenaean religion, that is, to what the Achaeans had assumed from the Minoan religion. However, the main texts describing the authentic rites, myths and practices of pre-Aryan Shivaism are found in other kinds of works, called Purânas (historical books), Âgamas (traditions) and Tantras (initiatory and magic rites). To these should be added the ancient Sânkhya (cosmology) and the texts on Yoga, a technique whose origin is Shivaite and pre-Aryan.

The question of the date of these texts is not so important. The translation into Sanskrit of the traditional learning such as we know it today depends on the period when it was more or less incorporated into official Hinduism, and has nothing to do with the contents. The date of Homer is not judged according to his first translation into English. A very important part of the rites and concepts of Shivaism is even today not accepted by the Brahmans and still retains its esoteric character. It is preserved by oral tradition, or in the form of manuscripts, the disclosure of which is, as a rule, forbidden.

Oral traditions remain an essential element in the handing down of rites and of the more abstract aspects of knowledge. Written texts are merely concise memoranda requiring a commentary which is usually oral. In the eighth century, which was a period of great Shivaite renewal, Shankarâchârya published his very important commentaries on the Upanishads, and the *Tirumurai*, the Shivaite canon in eleven books, was compiled in Tamil. Certain information on more ancient periods is sometimes given by the opponents of Shivaism, as is the case with the Dionysian rites and, later on, with their survival in the Christian world.

In the last hundred years, important commentaries on Shivaite doctrine and rites have been published in various Indian languages, thus making available to a much wider public those teachings which had been previously reserved for initiates. It is not possible to interpret the texts or get to know the practice of the rites without the aid of these documents.

The Purânas

The Purânas (Ancient Chronicles) are enormous texts, rather similar to the Bible, in which are transcribed and summarized oral traditions stretching back to the far distant past, such as the history of the Flood, the domestication of fire, and the migration of peoples.

These texts contain historical and geographical elements, genealogies sometimes reaching back to the sixth millennium B.C., mythological accounts, ritual or technical teachings (medicine, architecture, painting, music, dancing, etc.), philosophical teachings, social and moral codes. They form a veritable encyclopaedia. When Shivaism and the autochthonous cults were incorporated into Vedism at a relatively late period in order to form present-day Hinduism, the Purânas were adapted and translated into Sanskrit from non-Aryan languages, which were probably Dravidian. Thirty-six Purânas exist, of which some are enormous works. Six of the most important of these are Shivaite: the Shiva Purâna, the Linga Purâna, the Skanda Purâna, the Matsya Purâna, the Kurma Purâna and the Brahmanda Purâna. Important data concerning Shivaite tradition is also found in the other Purânas, and in particular in the Agni Purâna and the Vâyu Purâna. The most important Purânas are divided into "books" called samhitâs. If to the Purânas is added the Mahâbhârata, the great epic poem which comes from the same source, we have in these texts, despite the many additions and compulsory references to the Vedas and to the Aryan gods, a considerable amount of material and very important information on pre-Aryan Shivaism.

The *Râmâyana* is different, since it is a literary work composed in Sanskrit, after an episode mentioned in several of the Purânas, somewhat like *The Bacchantes* of Euripides or the *Dionysia* of Nonnos. It contains but little information on ancient civilization and beliefs, even though it refers to very ancient times. We see, for example, that the confluence of the Ganges and the Jumna is in a forest, whilst in the *Mahâbhârata* it is already the site of a great city.

Âgamas and Tantras

The Âgamas (Traditions) explain the rules of behaviour of the Shivaite sects, referring to traditions existing since time immemorial, and their content, if not their form, is considered as being more ancient than the Vedas. From the Shivaite point of view, they are revelation, whereas the Vedas are only writings of human origin.

There are twenty-eight principal Shivaite Âgamas and more than two hundred secondary Âgamas. These works have, however, never been effectively incorporated into the sacred texts of Aryanized Hinduism. Considered as texts for initiates, they were never widely divulged. Many of them have still not been published and are kept secret. Their handing-down by oral means is still regarded as being the only valid method. The written form is, in many cases, if not forbidden, at least considered dangerous, as certain teachings must not be imparted except to those who are worthy. Writing has no value in transmitting magical formulae. In the West, this view was also shared by the Druids and is still the case in all religions for ritual and magical formulae, including the words of consecration in the mass.

"During this long period of time [when Shivaism was banished], the Shiva Âgamas must have been composed, so that the Shivaites might have for themselves something as sacred as the Vedas of the orthodox, and also so that they might have well-established rules and regulations relating to their order." (C. V. Narayana Ayyar, *Shaivism in South India*, p. 71.) The rites taught by the Âgamas include gestures (*mudras*), symbolic diagrams (*yantras*), and other practices which do not exist in Vedic ritual.

The Tantras are works of an esoteric nature which are analogous to the Âgamas. They deal with all ritual aspects, especially those concerning the cult of the goddess. They also deal with Yoga, cosmology, alchemy, rules of behaviour, magic and sacrifices. For the purpose of erotico-magic and spiritual realization, the Tantras summarize the millenial experience of Shivaite India as to the nature of the cosmos and its relationship to the subtle structures of man. The Tantras are an applied method based on the principles of Sânkhya (cosmology). or macrocosmic science on the one hand, and of Yoga, the science of the human being or microcosm, on the other. These are the basic sciences of Shivaite tradition. Tantra, the science of rites and magical powers, defines the possibilities of realization, based on the relationship between the macrocosm and microcosm, which is the result of Sânkhya and Yoga.

As a rule, each Tantra is divided into four parts: doctrine, Yoga, ritual, and rules of life. Without the Tantras and Âgamas, it is impossible to understand the symbolism of rites and also of sacred architecture and iconography. This is true not only of the Hindu temple, but of all religious architecture, which throughout the world observes the same rules of orientation, whether it be megalithic monuments, Egyptian and Greek temples, or the Christian cathedrals of the Middle Ages.

Greek and Latin texts

We have no texts explaining the rites and ceremonial of the Dionysiac mysteries in the Greco-Etrusco-Roman world, although there are allusions which can often be clarified with the aid of Indian texts. Homer, Plato, Euripides, Aeschylus, Nonnos and Apollodorus, all make reference to Dionysiac rites. Furthermore, there are many modern studies of the Greek and Cretan religion, largely based on monuments, graphic representation, vases and painting.

Apart from these references, Livy's account is practically the only ancient literary document about the Dionysiac mysteries. Due to his hostile attitude, however, Livy's descriptions must be treated with caution, as his aim was to discredit them. His assertion that these rites were introduced into Etruria in the second century B.C. by a *Graecus ignobilis* is clearly fallacious.

The crimes imputed to the Dionysiac sects, such as incest, the murder of new-born children in order to eat their flesh and drink their blood, etc., were later ascribed to the early Christians. The same accusations were made at the trials of heretics during the Middle Ages. Initiatory societies are always represented by their persecutors as covens of witches, but closer examination will often yield some interesting information. By studying Shivaite rites, the only ones which have continued down to our own times, the real practices of the Dionysiac rites and "mysteries" may be reconstructed.

Archaeological Data

Apart from the texts mentioned above, there are numerous archaeological documents, symbols, statues of gods and representations of ceremonies which permit us to reconstruct the rites and beliefs to which they refer. For this kind of reconstruction, the vast amount of Indian literature, which describes the rites in such minute detail, supplies us with precious elements to explain the great abundance of Cretan, Greek and Roman imagery.

When considering "prehistoric" remains, it is important to remember that they belong to the period of a civilization using wood, and can on no account be taken as representative of the cultural or artistic level of their era. They were probably the work of shepherds or peasants and often resemble the graffiti of modern prisons. The Valcamonica drawings belonging to the Roman or medieval period, are just as primitive as those of the Neolithic Age.

The most ancient stone monuments reproduce wooden architecture, which was often very elaborate. The cultural level of a people, whether ancient or recent, cannot therefore be judged by the rare remains which have survived. Stonehenge and Carnac are contemporary with the most refined period of Cretan paintings, and thus with the end of the Egyptian Middle Empire, and with the sanctuaries of Malta. Climatic conditions have erased the fragile structures of cities built of wood and daub. However, as the religious symbols are the same, it would seem absurd to say that no contacts existed, and that the European continent was in the hands of a primitive civilization. The primitive peoples, in fact, came later on: these were the Barbarians who destroyed the ancient civilizations. Miraculous catastrophes like those of Santorini and Mohenjo Daro were needed to preserve some physical vestiges of the civilizations of that period until our own times.

Chapter 2

ASPECTS AND LEGENDS OF THE GOD

The Sacrifice of Daksha

Whatever the original character of Vedism, once this Aryan religion was established in India, Iran and Greece, it became the religion of the governing classes of the cities. They reduced the ancient populations to slavery – despising their gods, rites and customs.

The sacrifice of Daksha evokes the conflict between city religion, as represented by Brahmanism and the Aryan rites, and ancient Shivaism, the religion of the people and of nature.

Daksha, a Vedic sovereign and sage, arranged a great sacrifice in honour of all the gods, except Shiva. Shiva was considered to be an unclean, non-Vedic divinity, even though Daksha had previously given him, for political reasons, the hand of his daughter Sati (Fidelity), in a union symbolizing the disputed acceptance of the ancient Dravidian god amongst the Aryan gods.

According to the version of the *Bhâgavata Purâna* (IV, chap. 2 to 7), Daksha says, "Against my own will, at the instigation of Brahmâ, I gave my daughter to this unclean being, the destroyer of rites and social barriers, who teaches the sacred texts to men of low birth, to the *shudras*. Like a madman, he haunts horrid cemeteries, surrounded with ghosts and evil spirits. He is naked, his hair in disorder. He laughs, he weeps, he smears himself with ashes and wears as his only ornament a necklace of skulls and human bones. He pretends he is 'of good omen' (*shiva*), but in reality he is 'of ill omen' (*ashiva*). He is mad, adored by madmen, and reigns over the spirits of darkness. May this so-called sovereign, the last of the gods, never receive a part of the offerings of sacrifice."

But, according to the *Shiva Purâna* (*Rudra Samhitâ, Sati Khanda,* chap. I, 22–23), Daksha is in his turn cursed by Nandi (Joyful), the bull, who is the companion and personification of Shiva in the animal world. "This ignorant mortal hates the sole god who does not return hate, and he refuses to recognize the truth. He worries only about his home life, with all the compromises it implies. In order to gratify his interests, he practises interminable rites with a mentality degraded by Vedic prescriptions. He forgets the nature of the soul, since he occupies himself with quite different things. The brutish Daksha, who thinks only of his wives, shall henceforth have the head of a he-goat. May this stupid being, swollen with the vanity he draws from his knowledge, together with all those who with him oppose the Great Archer Shiva, continue to live in their ignorant ritualism.

"May the enemies of 'Him who soothes pain', whose spirit is troubled by the odour of the sacrifices and the flowery words of the Vedas, continue to live with their illusions. May all these priests, who think only of eating, who neglect knowledge except in their own interest, who practise austerities and ceremonies only to earn their living, who seek only riches and honours, end up as beggars."

The Vedic sage Bhrigu, who presided over the sacrifice, replied, "All those who practise the rites of Shiva and follow him are but heretics who oppose the true faith. They have renounced ritual purity. They live in error. Their hair is tangled; they wear necklaces of bones and smear themselves with ash. They practise the initiation rites of Shiva, during which the use of intoxicating liquor is considered to be sacred. Since they despise the Vedas and the Brahmans – the pillars of social order – they are heretics. The Vedas are the only way of virtue. May they follow their god then, the king of evil spirits."

The priest-king, the proud Daksha, who had invited Vishnu and the other gods to participate in the rites of sacrifice, invited neither Shiva nor his own daughter, Sati. Although not summoned by her father, Sati returned to her home. Seeing that no part of the offerings had been set aside for her husband, and insulted by her father, she killed herself.

"Then Shiva, in his affliction, created a terrifying spirit called Virabhadra who, at the head of Shiva's companions, the Ganas, destroyed all those at the sacrifice, sparing none. Having cut off the head of Daksha, he threw it into the fire." (*Shiva Purâna, Rudra Samhitâ, Sati Khanda*, chap. 1, 23.)

Shiva himself tore out the beard of the sage Bhrigu, who poured the oblations onto the sacred fire, he squeezed out the eyes of Bhaga (the Aryan god of inherited goods) and broke the teeth of Pushân (god of acquired riches).

The same ostracism of the god is found in the Dionysian tradition. Dionysus is insulted and expelled by Lycurgus, King of the Edones (Apollodorus, III, V, 1–3). Moreover, according to a fragment of *The*

Cretans by Euripides, it was due to the impiety of Minos, who had refused to sacrifice a bull to the god, that the latter drove his wife Pasiphae mad and she became enamoured of a bull. This is how the Minotaur was conceived.

Names and aspects of the god

In the forest, the name of the tiger is never spoken; in the same way, the name of a god is never used openly. He is only named indirectly by using adjectives. The French word "dieu" comes from the root *div* which means "radiant". The Germanic *Gott* and English *God* come from another Indo-European root, *Go*, which surprisingly means "the bull".

In the *Aitareya Brâhmana* (II, chap. 34, 7), it is prescribed that a formula must be altered in order to avoid the direct mention of the name of the god. References to the god must always be indirect, suggested by mentioning one of his qualities or attributes. For this reason, in all mythologies the different aspects of the divine have multifarious names.

It seems that, in prehistoric India, Shiva (the Benevolent) was called "Ann", a name also attributed to the goddess, the meaning of which is not known, but may be compared with the Hittite Ann, Canaanite Anat and Celtic Ana (who became Saint Anne in Brittany). In the Vedic pantheon, Rudra ("he who causes tears")[1] refers to his terrifying aspect. A text of the *Shiva Purâna* commented on in a Sanskrit treatise, the *Shiva Sahasra Nâma*, explains the meaning of about one thousand names of the god. According to the aspect of the god preferred by his votary, the secret and magic formula is established. It is then communicated to the apprentice at his initiation, to be his constant companion and refuge throughout his life.

There is no word which is expressive of divine majesty. The gods are called by their attributes, or qualities, as manifested in creation. Godhead cannot be encompassed or defined by a form or word. The thousand names of Shiva are merely epithets referring to the various aspects of his manifestation.

Dionysus also appears under manifold aspects: he is a bull-god, a dying god, an infant god, a god abandoned by his mother, the god of a double-birth. In Crete, coins from Kydonia portray a youthful Dionysus;

---

[1] According to another etymology given in the *Shiva Purâna* (*Vâyaviya Samhitâ*, chap. 12, 30), Rudra means "the Howler".

others, from Polyrhenia, a horned Dionysus; the ones from Sybrita show a bearded Dionysus holding a thyrsus; elsewhere, a young Dionysus riding on a galloping panther. The god appears in each region with a different name and in a different guise.

The parallels between the names and legends of Shiva, Osiris and Dionysus are so numerous that there can be little doubt as to their original sameness.

Skanda, the "son" of Shiva, similar to the second Dionysus, is called Agnibhû (Fire-born), while Dionysus is Pyrigenes (Fire-born). He is Karttikeya (Son of the Pleiades): Dionysus is Briseus (Son of the Nymphs). Skanda is Sarajanma (Born in the reeds), Dionysus is Limnaios ("of the marsh"). Dionysus is Protogonos (the First-born), like Shiva, who is Prathamajâ (First-born), the "oldest of the gods". He is also called Bhâskara (Luminous), or Phanes (He who illuminates) in the Orphic tradition. This god, who teaches the basic unity of all things, is called Shiva (Benevolent) or Meilichios (the Benevolent). He is Nisah (Blessedness), the god of Naxos or Nysa. The very name Dionysus most probably means "the god of Nysa" (the sacred mountain of Shiva), just as Zagreus is the god of Mount Zagron. Shiva-Dionysus is also Bhairava (the Terrible) or Bromios (the Boisterous), Rudra or Eriboas (the Howler). His feminine aspect is the "Lady of the Mountains" (Pârvatî, or Rhea, or Cybele), also called the "White Lady" (Gaurî or Leucothea). Shiva is Shankara (the Pacifier) and he is Isha[1] (the Lord), Pashupati (the protector of animals), Kâla or Kronos (Time which destroys all things, the Lord of Death). He is Skanda (the Jet of Sperm), the god of Beauty and of Mysteries, Murugan or Kumâra (the Adolescent), the equivalent of the Cretan Kouros (Boy), also called Guha (the Mysterious), whom the Greeks called Hermes.

Cretan Zeus is accompanied by the Korybantes, the servants of the goddess. The chief of the companions (Ganas) of Shiva is Ganapati, created as guardian of the goddess' gate. He is the god of Gates and thus corresponds to Apulunas, the god of Gates in Anatolia. Ganapati is called Mushaka-vâhana, "the mouse-rider", much as Apollo is called Smintheus, ("of the mice"). As Lord of the Mountains, Shiva's title is Kolônatas or Girisha (lord of the mountains). He is Bhava (the King), Agrionos (the Hunter) or Sharva (the Archer), and Mahâdeva

[1] In Aramaic and Oriental languages, the name we pronounce as Jesus is pronounced Isha.

(Supreme God). In his wanderings as a madman, he is called the Hermaphrodite (Ardhanarîshvara), corresponding to the Greek Erikepaios. As the principle of all life, his symbol is the phallus (*Linga* or Priapus). Represented as a pillar, or standing stone, he is called Sthanu (Pillar) or Perikinos ("of the column"). As Lord of Yoga, Shiva is named Yogendra, Yogeshvara, Mahâyogi, since it is he who taught the world the Yoga method through which man can know himself, realize himself and communicate with subtle beings, beasts, plants and gods. He also teaches the dance and the music which leads to ecstasy, the intoxication which takes man out of himself. He is Melpomenos (the Singer) or Natarâja, the "king of dance and of the theatre". It is by means of ecstatic and sacred dances that the god's followers, the *bhaktas*, or Bacchants, make contact with him and receive the message of wisdom. His festivals are those of the Spring, of the Renewal of Life, and of creative Eroticism. He is Bhûpati (lord of the earth), Phlios (the Verdant), Setaneios, the god of the New Crop. The Romans usually called Dionysus, Liber. Some texts speak of Dionysus' incessant vagabondage over hills and dales. His steed is the bull; he himself is the bull-god, and the bull is his manifestation in the animal kingdom. He is incarnate in the most male and most noble of animals, through which he brings redemption to the world on the altar of sacrifice. The image of the bull is often substituted for his anthropomorphic image. The god is also manifest in the sacred fig tree and in precious stones. His necklace is a serpent, and he is called Vyâlin (snake-girded). He is naked, libidinous, and preaches rapture, love, detachment, and friendship with nature. God of Sensual Pleasure and of Death, he is present in the forest and at the funeral pyre. Shiva is at the same time benevolent (Shambhu) and terrible (Bhîma). Dionysus, too, is gentle with those who worship him and terrible to his enemies. He is the charming ephebe who lures the young King of Thebes into the mountains and has him torn to pieces alive by his Bacchants. Whoever does not worship the divine phallus, the source of all life, is doomed to destruction, to error, madness and physical and spiritual death.

Just as the god's name must not be spoken, neither should he be looked on. The Greeks' fear of looking on the gods comes from their Minoan heritage. According to Callimachus, Tiresias lost his sight for having seen Pallas bathing. In order to allow Heracles to behold him, Zeus had to wrap himself in a goat-skin. In India, the power of lightning is attributed to the glance of a god. Kâma, the god of Love, is reduced to cinders by one look from Shiva. Ganesha is beheaded by the glance of Saturn. The Sun-god must not be gazed on either at his rising or setting.

Pashupati, Lord of the animals

"Rudra lives in forests and jungles. He is called Pashupati, Lord of the wild beasts." (*Shatapatha Brâhmana*, XII, 7, 3, 20.) Shiva's flock comprises all living beings, including man. The difference between beasts, men and gods is only one of rôle and level in a continuous hierarchy. The various aspects of being are present in varying degrees in all forms of existence. No god is without animality, no animal without humanity, no man without a part of divinity. Three components are distinguishable in all men: *pati, pashu* and *pâsha*. Those in whom the *pati* (master) element is dominant are the wise, who are close to the gods, understand the rules of divine activity and creation, and take part in it. Men in whom the animal element predominates are called *pashu* (cattle). The abstract element, *pâsha* (bond or snare), expresses the unity and interdependence of all forms of life. *Pâsha*, the bond, is the body of laws connecting the various elements of matter and living being bound up in creation.

There is no morality other than that of respecting the *pâsha*, or bond, meaning the interdependence of the animal world, the divine and ourselves, and of realizing the place we occupy in the overall plan of the divine work, the affinities which bind us to the animal and vegetable species and the responsibilities which are implicated thereby. *Pâsha* may be defined as the natural law, which is divine law. All other moral law is only social convention, which can have no value on a universal level. All true morality must conform to these basic laws on which creation is founded. Social conventions established by human laws have nothing to do with religion. Wherever the influence of the Shiva-Dionysus cult has spread, great importance is given to the animal and vegetable world. This aspect of religious history seems often to have escaped modern scholars of the ancient world.

"One of the most conspicuous features of Greek culture – the part played in myth by plants and animals – is left unexplained." (R. F. Willetts, *Cretan Cults and Festivals*, p. 60.)

"Shiva looked at the gods and said, 'I am the Lord of the Animals... The courageous Titans, the Asuras, can only be destroyed if each of the gods and other beings assumes his animal nature'. The gods hesitated to recognize their animal aspect. Shiva said to them, 'It is not a disgrace to recognize your own animal [the species of the animal kingdom corresponding to the principle which each god embodies on the universal plane]. Only those who practise the rites of the brothers of the animals, the *Pashupâtas*, will be able to overcome their animal nature'. It was thus that all the gods and the Titans recognized that they were the Lord's cattle and that he is known by the name of Pashupati, the Lord of the Animals." (*Shiva Purâna*, *Rudra Samhitâ*, V, chap. 9, p. 13–21.)

In order to watch over beasts, plants and men, Shiva created the *Vidyeshvaras* (masters of knowledge), who appear as forest spirits, satyrs, nymphs, fairies, or guardian angels, the protective spirits of creation. Pashupati is the head of these spirits and through them is revealed in all the aspects of the natural world. Shiva lives in the mountains and forests, where his mysterious presence is felt, and where his sanctuaries are built and offerings are brought, in caves and isolated places.

"In Roman contexts, the horned god was likened to Mercury, no doubt in his earlier rôle as the protector of the flocks and herds... The sinuous serpent winding round his caduceus is... in accordance with Celtic tradition... Again, the horned god appears as a kind of native Silvanus, god of the woods, naked and without attribute apart from his huge penis. In north Britain, another type of naked phallic god is figured, but without horns, therefore presumably of the Cerne giant type... A deity of similar type, fierce and aggressively phallic, comes from Maastricht, Holland... A remarkable group of figures from the Caucasian mountains testifies to the widespread cult of ithyphallic deities or heroes in prehistoric Europe as elsewhere... The combination of horned beasts, ithyphallic men and other symbols, together with the close association of a spring and probably a pool, indicate an ancient Caucasian fertility rite somewhere between 1000 and 600 B.C." (Anne Ross, *Primitive Erotic Art*, pp. 83–85.)

The character of Shiva as protector and charmer of animals has often been transferred to other divinities such as Gopâla-Krishna, Pan, Orpheus, and even Jesus, the Good Shepherd.

"All the divinities are called *Pashupâtas* (brothers of the beasts), since they belong to the flock of Pashupati. All those who consider the Lord of the Animals as their god become brothers of the beasts." (*Linga Purâna*, chap. 80, 56–57.) They then become part of the god's flock and receive his teaching.

"Shiva said, 'the most sacred *Pashupâta* Yoga, the Yoga of the brothers of the animals [through which the unity of living beings is realized], and the Sânkhya (Cosmology) [explaining the structure of the world] were taught by me... Knowing that the things of this world are ephemeral, the Yoga of the Lord of the Animals should always be practised'." (*Linga Purâna*, chap. 34, 11–23.)

The modern conception of ecology may appear as an attempt to return to a true ethic, even though it may be anthropocentric. It is not only a question of preserving nature for the service of mankind, but rather of rediscovering man's rôle in nature, as a co-operator in the work of the gods. A religion which does not respect the indissoluble oneness of creation, and which is not fundamentally ecological, is nothing but a fraud. It serves as an excuse for human depradations, and cannot claim to have any divine origin. Man is but one element of the whole, and it is the whole which is the work of God.

The forest spirit, the lustful and naked god
The identification of god and man with nature implies nakedness. Man was born naked. Only the hypocritical and pharisaical religion of the city requires man to be clothed. Shiva is naked. The Shivaite sage and monk wander through the world naked and without ties. In India, nakedness is synonymous with freedom, virtue, truth and holiness. The ancient atheist religion of India, Jainism, which was in other respects the rival of Shivaism, also required nakedness of its followers. The Greek world was familiar with the gymnosophists, the naked ascetics from India, and the soldiers of Alexander who in India wished to follow the philosophers' teachings also had to go naked. Nakedness has a magic and sacred value. "Sow naked, plough naked, reap naked, if you wish in due time to accomplish all the works of Demeter, so that each of her fruits will grow for you also in due time." (Hesiod, *Works and Days*, pp. 390–395.)

"Ritual nakedness is... well-known and widespread in early religions, and many examples of it occur in the Celtic literatures. In the Irish mythological story, 'The Destruction of Da Derga's Hostel'. ... [the king's] bird-father told him...: 'A man stark naked, who shall go at the end of the night along one of the roads of Tara, having a sling and a stone, he shall be king'." (A. Ross, *Primitive Erotic Art*, p. 81.)

Dionysus is also represented naked with long hair, when he does not wear the saffron-coloured monastic robe. "The gods and sages were created naked. The other human beings were also created naked." (*Linga Purâna*, I, chap. 34, 13.) The Purâna legends portray

Shiva as a libidinous adolescent roaming naked in the forest, charming the wives of the proud ascetics who wish to conquer heaven by their will-power. Shiva humiliates the ascetics, seduces their wives and, scattering his seed here and there, makes precious stones and holy places appear on the earth.

"On the mountain there is a wonderful forest called the forest of Dâru, where many sages live... Shiva himself, assuming a strange form, came there to put their faith to the test. He was magnificent, completely naked, his only ornament the ash with which his whole body was smeared. Walking about, holding his penis in his hand, he showed off with the most depraved tricks." (*Shiva Purâna, Koti Rudra Samhitâ*, chap. 12, 6–10.)

"The lord appeared as a man of low extraction. He waved a flaming brand in his hands. His eyes were red and brown. Sometimes he laughed violently; sometimes he sang in an astonishing manner. Sometimes he danced lasciviously; sometimes he uttered cries. He wandered around the hermitages like a beggar. Despite the dark colour of his skin, his beauty was astounding. He laughed and sang, threw winks which seduced the women. He, who had vanquished the god of Love, inspired desire by his beauty alone. Despite his strange appearance and tanned colour, the most chaste women were attracted to him." (*Linga Purâna*, 1, chap. 29, 7, 10, 12 and chap. 31, 28–32.)

"It was in order to make sport of those who lived in the forest that Shiva came personally to these woods. Some of the sages' wives were frightened at the sight of him; other women, amazed and excited, drew near to the lord. Some embraced him, others grasped his hands. They argued amongst themselves in order to touch him." (*Shiva Purâna, Kothi Rudra Samhitâ*, chap. 12, 9.) "At his smile, those women who were in front of their huts in the forest, or who dwelt high in the trees, left their tasks. They rent their clothes and let their hair fall loose. Some rolled on the ground. They clung to each other and, barring Rudra's path, they made wanton gestures at him, even in the presence of their husbands. The Lord Rudra said nothing to them, neither good nor bad." (*Linga Purâna*, 1, chap. 29, 7–9.) Here we find the same behaviour as that of the Maenads, and the name of Gynaimanes (He who maddens the women), which was given to Dionysus. "In the meantime, the great sages arrived. They were shocked to see the god abandon himself in obscene acts. Scandalized, they cried, 'Who is this?', 'Who is this?' But the naked one gave them no reply." (*Shiva Purâna, Kothi Rudra Samhitâ*, chap. 12, 14.)

"The priests and sages used indignant language, but the power of their virtue could not prevail against Rudra, just as the brightness of the stars cannot prevail against the light of the sun." *Linga Purâna*, I, 29, 9, 24.) "The sages cried, 'This Shiva who carries a trident has a body of ill omen. He has no modesty. He has neither dwelling nor known ancestors. He is naked and ill-made. He lives in the company of evil spirits and wicked goblins . . . If he had money, he would not go naked. He rides on a bull and has no other conveyance. His caste is unknown; he is neither a scholar nor a sage. He has only evil spirits for a retinue. He has poison even in his neck. Compare your necklaces to the garland of skulls he wears, your unguents to the ash of the funeral pyre with which he smears his body'." (*Shiva Purâna, Rudra Samhitâ*, chap. 24, 45–47, and chap. 27, 36.)

The "Linga", principle of life

Shiva's symbol is the *Linga*, or phallus. The penis is, in fact, the mysterious organ by which the creative principle manifests itself in giving life to a new creature. It is thus the organ by which the creative principle is visibly represented in a particular species. The sperm, which potentially contains the whole of ancestral and racial heritage and the genetic characteristics of the future human being, is called *bindu* (limit point). It is, in fact, the infinitesimal and mysterious transition between non-existence and existence. The penis is therefore the organ through which a link is established between man (or animal, or flower) and the creative force which is the nature of the divine. It is the most perfect example of a symbol.

"Shiva said, 'I am not distinct from the phallus. The phallus is identical with me. It draws my faithful to me, and therefore must be worshipped. My well-beloved! Wherever there is an upright male organ, I myself am present, even if there is no other representation of me'." (*Shiva Purâna, Vidyeshvara Samhitâ*, I, chap. 9, 43–44.) "The basis of the entire world is the phallus. Everything is born of the *Linga*. He who desires perfection of soul must worship the *Linga*." (*Linga Purâna*, I, chap. 3, 7.) "The Lord is the source of all enjoyment . . . For existence to be a perpetual joy, the follower must worship the phallus which is the god Shiva himself, the sun which gives birth to the world and upholds it. It is the symbol of the origin of all things. Shiva, the origin of all things, should be worshipped in the form of the phallus, through which the male principle is recognizable. The phallus is thus the symbol of the god." (*Shiva Purâna, Vidyeshvara*

Samhitâ, I, chap. 16, 103–106.) Wherever the cult of Shiva has spread, the phallic emblem and the cult of the phallus play an essential rôle.

The veneration of the phallus is found in the Mediterranean and north of the Western World since prehistory, and in the Dionysiac cult up to the sixth century A.D. In Greece, it played an important part in the ceremonies in honour of Dionysus. In Egypt, special honours were given to the sexual organs of the dismembered Osiris. The veneration of the holy foreskin of Christ, still practised in Italy, may be a survival of this ancient cult.

Everything in living human beings or animals, as in plants, is centred on the procreative organ. Man is only a "phallus-bearer" (*Linga-dhara*), the servant of his sexual organ. The notion of a father-god is a puritan transposition of the notion of the *Linga*. The father is in fact the one whose sexual organ discharges seed into the receptacle, the *arghia* or vagina.

According to the Shivaite concept, pleasure is the image of the divine state. This is why, when the god is shown in his procreative aspect, he is also shown under the aspect of pleasure. The sexual organ has therefore a double rôle: the lesser rôle of procreation, and the higher rôle by which it becomes a means of contact with the divine state, the ecstasy of sensual pleasure (*ânanda*). Sensual enjoyment is a "sensation of the divine". While paternity ties man to the things of the earth, the ecstasy of pleasure can reveal divine reality to him, and lead him to detachment and spiritual realization. "The phallus is the source of pleasure. It is the only means of obtaining earthly pleasure and salvation. By looking at it, touching it and meditating on it, living beings can free themselves from the cycle of future lives." (*Shiva Purâna, Vidyeshvara Samhitâ*, I, chap. 9, 20.)

From the point of view of Shivaite mysticism, as is also the case with Dionysiac orgiasm, erotic ecstasy is not a means of reproduction, but purely a seeking after pleasure. "In order to please the Lord, his symbol must be venerated, independently of its physical function. Its function being to give birth, giving birth is excluded." (*Shiva Purâna, Vidyeshvara Samhitâ*, I, chap. 16, 108.)

The union of Shiva and his lover, Shakti, Pârvâti, or Sati, is not procreative. The children of the one and the other are begotten separately. Skanda, the god of Beauty and head of the gods' army, was born of the sperm of Shiva falling into the mouth of the sacrificial fire and from there into the waters of the Ganges. Ganapati, the elephant-headed god who is worshipped before undertaking any enterprise and who protects the entrance of the home, is the son of the goddess, formed from fragments of her skin which fell as she was bathing.

"The *Linga* is an outward sign, or symbol." However, the *Linga* must be considered as being of two sorts, external and internal. The material organ is external, the subtle organ internal. Simple people worship the external *Linga* and carry out rites and sacrifices. The purpose of the phallic image is to stir the faithful to knowledge. The intangible *Linga* is not perceived by those who only see external things; the subtle and eternal *Linga* is only perceptible to those who have attained knowledge." (*Linga Purâna*, I, chap. 75, 19–22.) "Those who practise ritual sacrifice and habitually worship the physical *Linga* are not capable of controlling their mental activity in meditating on its subtle aspect... Those who are not yet conscious of the mental, or subtle sexual organ, must worship the physical sexual organ, and not the contrary." (*Shiva Purâna, Rudra Sambitâ*, I, chap. 12, 51–52.)

The *Linga* is worshipped in the form of an upright stone (sailaja), or on an ithyphallic image of the god. It is also represented inserted in the *Yoni*, or female organ, and it is in this form that it appears in the sanctuary of the Shivaite temple. The word *Linga* simply means "distinctive sign". The god's presence is sometimes felt in apparently formless objects, which are then considered as *Lingas*. This is the case of the rough stone, adored under the name of Eros, which Pausanias (IX, chap. 27, p. 1) saw at Thespies. It is also the case of the Black Stone at Mecca, the Makheshvara of the ancient Hindus. In the grotto of Amarnâtha in Kashmir, there is a pillar of ice, which is venerated as a self-born (*svayambhu*) *Linga*, a direct manifestation of the god.

The *Linga* is sometimes simply in the form of a pillar, as found almost everywhere in the world. At Knossos, as at Thebes or Malta, the god was honoured in the form of a column. Orthos, the "Erect", represents Dionysus the Pillar or Priapic-Dionysus. Shiva is *urdhva-linga*, "of the erect sex". He is called Sthanu (Column), as Dionysus is called Perikionios ("of the Column"). The ancient Xoanon was the pillar-idol of the mistress of the Heraion. According to Evans, Minoan pillars are non-figurative images of the god.

"Agyieus was defined... as a pointed or a conical pillar... For Hesychios, Agyieus was 'the pillar-shaped altar, standing before the doors'... Agyieus worship, predominantly but not exclusively associated with Apollo, developed out of the cult of the Agyieus-pillar... and was thus fused with the Minoan pillar-worship... The omphalos persists in association with Apollo in the Cretan coinage. There is even some evidence to suggest that the cult of the sacred stone side by side with the cult of the guardian of gates and ways, which formed the essence of the conception of Agyieus in ancient Greece, was paralleled at an earlier date in Anatolia in a way which confirms the Oriental origin of Apollo... Although the epithet [of Agyieus] was normally regarded as proper to Apollo, it was sometimes associated with Dionysus and Zeus. This... indicates that the cult of the pillar antedates the association with Apollo." (R. F. Willetts, *Cretan Cults and Festivals*, pp. 259–260.) In Etruscan tombs, the phallus is the symbol for a man, and the house that for a woman.

The raising of a stone phallus is a meritorious act. It should be raised preferably in isolated places or on mountains. The ancient sanctuaries of Shiva, like those of Dionysus, are usually found outside cities.

The same is true of the megaliths found in England, Brittany, Corsica, and all over the world, from India to the extreme west. Although there is very little information concerning the megalithic monuments of the West, Hindu texts contain the entire ritual for setting them up, and for the orientation of sanctuaries, etc. All studies on European prehistoric religions should thus be based on the Indian documents available.

"The sexual significance of the menhirs is universally vouched for... Belief in the fertilizing virtue of the menhirs was still held by European peasants at the beginning of the century... Megalithic complexes must have been derived from a single centre, very probably in the Eastern Mediterranean... connected with Tantrism... Stonehenge (before 2100) is pre-Mycenaean." (Mircea Eliade, *Histoire des croyances et des idées religieuses*, pp. 130 and 135.)

Erect phalli with a face are found throughout the Western world, in Greece and also India. The Celts raised phallic-shaped stones surmounted by a human head or with a face carved on the glans. The "face of glory" (*kirti-mukha*), placed above the sanctuary of the Shivaite temple, is an elaborate form of the same symbol: the whole universe issuing from the mouth of the "face of glory" at the summit of the phallic tower.

In certain images, an entire person appears to be embedded in the phallic column. In the South of India, the *gundimallam-linga*, from which a human form stands out, and which dates from the second century B.C., is still worshipped. Similar statues are found up to the time of Medieval Europe.

Shivaites wear a small *Linga* around their neck, as did the ancient Romans. Numerous examples of these can be seen at Pompei. In India, a stone *Linga* is worshipped in each household. Large wooden phalli are carried in the processions of the god. Herodotus, speaking of the identity of Dionysus and Osiris, mentions the carrying of phallic emblems in the processions of both gods. The god Priapus reigns over the phallophoria of both gods. Both sexes took part in the erotic songs and orgies. In the agrarian cycle of Athens, phallic- or snake-shaped cakes were baked, whose crumbs were mixed with the seed-corn.

"Until very recently... phallic cakes were baked by German French and Italian peasants at Easter to be carried in procession to the church." (Philip Rawson, *Primitive Erotic Art*, p. 53.) "At Trani, by Naples, a huge wooden phallic image called *Il Santo Membro* was carried in procession annually until the eighteenth century." (*Ibid.* p. 75.)

A phallic meaning has often been attributed to certain objects or animals, thus allowing the sexual organ to be mentioned allegorically following a similar principle to that of not pronouncing the name of the god.

"[From] *c.* 6500–2000 B.C. in Western Europe... the penis becomes plough, axe, dagger and sword: semen the seed, rain, sun snake and bird," [fish and water.] (P. Rawson, *ibid.*, p. 45.)

"Some Greek vases illustrate festivals in which the huge phalli are shaped like fish... [The] relationship between fish and penis can indicate how early established was this analogy, which later became so universal... The winged phalli of ancient Greece... [are] still standing in the sanctuary at Delos... Such phallic birds, imagined either as live cocks (!) or geese... feature large in the folk and erotic art of Europe." (P. Rawson, *ibid.*, pp. 21, 53, 71.) In popular Italian usage, the male organ is frequently called *uccello* (bird) or *pesce* (fish) This is clearly a survival from ritual terminology. Man preserves in his own body certain memories of his own long evolution. He was first a fish, then a bird, and lastly a mammal. This is recalled in certain Tantric rites. In the offering of sperm by masturbatory practices, man is a fish. In initiatory rites involving anal penetration he becomes a bird (the bird is always a symbol of esoteric significance)

In rites of fecundation and sexual union, he is a bull. Some of these aspects will be dealt with in speaking of initiatory rites.

The phallus brings good luck, averts danger and the powers of evil, and also plays an important part in rites of initiation. "In antiquity, in the temples of Egypt and the Greco-Roman world, it was attributed with the ability to inhibit and avert the powers of darkness and demons." (Julius Evola, *Le Yoga tantrique*, p. 112.)

"Those who always worship the Great God under the physical guise of the *Linga* are free from fear, birth and death." (*Linga Purâna*, II, chap. 6, 40.) In India, the image of the *Linga* and representations of sexual coupling protect both temple and house against lightning and other calamities.

"[Figures which were used to conjure sexual potency, strength, and prowess are frequently encountered in the Celtic countries of Europe.] They consist of representations of emphatically phallic men engaged in some activity such as hunting, fishing, sorcery or ball-games... Belonging to the early Romano-British period is the famous chalk-cut figure on the hill above Cerne Abbas, Dorset. Known as the Cerne Abbas giant, this British 'Hercules' with his all-conquering club, like that of the great Irish god the Dagda, and his huge penis and testicles, has survived through the centuries, dominating the surrounding countryside, defying the Church... Young couples, about to be married, still resort to him, and it was believed in the district that to have sexual intercourse within the hollow of the vast phallus could only have beneficial results." (A. Ross, in *Primitive Erotic Art*, pp. 80–82.)

"There are numerous references... in European literature to the fact that... actual human genitals were felt to have a magical power, especially in averting all kinds of misfortune..." (P. Rawson, *Primitive Erotic Art*, p. 76.)

According to common practice still widespread in Mediterranean countries, men touch their sexual organs to avert the evil eye. "Emblems of the male organ, either realistic or purely symbolic, were often planted in their fields by agricultural peoples... In the fields of southern Italy, crude phallic boundary stones survived long into modern times... These were block-like stones with projecting phalli, sometimes also with human heads, which came to be 'named' as Priapus, Hermes, Liber, Tutunus, or Mutunus." (P. Rawson, *Primitive Erotic Art*, pp. 52 and 72.)

In Shivaite texts, the vault of heaven is considered as an immense phallus (*âkâsha Linga*) resting on the earth, which is the female organ, or matrix of the world. Rain is the seed which fertilizes the earth, lightning the orgasm. This symbolism is found in the Celtic religion: "Since the fluid semen came to be identified as the generic cause of fertility... the identification of the sky as male, moistening and fertilizing a female earth... took place in the very early stages of agriculture." (P. Rawson, *Primitive Erotic Art*, p. 50.)

According to the Etruscan History of Italy by Prometheus, quoted by Plutarch, a phallus appeared in the fireplace of the King of the Albani. He commanded his daughter to couple with the phallus, but she refused and sent her maid-servant instead. From the latter were born Romulus and Remus, who were abandoned in the forest and fed by a she-wolf. "In Celtic mythology, the powerful Fergus mac Roich, 'Fergus son of Great Horse', [represents the male principle]. His penis is described as being seven fingers in length; he mates with the great divine queen Mebd, 'Drunk Woman', whose own sexuality is boundless." (Anne Ross, *Primitive Erotic Art*, p. 83.)

In the *Skanda Purâna* (*Kedara Khanda*) and *Shiva Purâna*, the sages curse Shiva, whose sexual organ falls to the ground under the effect of the curse. But immediately, the god's sexual organ becomes an immense pillar which transpierces and fills all the three worlds. "Shocked by the appearance and behaviour of Shiva, the sages of the forest said to him, 'You have acted perversely. That is contrary to the Scriptures. Your sexual organ will fall to the ground'. When they had thus spoken, the sexual organ of this messenger of Heaven, who was none other than Shiva of the marvellous forms, at once fell to the ground. The phallus burned everything before it; wherever it went, all was consumed. It travelled through the under-world, in heaven and on the earth, never staying in one place. All the worlds and their inhabitants lived in anguish. The sages were struck with dismay. The gods and the sages knew neither peace nor pleasure any more." (*Shiva Purâna, Kothi Rudra Samhitâ*, chap. 12, 17–22.) Hesiod's account of the emasculation of phallic heaven (*Theogony*, p. 180) uses the same symbolism.

"Rudra disappeared and the sages betook themselves to the god Brahmâ, who said to them, 'How stupid you are! In a single moment, you have destroyed all the merits acquired by your austerities. The man with the erect sexual organ whom you saw, impotent men that you are, is the Supreme Lord in person'." (*Linga Purâna*, I, chap. 29, 9–25.) "And Brahmâ continued, 'As long as this phallus is not in a fixed position, no good can come to any of the three worlds. In order to calm its wrath, you must sprinkle this divine sexual organ with holy water, build a pedestal in the form of a vagina and shaft (symbol of the goddess), and install it with prayers, offerings, prostrations, hymns and chants accompanied by musical instruments. Then you shall invoke the god, saying, 'You are the source of the universe, the origin of the universe. You are present in everything that exists. The universe is but the form of yourself. O Benevolent One! calm yourself and protect the world'.' The sages therefore reverently approached Shiva who said to them, 'The world shall not find peace until a receptacle is found for my sexual organ. No other being except the Lady of the Mountain may seize hold of my sexual organ. If she takes hold of it, it will immediately become calm'." (*Shiva Purâna, Kothi Rudra Samhitâ*, chap. 12, 22–46.)

The Hermaphrodite (Ardhanarîshvara)

One of the principal aspects of Shiva is the Ardhanarîshvara, the hermaphrodite. In the process of creation, "the power to conceive (*vimarsha*) and the power to fulfil (*prakâsha*), when reunited, are immediately manifested as a limit point (*bindu*), or localization which is the starting point of space and time. From this point starts the vibration or sound (*nâda*) which is the substance of the universe. Space is a female principle, a receptacle, while time is an active, male principle. Their union, symbolized by the divine hermaphrodite, represents the Eros (*Kâma*), the creative impulse." (Karpâtrî, *Shri Shiva tattva*, quoted by Alain Daniélou, *Hindu Polytheism*, p. 205.)

Primordial divinity is essentially bisexual. The division of this principle into two opposing poles which give life to the world is merely apparent. The divine is defined in the Upanishads as "that in which opposites coexist". "When Shiva and Shakti are united, their union is sensual delight. Delight is their reality; their separate existence is only a fiction." (Karpâtrî, *Lingopasanâ rahasya*, quoted in *Hindu Polytheism*, p. 203.)

The reality of the world is therefore seen as sensual delight, the spark produced by the union of opposites. The hermaphrodite, the image of the non-division of opposites, represents sheer sensual delight, which is permanent, absolute, and thus divine nature itself. "Divine bisexuality is one of the many formulae for the totality-unity signified by the union of couples of opposites: masculine-feminine, visible-invisible, heaven-earth, light-darkness, as also goodness-wickedness, creation-destruction, etc." (M. Eliade, *Histoire des croyances et des idées religieuses*, p. 178.)

"The first creation consisted of spirits, goblins, and demons, which issued from the mouth of the uncreated being, like a materialization of its vital breath (*prâna*). Rudra appeared first, shining like the rising sun. He was androgynous... The immensity, seeing this divine hermaphrodite, said to him, 'Divide yourself'. Thus, with the left side of the god was created a goddess, who became his companion. It was she who was later incarnate in the daughter of the priest-king Daksha. Taking the name of Sati (Fidelity), she became the lover of Rudra." (*Linga Purâna*, chap. 41, 41–42, and chap. 99, 15–19.)

Thus, to create a world outside himself, the god divides himself, and the two poles diverge. The state of absolute bliss disappears and is only recreated by the union of opposites, by love. The divine hermaphrodite "divided his body into two halves, the one male, the other female; the male in this female procreated the universe". (*Manu Smriti*, I, 32.)

The Prime Cause may be conceived as masculine or feminine, as a god or a goddess, but in both cases it is an androgynous or transexual being.

According to the Phrygian tradition recounted by Pausanias (VII, chap. 17, 10–12), Papas (Zeus) fertilized a stone phallus named Agdos, which engendered a hermaphrodite being, Agditis. The gods, having castrated Agditis, transformed him into the goddess Cybele who is the equivalent of Pârvatî, the Lady of the Mountains, and the female counterpart of Shiva. Anat, the goddess of the Ugaritic Canaanites, like other goddesses of love and war, is provided with male attributes and is considered bisexual. This is also the case with the Etruscan goddess. The Hurrite god Kumarbi is bisexual, as are the Akkadian gods Tiamat and Zarvan. The Hittite Teshub is the son of the celestial god Anu and is also an androgynous divinity. The statues of hermaphrodite and ithyphallic divinities are found in all parts of the world, beginning from the Neolithic Age. The carved wooden image found in Somerset, England, is a typical example.

All degrees of bisexuality appear in the various aspects of the god: virile in his terrible form, effeminate in his happy and benevolent aspects. In the same way, the goddess appears virile and aggressive as Bhairavî or Kâlî, the power of destruction. In this case, she plays the active rôle in her relations with Shiva, with whom she practises *Viparita maithuna*, inverse copulation. On the other hand, the goddess is feminine, modest and gentle in her rôle as Lady of the Mountain (Pârvatî) or Sati (Fidelity).

The same is true of Dionysus, sometimes shown as a bearded male in the strength of his maturity, and sometimes as an effeminate adolescent. "When the time was up, Zeus undid the stitches in his thigh and gave birth to Dionysus, whom he entrusted to Hermes and sent to Ino and Athanas, charging them to raise him as a girl." (Apollodorus, *Bibliotheke*, III, IV, 3.) When captured by a barbarian king, Dionysus is jeered at by him for his feminine appearance. According to Nicander, it was in the form of a girl that Dionysus warned the Minyads, who were excessively hard-working and virtuous, not to neglect his rites of initiation. In one of the texts of Aeschylus (fragment 61), the king shouts when he sees him, "'Where do you come from, man-woman, and where is your homeland? What clothing is this?' He takes from him the clothes symbolizing his double nature: the saffron veil, the girdle, and the golden *mitre*. He strips him naked, and although he is not deprived of his virility, he is too frail to put it to good account." Heracles, the most virile of heroes, changes clothes with Omphale. Arjuna, the valorous prince of the Mahâbhârata, during his exile, disguised himself as a eunuch and teaches music and dancing to the daughter of King Virata.

In the myth mentioned by Aristophanes and taken up by Plato in *The Symposium*, the first men were androgynous. In order to punish them for having rebelled against him, Zeus divided them in two. Likewise, according to the Purânas, the first men were sages who were still close to the divine and who engendered sons by a sort of mental projection. It was to destroy their power, which threatened that of the celestial beings, that God created woman and reproduction by means of the union of the sexes. In Genesis, the creation of woman from Adam's rib implicates androgyny in original man created in the image of the divine hermaphrodite.

Like Shiva, the first man (Adam) was male on his right side and female on his left. All Tantric rites in which women take part are known as Left-Hand rites. The left side is considered the weak side of man, reserved for humble or unclean tasks. It is for this reason that the left hand is never proferred. To offer something with the left hand is a sign of contempt. The circumambulation of a god's statue must be performed keeping it always to the right, i.e., clockwise. In Tantric magic when the feminine aspect of the god is invoked, this is performed in an anti-clockwise direction. The hermaphrodite, the homosexual, and the transvestite have a symbolic value and are considered privileged beings, images of the *Ardhanarishvara*. In this connection, they play a special part in magical and Tantric rites, as they do also in Shamanism. "The final goal of Tantrism is to reunite the two polar principles, Shiva and Shakti, in one's own body... Initiatory androgyny does not always involve an operation, as with the Australian aborigines. In many cases, it is suggested by disguising boys as girls, and, vice versa, girls as boys... Homosexual practices, as borne out by several types of initiation, can probably be explained by a similar belief: that the neophytes, during their initiatory instruction, combine the two sexes." (M. Eliade, *Méphistophélès et l'Androgyne*, pp. 139 and 149.)

With Shamans, divinatory power is connected with bisexuality. With the ritual gesture of *Anasyrma*, the magician, dressed as a woman, raises his robes to expose his sexual organ, thus appearing as a hermaphrodite. The Etruscan prophetess wore a phallus attached to her girdle. In the mysteries of Hercules Victor, in Italy, both the god and the initiates were dressed as women. Transvestism in Roman cults was intended to promote health, youth, vigour, and long life.

"In Siberian Shamanism, the Shaman symbolically combines the two sexes... the Shaman behaves as a woman, wears female clothing, and sometimes even takes a husband. This ritual bisexuality – or asexuality – is considered to be, at the same time, a sign of spirituality, of dealings with the gods and spirits, as well as a source of sacred power... The Shaman symbolically restores the unity of heaven and earth, and, as a consequence, assures communication between gods and men. Such bisexuality is lived ritually and ecstatically, and is assumed to be an indispensable condition for overcoming the status of profane men... Siberian and Indonesian Shamans reverse their sexual behaviour in order to live *in concreto* their ritual androgyny." (M. Eliade, *Méphistophélès et l'Adrogyne*, pp. 144–145.)

In Greece, in a very extreme rite, the servants of Attis and Rhea mutilated themselves and laid their sexual organs before the altar of the gods. "It is not possible to become a sexually adult male without having known the coexistence of the two sexes, which is androgyny; in other words, a particular and well-defined mode of being cannot be reached before having known the complete mode of being." (M. Eliade, *ibid.*, p. 138.)

The goal of the human race is thus the progressive reintegration of the sexes until adrogyny is achieved, more evolved human beings tending towards bisexuality. According to recent research on the brain, it appears that the intuitive, sensitive and receptive element in man is connected with the left side (the feminine side, corresponding to the right half of the brain); the logical, active, aggressive, male element is connected with the right side (the brain's left side). In the bisexual being, communication between the two sides of the brain is especially developed. This is why the creative artist is often bisexual, as is the magus, or medium, whence the rôle of so-called "inverts" in magical rites and the importance given to left-hand rites in Trantric practices. The myth of the divine hermaphrodite is symbolically represented by the Phoenix which recreates itself, thus representing Immortality. When Christianity was established in Rome, the Phoenix became associated with the person of Christ. When the Universe is reabsorbed, the two opposing principles will be reunited and the hermaphrodite will be restored, first of all in the creatures, and then in the godhead itself.

Vishnu and Apollo

In Indian cosmology, the explosive centrifugal force which gave birth to the universe is called Shiva; the contrary cohesive force, a centripetal force permitting the formation of the solar systems and stars, is called Shakti (Energy). This opposition is found in all aspects of existence, either in matter or life. In Aryanized Indian or Mycenaean Shivaism, Vishnu-Apollo gradually took the place of the goddess in a relatively ancient period. He is a masculine representation of the principle which Shivaite cosmology considers as feminine. He is often represented under a graceful and youthful form, and sometimes transforms himself into a woman. But, like the goddess, he can also have terrible aspects, like that of the man-lion. It is he who becomes incarnate to protect both world and city from destruction. Vishnu is the conservative principle, inseparable from and yet opposed to Shiva. His cult is easily acceptable to the religious concepts of the city, which tries to dissimulate its own malpractices under the guise of sentimental piety. His cult is the one preferred by women and merchants attached to material goods.

In the Greek world, Apollo appears as the brother and counterpart of Dionysus. "Dionysus, who concentrates all contradictions within himself, is the same as Apollo, who is his contrary." (Giorgio Colli, *La Sapienza greca*, p. 25.) The contrasts and affinities between Apollo and Dionysus recall those of Vishnu and Shiva. In rites, Apollo replaces the goddess. The serpent Python, which guarded the Delphic sanctuary, was killed by Apollo, who appropriated the oracle of the earth-goddess, herself similar to the Minoan goddess. This myth symbolizes the change-over from a feminine to a masculine represent- ation of the principle of protection and cohesion in the Mycenaean religion in which male gods predominate.

The opposition and complementarity of the cults of Shiva and Vishnu, as well as the interchangeability of Vishnu and the goddess, appear very early in Aryanized Shivaism as also in Creto-Mycenaean religion. The temple of Pythian Apollo at Gortyna in Crete is extremely ancient. The cult of Apollo probably came to Crete from Asia Minor. In the Greek world, the god was attributed with a Lydian origin.

In Dionysus' absence, Apollo reigns at Delphi as master of the oracle. In Greece, the male god Apollo replaced the goddess in a great number of sanctuaries.

Orpheus is the priest of Apollo, and even called his son. He also shares the Apollonian ambiguity, and is sometimes considered homo- sexual. In a Neoplatonic text quoted by Colli (*La Sapienza greca*, p. 233), "Orpheus died torn apart by the women of Thrace and Macedonia because he had forbidden them to take part in the secret rites, but also for another reason. It is said . . . that he held the whole female race in abhorrence . . . The women, driven by anger at his contempt for them, killed all those who tried to shun them and cut Orpheus into pieces which they threw into the sea." Phanes, who is an invention of Orphic poetry, is also a god who is at the same time both male and female. According to Nonno Abate (quoted by Colli, *ibid.*, p. 257), Phanes' sexual organs were in the same place as his anus.

In the form of the Enchantress (Mohini), Vishnu assumes his feminine aspect to seduce Shiva. "One day, Shiva, with his marvellous games, caught a glimpse of Vishnu who had taken the form of the enchantress Mohini of dazzling beauty. Struck by the arrows of Eros, Shiva let his sperm spurt out . . . The seven sages gathered his seed on a leaf and poured it into the ear of Anjani, the daughter of Gautama. She became pregnant, and thus Shiva was incarnate in the form of the monkey Hanuman, renowned for his strength and his exploits." (*Shiva Purâna, Shatarudra Samhitâ*, chap. 20, 3–7.) It was also in female form that Vishnu seduced the Titans, the Asuras, and stole from them the nectar they had seized, thus depriving them of Immortality.

According to the Tamil *Kanda purânam*, "The hermits of the Târuka forest, who were hostile to the lord, practised austerities and made sacrifices in order to conquer heaven. Shiva went to Târuka accompanied by Vishnu whom he commanded to take the form of a courtesan, which he had already done on another occasion in order to seduce him. He himself took the form of a splendid naked boy. In his hands he carried a trident and a beggar's bowl. When they reached the forest, he told Mâl (Vishnu) to go and seduce the hermits and discourage them from their austerities. At the sight of the courtesan, the hermits fell in love with her. They abandoned their ascetic practices and followed her everywhere she went. The ardour of desire made them lose all dignity. Meanwhile, Shiva, disguised as a beggar, walked in front of the dwellings of the hermits' wives, singing hymns. The women came out and were excited on seeing him. Beside themselves, they let themselves be stripped of their clothing, and their bracelets slid from their arms. The beggar wandered from one house to another. The women followed him and lost their chastity... The courtesan, followed by the hermits, and the beggar accompanied by their wives, met in the forest. The hermits, seeing their wives half-naked, unashamedly accompanying a beggar, were astonished. They took council together and finally realized that the beggar and the courtesan, who in the meantime had disappeared, were none other than Shiva and Vishnu, and that Shiva was the cause of their misadventure. Having lectured their wives, they sent them back to their dwellings... However, the hermits were furious with Shiva and sought some way of killing him. They offered up a great sacrifice. From the centre of the sacrifice there came a furious tiger which they commanded to go and kill the lord. The tiger, roaring ferociously, sprang upon the god, who seized and killed it, tearing off its skin for a garment. From the fire there came a trident, which the god seized, then an antelope, which he took with his left hand, and snakes which he used to adorn his head-dress. A Lord of demons then appeared who sprang at 'Him who gives peace' (Shankara). With a movement of his hand, Shiva calmed their fury and commanded them to form an army in his service. They obeyed him. Then a death's head appeared which the hermits threw at Shiva. He seized it and placed it in his hair. The ascetics of the Târuka forest, outraged at being baulked, then tried their magic spells. These united and took the form of a terrifying sound issuing from a horn. The god seized the horn and kept it in his hand. The ascetics then offered a new sacrifice, from which came a powerful spirit called Muyalakan (Epilepsy). They commanded it, and the fire, to go and kill the god. The god seized the fire in his hand, threw the spirit on the ground and stood on its back.

"The hermits shouted curses at Shiva. None of them was efficacious. Muyalakan, crushed by the master's feet, struggled and turned his head from side to side. The god began to dance on him. The whole universe trembled. When the dance ceased, the hermits of Târuka prostrated themselves at the god's feet and sang his praises. He commanded them henceforth to practise the rites of his cult and to continue their lives of austerity. After this, he set out again for his white mountain covered with snow." (Tamil *Kanda purânam*, II, chap. 13, 30–127.)

In another passage of the *Kanda purânam* (II, chap. 32), "Vishnu, in the form of the Enchantress (Mohini), had gone to rest by the ocean of milk. Shiva wished to show the world that Vishnu was merely one of his four wives. He approached him and manifested his desire to unite with him. The illusory woman tried to refuse, saying that a union between persons of the same sex was unfruitful. The lord made him admit that he was only the incarnation of one of his powers and that it was for this reason that he had already been able to give birth to Brahmâ (the god of Space) and to take the form of a woman in the Târuka forest.

"As Vishnu remained stubborn, the lord took him in his arms and brought him to the shade of a *châlam* tree by the side of the sea, to the north of the continent of the rose-apple tree. There he united with him, still in the form of the Enchantress. The sap which they spilled was transformed into a river which took the name of Ganges... From the union of the Lord and the dark-skinned god was born a child with a black body and red hair, carrying a bouquet in his hand. The three-eyed god gave him the name of Son of Shiva-Vishnu (Arikaraputtiran). He granted him many gifts... He also granted him the sovereignty of one of the worlds... When Arikaraputtiran appeared before the king of heaven (Indra), seated on a white elephant and surrounded by Shiva's rogues, Indra prostrated himself before him." (*Kanda purânam*, II, chap. 32, 27–60.)

At the end of the world, Vishnu will fall asleep. The cohesive force will cease to function, and the universe, from atom to galaxies, will dissolve.

The God of the humble

Shiva, the god of the pre-Aryan populations, remained their favourite divinity, even after they were subjected and reduced to the status of working castes in a world dominated by the Aryan invaders. The *Hymn to the Hundred Rudras* in the *Vâjaseneyî Samhitâ* (*Yajur Veda*, chap. 16, 1) invokes him as the patron of artisans, cartwrights, carpenters, smiths, potters, hunters, water-carriers and foresters. He is the god of soldiers, mercenaries, and intrepid charioteers. He is the chief of thieves and plunderers. Skanda, Shiva's son, is also the god of thieves, as mentioned in Shudraka's poem, *The Small Terracotta Wagon*. A treatise on the art of Stealing, the *Sanmukhakalpa* ("Manual of the six-faced god"), is attributed to Skanda. Shiva is also the god of the *vratyas*, the begging and wanderings ascetics (see P. Banerjee, *Early Indian Religions*, p. 41.) "In Shivaism, transcendency in relation to the norms of ordinary life is illustrated at a popular level by the fact that Shiva, amongst others, is represented as the god or 'patron' of those who do not lead a normal life, and even of outlaws." (Julius Evola, *Le Yoga tantrique*, p. 91).

As the god of the humble, Shiva's teachings are addressed to all mankind. The Brahmanic texts reproach him with having taught the lower classes the secrets of mythology, rites, and the highest knowledge, and with having opened to them the ways of initiation. The *Shatapatha Brâhmana* (V, chap. 3, 2) mentions the *shudras* or artisans as participants at the sacrifices of Shiva and at the *soma*, the sacred drink representing the god's sperm. Even today, in the most important Shivaite sanctuaries, the cult is performed alternately by Aryan Brahman priests and *shudra* worker-priests. Thus, a non-Aryan priesthood has survived through the centuries, despite four thousand years of Aryan domination. "In Mahratta country where Shivaites greatly prevail, the Brâhmanas do not officiate in the Linga temples. There is a caste separate for that known as Gurava, a distinct order of men being originally of Shudra [non-Aryan] stock." (P. Banerjee, *Early Indian Religions*, p. 41). The traditions of these non-Aryan priests are little known in the Hindu world which is dominated by the Aryan or Aryanized high castes. It appears that no modern research has been carried out on this subject.

The festivals of Shiva are always those of the humble classes. At Holi, the Spring festival, corresponding to the Dionysia and still surviving as carnivals, the artisans and servants have the right to insult and ill-treat their masters, the nobles and priests, which they do with an abundance of abuse and obscenity, as do also the Ganas, Shiva's rogues, to the gods, the sages and Brahmans. This aspect will be dealt with later on, in examining Shivaite festivals.

The Healer

As god of the vegetable world, Rudra-Shiva knows all remedies. He is described as the greatest of physicians (*Rig Veda*, I, 43, 4; I, 114, 5; II, 33, 2, 4, 7, 12, 13, etc.) Poisons are at his disposal, but he himself does not fear them. When the gods and Titans gave birth to the world by churning the cosmic ocean, nectar came out, but also poison. Shiva drank the poison in order to protect the world. The poison remained in the god's neck, which became blue. This is why Shiva is also called the blue-necked god (*nîlakanta*). Medicine heals through the prudent use of poisons. The snake is the carrier of the most virulent types of poison, and forms the necklace of Shiva, who is always associated with snakes. This aspect of the god is also found in Asclepios. "The cult of Asklepios deserves special notice among the historical cults of Crete... The snake, which is the constant companion of Asklepios, represents a familiar element of continuity with a much earlier phase of Cretan religion, as we recall the prominence of the Minoan snake-cult... The respect shown to the Asklepios cult..., with its... miracle cures and genuine medical lore,... [was so great] that in the late pagan period, this god was looked upon as the chief opponent of Christ." (R. F. Willetts, *Cretan Cults and Festivals*, p. 224).

We shall deal later with the snake-goddess cult.

The caduceus of Mercury, entwined with two snakes, is the symbol of modern medical services.

The sovereign of the directions of space

Shiva is the sovereign of the universe. His various aspects are connected with the gods who reign over the directions of space, to whom an important symbolism is attributed, as well as a direct influence on life. The symbolism of the directions of space is found in Crete, Egypt, in the megalithic cultures, in Greek and Roman religion, and up to the Christian Middle Ages. It plays an essential rôle in the orientation of sanctuaries, Yoga positions, and the position of participants in ritual ceremonies.

The *Atharva Veda* and *Brâhmanas* mention the aspects of the god who rules the directions of space (see P. Banerjee, *Early Indian*

Religions, p. 30).

As Bhava (the Origin of things), Shiva rules over the East, the direction of beauty and of the sun. He protects the *vrâtyas* (the humble, the wanderers, the excommunicated, the excluded).

As Sharva (the Archer), he rules over the South, the direction of death and of the ancestors. He is the lord of ghosts, the king of the infernal regions.

As Pashupati (Lord of the Animals), he rules over the West, direction of the night, of magic and celestial waters. He is the god of Forests.

As Ugra (the Terrible), he rules the North, the direction of the moon, where the intoxicating cup of *soma* is to be found. He is the god of Inebriety and Wine.

As Rudra (Lord of Tears) or Agni (the Fire), he rules over the nether regions, the world of Titans and demons.

As Ishâna (the Supreme Sovereign), he rules over the vault of heaven and the gods. He is the god of love.

Rudra (the Howler), Sharva (the Archer), Ugra (the Terrible) and Asani (the Thunderbolt) are the destructive aspects of Shiva, whilst Bhava (the Source), Pashupati (Lord of the Animals), Mahâdeva (the Great God) and Ishâna (the Sovereign) are his benevolent aspects.

In dealing with rites, we shall see the importance of the proper placing of the participants. Orientation must be strictly observed in all architecture, whether sanctuaries, temples, or individual houses, as well as in the planning of towns. Temples dedicated to the beneficent aspects of the gods, always open to the East. The West is the direction of magic rites, the South, the direction of the dead and of tombs (cf. the Appian Way in Rome). Even inside the house, the use to which rooms are put is determined by their orientation: rooms destined for the kitchen, the bathroom, for eating, meeting or sleeping. The "love room", under the sign of Ishâna (the Zenith), is built on terraces on top of the house.[1]

For practising Yoga and performing beneficent rites, one must always face East. The rules of orientation were observed for Christian sanctuaries up to the end of the Middle Ages. The recent change of the priest's position during the Catholic mass should, in principle, make the rite maleficent.

---

[1] For a more detailed explanation of the significance of the directions of space, see *Le Temple hindou* by A. Daniélou.

The God of Death

Everything which is born must die. The principle of life is thus associated with time, which is to say, with the principle of death. The creator god is also a destroyer god. Life feeds on death. Nothing can live, save by the destruction and devouring of other lives. Thus Shiva also has a terrifying aspect (Bhairava). He is called Kâla or Kronos (Time), or Rudra, the Lord of Tears. To flatter him, he is called by the euphemism Aghora (Not-Terrible). Under this aspect, "He has three eyes. His crown is made of a serpent. He is covered with rich jewels. His face is covered with the ash of funeral pyres. He is accompanied by ghosts, gnomes, evil spirits, witches and demons. He is clothed with an elephant's skin. He adorns himself with snakes and scorpions. His voice resounds like thunder on a stormy day. He looks like a mountain of dark-blue kohl or eye-black. A lion skin is on his shoulder. He is terrifying. His statue is erected near funeral pyres or in cemeteries." (*Linga Purâna*, II, chap. 50, 23–26.)

The members of certain Shivaite sects of wandering monks imitate the god, living naked, their bodies smeared with ash, their unkempt hair bleached with lime. They practise meditation on the places of cremation. "Shiva is the destroyer. He likes cremation grounds. But what does he destroy? Not merely the heavens and the earth at the end of the cycle, but the chains that bind the individual soul. What *is* the cremation ground? It is not the place where the mortal remains are burnt, but the heart of his faithful reduced to a desert. The place where the ego is destroyed represents the state where illusion and action are reduced to ashes. It is there that the Nalarâja dances." (see A. Coomaraswany, *The Dance of Shiva*.)

Shiva is called Mahâkâla, the Time of time, the Great Destroyer. He is worshipped especially under the aspect of his manifested energy, Kâlî, who is the "Power of time", the terrible goddess. Shiva is always present at the funeral pyre. He reigns over the subterranean world of the dead. Like him, "Dionysus is a chthonian deity..., a subterranean god who reveals himself during the winter period or perhaps at the time when the souls of the dead return... It is to this god that the sepulchre is appropriate, the sepulchre whose presence we find in the sanctuaries of a god who has a horror of contact with death... He rules over the night, since, during the day, the sun is called Apollo, but during the night, Dionysus." (H. Jeanmaire, *Dionysos*, pp. 195–196.) In the same way, Osiris ruled over the world of the dead.

Dionysus is *nyktipolos*, "the night prowler". Shiva too is called Nishichâra (night prowler). He holds a severed head in his hand, and wears a necklace of skulls.

Ash and the saffron-coloured garment

Ash represents the remains of a world destroyed, especially the ash of funeral pyres. Only Shiva exists beyond death. He is "clothed with ashes", his body is smeared with ash. It is from ash that a new world will be born. All new life is born from a life destroyed. Shiva said, "My seed, my creative power, is nourished on the ashes of what has been destroyed. This is why ash protects. In the hour of danger, but even when asleep, under shelter, or in a house, ash will protect you. He who has purified himself by rubbing himself with ashes, who has overcome violence and the impulse of his senses, will no longer regress after coming to me." (*Linga Purâna*, chap. 34, 8–10.)

The followers of the god smear their bodies with ash as a sign of detachment, since for them the illusory world of appearances is already destroyed. Sometimes they also use whitewash as a symbol of ash. "Purification, *Catharmos*, consists of rubbing the new member's body with a coating of clay and flour, substances which are attributed, perhaps due to their whiteness, with a symbolic value. The initiation period which, according to Aristophanes, signifies the reception by Socrates of a new disciple, confirms this kind of ablution." (H. Jeanmaire, *Dionysos*, p. 96.) In India, the actors playing the part of the god in Shivaite processions, cover their body with plaster or ash. Only extremist sects of comparatively recent origin use ashes from funeral pyres. In ancient times, the Shivaites did not burn their dead.

In India, the colour of mourning is saffron, as it is also in the Celtic world. When not naked, the garment of Shivaite monks is saffron-coloured. This practice was taken over by the Buddhist monks. A saffron-coloured robe is also attributed to Dionysus. When black became the colour of mourning in the Christian world, priests wore a black robe, since they are, to the worldly view, living-dead.

Saffron or ochre is the colour which is sacred to Shiva. "The wide-spread practice of smearing adepts or people with red ochre is a symbol of the renewal of life. In tombs of the higher Palaeolithic, the bones of the dead are smeared with red ochres." (see F. C. Hawkes, *The Prehistoric Foundations of Europe*.)

Chapter 3

THE GODDESS:

power, lover and mother

The Goddess

Shiva is the deviser of the world. In order to accomplish his plan he requires an executive, a material force or "energy". Energy (Shakti) is thus his first manifestation, or complement, the issue of himself. Cosmology (sânkhya) represents this power of materialization, both as a cohesive or centripetal force allowing matter to be organized, which is called Vishnu (the Immanent), and as the female counterpart of the god. The goddess is the "receptacle", or raw material, made of energetic elements, which is the indispensable support for all apparent manifestations.

Without the creative energy represented by the goddess, Shiva is like a corpse (*shava*), incapable of acting, of revealing himself, of accomplishing his ideation of the world. The representation of the Prime Cause of the world as being either masculine or feminine is purely a question of approach or viewpoint. Tantrism considers the female principle as the efficacious aspect, which is for man the divine reality. It follows that the goddess is the central object of the cult although occasionally she is replaced by Vishnu-Apollo.

The manifestation of a world whose nature is energy requires opposing poles. Substance – the material of the world – is the current which unites the poles. Matter is not stable, but is pure energy organized in space-time. In the primodial Trinity, neither Shiva nor Shakti is the substance of the created; it is the spark which flies between them: attraction (*râga*), delight (*ânanda*), pleasure (*kâma*), love. Three is the first of numbers. The echo of this concept is found in Hesiod, who states, "First there was the Abyss (the formless), then the Earth (matter), then Love". A symbolic but precise image of the process of creation is the union of the sexes, perceived essentially as pleasure. Delight is the substance of the world, and is what brings us near to the divine state. Reproduction and fecundity are only occasional accidents of the union of the sexes. The myths and symbols of sexual union should not be interpreted in terms of fecundity. The world is a spark of pleasure. It is not one of the principles which makes the other fertile. "Aphrodite will never become the goddess of fertility *par excellence*. It is physical love, carnal union, which she inspires, exalts and defends... Under the disguise of a frivolous divinity, is hidden one of the deepest sources of religious experience: the revelation of sexuality as transcendency and mystery." (M. Eliade, *Histoire des croyances et des idées religieuses*, p. 296.)

In the most ancient Greek theogonies, the divine beings, whether male, neuter, or female, procreate by parthenogenesis. The union of god and goddess is sterile. Each procreates on his own, independently of the other. Shiva is represented in permanent coition with a goddess, lasting thousands of years, but he only gives birth to his son Skanda when the coition is interrupted and the divine sperm falls into the mouth of the sacrificial fire. The goddess also procreates by herself, independently of the god. "Hera gave birth to the illustrious Hephaistos without the union of love, but out of anger and defiance hurled at her husband." (Hesiod, *The Theogony*, p. 927.)

The union of Zeus and Hera, the patrons of marriage, is infertile. Zeus is father of many children, but Hera is not their mother. Hera likewise has children, but Zeus is not their father. In the Christian religion we find the myth of the Virgin who gives birth to the god without any male intervention.

The preference given to the cult of the goddess, Shaktism, is of extremely ancient origin and is not peculiar to India. It is connected with the living being's affective relations with his mother, the vagina, or cavern, from which he came. "Shaktism reflects a mine of spirituality which offers visible analogies with the proto-historic, Pelasgian and pre-Hellenic Mediterranean world. The Hindu 'black goddesses' (such as Kâli and Durgâ) and the Palaeo-Mediterranean goddesses (Demeter, Melaina, Cybele, Diana of Ephesus and Tauris, and even including the Christian 'black Madonnas') all reflect a single prototype. Precisely in the substratum belonging to the Dravidian populations of India and, in part, to the layers and cycles of still more ancient civilizations, like those discovered by the excavations at Mohenjo Daro and Harappa. The cult of a Great Goddess or Universal Mother (*Magna Mater*) formed a central theme and assumed an importance completely ignored by the Aryo-Vedic tradition and its essentially virile and patriarchal tendencies. It was this cult which, remaining underground during the period of Aryan (Indo-European) conquest and colonization, emerged once more in Tantrism." (J. Evola, *Le Yoga tantrique*, p. 17.)

The multiple aspects of the goddess

As the source of all aspects of manifestation, the goddess is one and many. Whatever aspect of the world we look at, we find that it is based on an energy, or *shakti*, which is one of the aspects of the universal *Shakti*. This is why the goddess has many names and many forms, which, from a ritual point of view, may appear as different or even contrary principles.

Thus, she is virgin and mother, benevolent and terrible, outside ourselves, or present within us. We can perceive innumerable *shaktis* and, at the same time, their oneness. This is not peculiar to Shivaism. The Greek goddesses are equally interchangeable. "A number of Celtic goddesses can be called divided 'functions' of the Mother Goddess. Such as Macha, the fertility goddess in whose honour orgies were held, later a war goddess; Anu, whose paps are seen in the mountains in County Kerry; and Brigitt, who became the Christian St. Bride, goddess of abundance and marriage." (P. Rawson, *Primitive Erotic Art*, p. 44.)

We always find a long prehistory for each aspect of the goddess. "[The name of Athena] appears to be of pre-Greek origin... Her familiar association with the snake, the olive and the owl is a feature common to the Minoan goddess, to the domestic snake-cult, the tree-cult and the bird-epiphanies of Minoan religion." (R. F. Willetts, *Cretan Cults and Festivals*, p. 278.) Sarasvatî, like Athena, is the protectress of science and art. She is the inspirer of artisans and, as such, is worshipped by them. During the Sarasvatî Pûjâ – the festival of the Goddess – all tools and work instruments, books, and musical instruments are placed on an altar and venerated as symbols of her.

In all rites whose purpose is one of immediate effectiveness, the popular cult prefers to pray to the goddess, the mother or lover. This is the Tantric point of view. It is the feminine element, present in all beings, which ties us to the material world. Yet, through this element it is possible to unbind the fetters which tie us to the world. The orgiastic rites of Tantrism and the exaltation of the Maenads call to mind the role of the female element in the Dionysiac or Shivaite mysteries.

It is through the goddess that the creative work is accomplished. She checks the god's imagination and his creative or destructive mania. She is the intercessor. It is she to whom man must pray. This role of intercession is to be found in all goddesses, and even in the Virgin in the Christian world. The cult of a mother-goddess appears to be prevalent in prehistoric religions. It yields gradually to the cult of the lover-goddess, with the expansion of Shivaism and Tantrism. The goddess is also revealed in masculino form. According to the *Bhaghavatî Tattva*,[1] Vishnu, Krishna, Râma, Ganesha, and the Sun, are all manifestations of the female principle. This explains many of the aspects of their cults.

The lady of the mountain

The principal name of the goddess is Pârvatî (she of the mountain), since the summits are considered as points through which terrestrial energy rises toward heaven. It is there that heaven and earth unite. The union of the heavenly vault, likened to the *Linga* or Shiva, with the terrestrial energy spurting from the mountain, somehow binds the god to the world of living beings. According to Herodotus (7, III), the oracle of Dionysus is found on the highest mountains. "The high mountains are the pleasant abode of the goddesses." (Hesiod, *The Theogony*, 128.) In legendary tradition, Pârvatî is the daughter of the King of the Mountains, Himâvat (the Snowy), Lord of the Himalayas. At Sumer, the god Bel and the goddess Nin-har-sag resided on the "Mountain of the East", and the goddess was the "Lady of the Mountain". In the Greek and Cretan world as in the Middle East, we also find the image of Pârvatî whom Euripides calls the "Mother of the Mountain". In Crete, Rhea is the goddess of the Mountains. The names Diktynna and Artemis call to mind the idea, respectively, of a mountain-Mother and a huntress. Diktynna is the goddess of the Mountain, the guardian of the initiates. Her name is derived from Mount Dikte. The name of Diktynnaios was given to the mountains in the northwest of Crete, in the area of Kydonia. The most ancient sanctuary of Diktynna was called Tityros (Satyr). According to Strabo, the *Tityroi*, the servants of the goddess and god, resembled the Korybantes. They correspond to the Ganas of Shiva, and belonged to the cycle of Greco-Phrygian tradition connected with the cult of infant Zeus in Crete and the Mother of the Gods in Phrygia and in the region of Trojan Ida.

A seal from Knossos shows the Lady of the Mountain inclining her sceptre towards an adoring male. The goddess is preceded by a lion, which is the vehicle of Pârvatî. At Ephesus, in a grotto of Cybele – the Mother of the Mountains – we see the goddess between two lions,

[1]   Translated by A. Daniélou in the *Journal of the Indian Society of Oriental Art*, Calcutta, 1945.

with a young companion near her who is the equivalent of Ganesha, the son and guardian of Pârvatî.

The power of time

Through her relation with Shiva, the goddess permits the revelation of the divine Eros. However, she may appear as the matrix or mother, from whom all things came forth and to whom everything will return at the end. In this case she is identified as Kâlî, the "Power of Time", or of death.

In his terrible aspect, Shiva is like Kâla (Time), who is the Greek Kronos. Kâli, the Power of Time, or of death, is also called Durgâ, the Inaccessible, representing the terrible aspect of the goddess. She appears, dancing on a world in ruins, with the attributes of Shiva the Destroyer, wearing a necklace of skulls and serpents. Surrounded by demons, she kills all who approach her. It is she who must be invoked to obtain a reprieve. Her cult, connected to Tantrism, is extremely widespread, and is a very important branch of Shivaism later taken up by Mahâyâna Buddhism. Eroticism and bloody sacrifices play a large role in the cult of the terrible goddess, who is the principal divinity worshipped today in certain regions of India, especially in Bengal. "The Irish Dagda, the great god of the early Irish mythological race known as the Tuatha Dê Danann, 'People of the Goddess Dann',... had intercourse... with the sinister war-raven goddess, the Mórrígan, whose sexual lust was as powerful as her desire for blood and carnage." (A. Ross, *Primitive Erotic Art*, p. 82) To her are offered the heads of enemy warriors killed in battle. The image of Kâlî, with her skull necklaces, is shown in erotic union with Shiva. Parallels of this exist in Egypt.

Carnage and cannibalism are characteristic traits of archaic goddesses. In the Ugaritic (Canaanite) myth of the third millennium, Anat, in a homicidal rage, slew the guards, soldiers and old men. The blood rose up to her knees. Like Kâlî, she is girded with the heads and hands of her victims.

Death is a return to the mother's womb, to the earth from which we came. Kâlî alone is invoked by her faithful as "Mother", the protectress. From whom else can mercy be implored, if not from the all-powerfulness of Time?

The white lady

Gauri, the White Goddess, is the benevolent aspect of the goddess.

She is the protectress and friend of men, a good fairy. For the Greeks, the White Lady (Leucothea) was the protectress of sailors. "Ino threw herself into the sea with the dead child Melicertes. She is called Leucothea and the boy Palaemon. At least, that is how sailors call them, when they come to their rescue during a storm." (Apollodorus, II, 4, 3.) According to John Lydus, (the Lydian, VI century), Leucothea takes the place of Proserpine as the mother of Dionysus. The cult of ancient Cretan Dionysus appears to have lasted a long time in the Greek islands, and the White Lady of the sea had an important cult there.

Sati (fidelity)

In Egyptian mythology, Isis is the symbol of fidelity. Sati (Fidelity) is the lover of Shiva, and her legend is distinct from that of Pârvatî, the Lady of the Mountains. Sati is the daughter of the Aryan priest-king Daksha. Her legend recalls the halt in the fusion of the Dravidian and Aryan pantheons, as well as one of the aspects of the female role, that of faithfulness to her husband and the abandoning of all ties with her family and clan of origin.

After the suicide of Sati, Shiva carries her body on his shoulder, letting pieces fall in different parts of the Earth. In the Osiris myth it is Isis who gathers the various parts of the god's body and buries them in different spots which then become holy places. In the myth of the Canaanites, who were bull-worshippers, the son of Baal Aliyan – the equivalent of Pashupati, the god of Springs and Forests – marries his sister, Anat. When Aliyan dies, Anat goes to find him in the Land of the Dead, carries him back on her shoulder and buries him on the top of Mount Saphon.

The mistress of the animals

Pârvatî, the Lady of the Mountain, appears as Mistress of the Animals. She is the counterpart of Pashupati, who is the Master of the Animals. For the whole of Mediterranean prehistory including Minoan Crete, the original Lady of the Mountains, Artomis, is the Mistress of wild beasts.

Artemis is the patron of hunters, wild beasts, and girls. It is she who rules over the sacredness of wild life. As a forest goddess, she is not a stranger to sexuality and childbirth, but rejects the social ties of marriage.

In Cretan religion, "female divinities – who are therefore by nature 'earthly' and 'secret' – had a predominant role. Amongst these, the best known through various monuments is a mistress-goddess of ferocious animals, Potnia Theron, depicted in the act of slaying or subjugating wild beasts, or else armed for the hunt." (Paolo Santarcangeli, *Le Livre des labyrinthes*, p. 101.)

She corresponds to the ancient pre-Celtic Mother of the Animals, whose image is found in the cave at Pech-Merle, in the southwest of France. "Fergus, [the Celtic great god, has for] his mate... Flidais, goddess of the woodlands and wild things. She was mistress of the animals..., a Celtic equivalent of the classical Diana, descended from and successor to the Palaeolithic prototypes." (A. Ross, *Primitive Erotic Art*, p. 83.)

Aphrodite, a goddess thought to have an oriental origin, was born from the seed of Uranos' sexual organs flung into the sea. This myth runs parallel to the one concerning the castration of Shiva. She is also the Mistress of Wild Beasts, like Pârvatî and Artemis. She sows desire amongst beasts, men and gods. "The goddess is represented in a rich variety of associations: with animals, birds and snakes; with the baetylic pillar and the sacred tree; with the poppy and the lily; with the sword and the double axe. She is a huntress and goddess of sports; she is armed and she presides over ritual dances... She has dominion over mountain, earth, sky and sea; over life and death;... Mother and Maid... She is both one and many." (R. F. Willetts, *Cretan Cults and Festivals*, p.75.)

The marriage of Shiva and Pârvatî

When the sages wished to persuade the vagabond god to take a wife, Shiva replied, "The only woman I can accept must be beautiful, she must practise Yoga and be able to withstand the ardour of my sperm. She must be a Yogi when I practise Yoga, and an amorous woman when I practise love. There is another condition. If she has not complete confidence in me and in my words, I shall abandon her." (*Shiva Purâna, Rudra Samhitâ*, chap. 17, 38–44.)

"Shiva, who is benevolent to his faithful, likes amusing himself with magic. So as to approach Menâ, the wife of the King of the Mountains, he took the form of a dancer. He held a horn in his right hand and a drum in his left. He wore a red garment, with a bag on his back. He danced marvellously and sang in a very gentle voice. He blew his horn and beat the melodious sounding drum. It was a marvellous spectacle. All the inhabitants of the place, men, women, and children, gathered to see him. They were in ecstasy.

"Pârvatî, the daughter of the King of the Mountains, saw the harmonious form of Shiva, who carries the trident and other attributes. His body was smeared with ash. A necklace of skulls was around his neck. His face was smiling; his three eyes shone. A snake served him for a sacred ribbon. Of dazzling whiteness, the beautiful Shiva, friend of the humble, ocean of goodness, repeated, 'Make your wish'. She bowed before him and said, 'Be my husband'.

"He granted her wish and continued his dance. Menâ wanted to offer him jewels and gold. But the dancer refused any present. He asked for the hand of Pârvatî, and continued dancing and singing. Menâ was outraged and wanted to have him thrown out by her servants... But there was nothing which could push him out. He was burning to the touch like the hottest fire. He illuminated everything around him. The beggar finally disappeared.

"The head of the Brahmans addressed the King of the Mountains, 'I heard that you wish to give Shiva your daughter for a wife; she is tender as a lotus flower, divinely beautiful, and accomplished in all things. But this Shiva has no home and no kin. He is ill-made, with no merits. He inhabits cremation grounds. He looks like a snake-charmer. He is only a naked Yogi. His limbs are misshapen. His only ornaments are snakes. The name of his family, his caste, and his origins are unknown to us. He is a badly-behaved boy, with no profession. His body is smeared with ashes. He is irascible and has no judgement. No one knows his age. His unkempt hair is wild. He is the companion of all kinds of worthless people. He is nothing but a beggar of evil disposition and systematically opposes the commandments of the Vedas'." (*Shiva Purâna, Rudra Samhitâ*, chap. 30, 26–52, and chap. 31, 43–47.)

According to the *Shiva Purâna* (*Rudra Samhitâ*, chap. 37 to 51, abridged):

"Urged by his wife and sons, the King of the Mountains had a letter of betrothal written by his scribe, and sent messengers with gifts to take it to Shiva. When they reached Kailâsa, the god's paradise, they gave him the message and placed the sacred mark on his forehead. Shiva treated them with honour and they returned home enchanted. The King of the Mountains then sent out invitations, and began to gather provisions and all that was necessary for the celebration. Vast quantities of rice, sugar and salt were piled up. Tanks were built for the milk, oil, curds, barley-cakes, and sweetmeats; others for wine, cane-juice, pastries and other sweets, as also for butter, intoxicating drinks, fruit-juices, and many other products. Spiced dishes and other appetizers were prepared to please Shiva's Ganas. Handsome robes were prepared, purified by fire, as well as jewels, precious stones, and gold and silver objects. The rites began on an auspicious day. The mountain women carried out Pârvatî's purification ceremonies.

"All the mountains came for the feast: the Mandara mountains and the mountains of East and West, the Malaya, Dardura, Vishâda, Gandhamadana, Karvira, Mahendra, Pâriyâtra, Krauncha, Purushottama, Nîla, Vindhyâ, Kalanjara, and Kailâsa mountains, as well as all the mountains of the other continents, who gathered in the dwelling of Himâvat (the snowy mountain).

"All the rivers also assembled, covered with jewels, The Godâvari, Yamunâ, Brahmastrî, Venîkâ, Ganges and Narmadâ, were seen arriving.

"The whole town was in a festive mood; banners, flags and garlands glittered everywhere. An immense, splendidly-furnished hall was built by Vishvakarma, the architect of the gods. Lions, storks and peacocks were sculpted in a most realistic manner. There were also artificial women who danced and dummy men who ogled them. Some superb guards, their bows stretched, were so life-like as to be mistaken for real men, elephants, chariots, and soldiers so natural as to appear alive. The goddess' statue was facing the entrance. She appeared to rise from an ocean of milk. A splendid apartment was prepared for Shiva.

"When he received the letter of invitation, Shiva burst into laughter. He had it read aloud and accepted the proposal. He said, 'I am always at the service of my admirers. By her devotion, Pârvatî has obtained the favour of having me for a husband. In seven days the wedding will take place'.

"Shiva called his bull and all his Ganas to accompany him, and also the horde of evil spirits (Bhûtas). They set off for the land of the snowy mountains for the marriage feast.

"The terrible Chandi, Shiva's sister, also came, sowing terror everywhere. She rode on a phantom and was covered with snakes. She wore a golden urn on her head. Thousands of gnomes accompanied her. The sound of drums was deafening, drowning everything that was not of good omen.

"The King of the Mountains, accompanied by all the mountains, came to bow down in front of Shiva, who was drawing near. Shiva was smiling, seated on his bull and covered with jewels. His beauty lit the four corners of space; his crown was resplendent. The snakes were transformed into precious garlands. A divine light emanated from his body. He was surrounded by gods fanning him and carrying fly-swats. He was received by the King of the Mountains with great honour and much ceremony.

"Menâ, the wife of the King of the Mountains, then demanded to see Shiva under his usual aspect, which destroys pride and vanity. From her balcony, she saw the arrival of the procession of Gandharvas, the musicians of heaven, magnificently dressed, mounted in their chariots, playing various musical instruments and accompanied by nymphs. When she saw the Chief of the gods of the Spheres (Vasu) arrive, she exclaimed, 'There is Shiva!' But she was told, 'No, it is only one of his ministers'. In the same way, seeing each new arrival, each more splendid than the last, Menâ would cry, 'There is Shiva!' And she had to be told, 'No! It is only an attendant'. She was dazzled.

"When Shiva appeared, seated on his bull, covered with ashes, his hair wild, a crescent moon on his forehead, a skull in his hand, a tiger-skin over his shoulder, carrying a bow and a trident, with his strange eyes, dirty and unkempt, surrounded by his vagabonds, devils and ghosts with terrifying forms, Menâ, terror-struck, fainted. When she revived, her fury knew no bounds, 'What shall I do? I am dishonoured! You have deceived me. A curse on my daughter, who wishes to exchange a jewel for a piece of glass, who prefers a jackal to a lion! May you all be accursed! Curse the day when I conceived that child. You have all plotted against me. Never shall my daughter marry that creature. I would rather kill her'. She ordered Himâvat, 'Seize your daughter; bind her; cast her into an abyss or into the depths of the sea. If you give your daughter to that creature, I will kill myself. I should prefer to poison my daughter, cut her into pieces, or drown her in the sea, rather than give her to Shiva. We have all been made to look ridiculous. This person has neither father, mother, brother, nor kin. He has neither beauty nor profession, nor even a house belonging to him, no clothes nor jewels; he is neither rich, nor young. He is filthy, ignorant, disgusting. What reason could I have to give him my daughter?'

"Reprimanded by the gods, Menâ became calmer, 'If he appears in a pleasing form, my daughter may be given to him. Otherwise not'. Shiva then showed himself to Menâ in his most charming aspect. Each part of his body shone with light. His garments were of many colours. He wore precious jewels. His skin was clear and shiny. The crescent moon added even more to his beauty.

"Menâ was dazzled and asked pardon for the insults she had cast on to the god. All the women left their occupations and hurried to see him, some half-dressed, others snatching their baby from their breast, or leaving their husband at the table without serving him. The men, like the women, were charmed by the god's beauty and congratulated Menâ. She then went down to meet her daughter's betrothed.

"After the rites of the bath, the King of the Mountains and Menâ decorated Pârvatî with the ornaments brought by Shiva. He himself performed the ceremonial ablutions and put on his splendid garments.

"A great feast was held. Conches were blown; they beat drums, such as the *pataha* (kettledrums) and *anaka* (double-drum). Marine shells (gomukha) were played. They sang songs of good omen to accompany the dancers.

"A priest began to perform the rites in an enclosure where an altar had been built. Pârvatî was seated on a raised platform. Grains of rice were thrown over the couple. The priest, according to the rules and in order to perform the rites, asked Shiva, 'Tell us now your genealogy, your caste, your family, your Vedic ancestors and the Vedas which you can recite'. There was a moment of embarrassment. Shiva turned his head aside. The sage Nârada began to play the vînâ. He said, 'Shiva is the Supreme Being. He has no ancestors, nor family; his only family is the divine word. He is the primordial Sound (Nâda)'.

"The King of the Mountains himself then spoke the ritual words, 'I give you my daughter as wife. Deign to accept her', and he placed Pârvatî's hand in Shiva's. He then offered a dowry of jewels and precious vases, a hundred thousand cows, one hundred harnessed horses, a hundred thousand tender young servants, chariots and elephants.

"Pârvatî, the daughter of the mountains, was so beautiful that the god Brahmâ, looking only at her toe-nails, was struck by Eros. He said, 'Troubled by Eros, I looked frequently at her limbs, and immediately my sperm flowed to the ground. I am an old man and felt ashamed of this emission of seed; so I pressed my sexual organ between my two feet'. But Shiva, having noticed what happened, was overcome by fury and wanted to kill Brahmâ. The other gods, however, so covered him with praise that he became calm. Brahmâ's seed, as a consequence of repeated pressure, spilled out in sparkling jets. Many sages were born from this seed, and are called *Vâlakhilya*.

"They were banished to the Mountain of Perfumes (Gandhamâdana) and became followers of Shiva. The couple were then led to the bridal chamber. The women of the 'City of the Snows' performed the rite of good omen. Then came the goddesses to bestow favours . . . Together with his wife, Shiva chewed betel and camphor."

The notion of the god whose sperm gives birth to living beings is also found in the Greek world. Erichthonios was born from the seed of Hephaistos which dropped on the ground when the god was pursuing Athena. Zeus, too, let flow his seed on seeing Persephone. "He had not known a passion so violent even when he fell enamoured of the Cyprian-born goddess, on which occasion, due to the impossible desire to possess her, he spurted his seed onto the ground, shooting out the burning foam of his love, which gushed forth spontaneously. It was thence, in hornèd Cyprus, their foster-mother, that the double-bodied race sprang, the hornèd Centaurs." (Nonnos, *Dionysia*, song V, (610–615).)

Chapter 4

THE SONS OF THE GODDESS
AND OF THE GOD

Ganesha, Korybas or Hermes, Lord of Obstacles, Guardian of Gates and Mysteries

"Pârvatî's companions complained to her, saying, 'The servants of Shiva do not refuse to carry out our orders, but they are not really at our service. They obey Shiva and guard our gate. We cannot trust them. We need someone who is really ours....'. When the goddess was taking her bath, Shiva thrust aside Nandi, the Minotaur who guarded the gate, and entered the apartment. The goddess was very embarrassed... She decided to create a servant for herself and, with the scrapings of her skin, fashioned a boy.

"He was a beautiful adolescent, well-proportioned, tall, strong and courageous. She said to him, 'You are my son and belong only to me'. He promised to obey her in all things. The goddess was overjoyed and covered him with caresses, clasping him in her arms. She placed him before her gate, armed with a club. When Shiva wanted to enter, the boy barred the way and, despite the god's injunctions, refused to let him pass. Shiva was furious and sent his Ganas to get rid of this troublesome intruder. Long palavers and interminable scuffles followed. The faithful guardian was always victorious... When she saw the army of gods join the Ganas to attack the valiant boy, the Mother of the World deputed two of her powers, two *shaktis* in the form of she-devils, to come to her son's aid. One of these she-devils, of terrifying aspect, remained standing. Her open mouth was as wide as the cavern of the Black Mountain. The other had the appearance of a thunder-bolt and innumerable arms. She was enormous and terrible, ready to strike all those who drew near. During the battle, the two *shaktis* caught with their mouth the projectiles cast by the gods and Ganas, and cast them back... When Vishnu tried to attack the son of the goddess, the two *shaktis* united with the boy's body, thus giving him extra strength. Even the army of the gods was vanquished by the courageous boy. Finally, when he was busy fighting Vishnu, Shiva himself treacherously cut off the boy's head with his trident. Seeing the grief of the goddess and in order to calm her, Shiva immediately ordered the young man's head to be replaced with that of the first living being encountered... This was an elephant, whose head was joined to the revived boy and, so as to console the goddess, Shiva named him Ganesha, chief of the Ganas." (*Shiva Purâna, Rudra Samhitâ*, chap. 13–18, abridged.)

According to another version, it is the maleficent glance of Saturn which decapitates the child. Invited together with the other planets to Ganesha's baptism, Saturn, who brings bad luck, could not resist the desire to glance furtively at the child, whose head at once burst asunder.

Ganesha is therefore the goddess' son. Like Hera's son Hephaistos, the magician, he was engendered by the goddess alone, without any male intervention. Ganesha is the leader of the Ganas, the "Vagabonds of Heaven", young people belonging to the world of spirits, who are Shiva's companions. Amongst these are the "Obstructors", who hinder any accomplishment and provoke the mistakes which make sacrifices inefficacious and virtues useless. Ganesha is thus the equivalent of the Cretan Korybas, the eponym of the Korybantes, the troupe of celestial youths who form Dionysus' escort. Korybas is the son of Cybele, the Goddess of the Mountain, just as Ganesha is the son of Pârvatî, the Lady of the Mountain.

Ganesha is called Vighneshvara, the master of obstacles. It is he who creates difficulties in all human or spiritual accomplishment. Only his benevolence allows them to be overcome. He is therefore the master of initiation and of mysteries, as well as of the rites by which obstacles can be evaded or overcome. "Those who do not worship the lord of obstacles, even if they are gods, shall never obtain the results they desire. Should anyone perform rites without having first rendered homage to the chief of the Ganas, the rites will be ineffective. Ganesha must be honoured by all, priests, warriors, farmers, or artisans, who shall offer him fine nourishment in order to obtain the fulfilment of their desires." (*Linga Purâna*, I, chap. 105, 23–28.)

Ganesha is invoked before any undertaking, so as to avoid the Ganas' hindering its accomplishment. The statue of Ganesha is also placed above the door of the house to protect its entrance, almost in the same way that a watchman from the caste of thieves is sometimes employed.

Symbolically, Ganesha represents the basic unity of the macrocosm and microcosm, the immense being (the elephant) and the individual being (man). This highly implausible identity is however a fundamental reality and the key to all mystic or ritual experience. as well as to Yogic possibilities. Without being aware of Genesha, and without worshipping him, no accomplishment is possible. He is the guardian of gates and mysteries. In Egypt, Osiris appears as the guardian of his mother's door. As guardian of gates, Ganesha guards the entrance to the labyrinth, the mysterious paths inside the human body which start from the energy coiled at the base of the spine. In Yoga practice, Ganesha's centre is situated in the region of the rectum.

The most ancient symbols of the Cretan labyrinth are the double axe (labrys) and the gammadion (the Indian swastika). Ganesha carries a double axe and his symbol is the gammadion. It should be noted that the graphic representation of Shiva's drum, in the shape of an hour-glass, is identical to the double axe. It is possible that there was a relationship between the two. Ganesha is known for his trickery and cheating, which allowed him to take advantage of his half-brother, Skanda, the son of Shiva. The Greeks attribute some of his characteristics to Hermes, brother of Apollo, the giver of good things. Hermes is the personification of devious and secret ways, implying trickery and cheating. He is the companion and patron of thieves, but is also the protector of herds, and of travellers who lose their way. Like Ganesha's, his is a world of greed, cheating, trickery and lying. It is through trickery and the perverse, irrational rites of the mysteries that both heaven and earth can be conquered.

Ganesha, like Hermes, is the god of Luck and Gambling. "Oracular consultation by means of dice was held in great respect by the Greeks, especially amongst herdsmen, for whom success was the result of invoking Hermes, the god of luck." (H. Jeanmaire, *Dionysus*, p. 190.)

When comparing him with Hermes, it should be remembered that Ganesha is not a monstrous god. He is a young god of dazzling beauty. His elephant's head is only a symbol of his greatness and mystery.

Ganesha's mount is the mouse (*mousa*), an animal which penetrates inside things and discovers their mystery. For the Greeks, it is Apollo, Hermes' brother, who is called Smintheus ("of the mouse"), from the Cretan word *sminthoi*, meaning "mouse", which, however, is not itself a Greek word.

Hermes is identified with Egyptian Thoth, the preserver and transmitter of tradition.

THE SONS OF THE GODDESS AND OF THE GOD

Kumâra or Kouros, the boy

The cult of Kumâra (the Boy), the infant-god fed by the nymphs, goes back to remote prehistory. His myths are inextricably entwined with those of Shiva-Dionysus, whether he is the god's son, the god himself, or a new Dionysus. In the ancient Dravidian religion, he originally appears as an independent divinity; in Shivaism, he is Shiva's son; in the Mediterranean world, he is the new Dionysus, son of the old god. His legend and attributes are much the same everywhere.

In south India and Ceylon, Tamil tradition, which stretches back beyond the Neolithic Age, gives an account of the cult of a young god called Murugan (the Boy), worshipped by primitive tribes known as Väddäs. His attributes are the cock and the hunting-spear. Representations of Murugan have been found at the prehistoric sites of Adiccanallûr, in southern India. He was offered animal sacrifices, and was originally associated with the snake-cult. Even nowadays, his priests are non-Brahmans. In Shivaism, this young god was born from Shiva's sperm. He is called Kumâra (the Boy) or Skanda (the Jet of Sperm). He also has other names which refer to the vicissitudes of his legends.

According to the *Shiva Purâna*, "For more than one thousand celestial years, Shiva remained in perpetual copulation with Pârvatî, indifferent to the problems of the world. Tormented by the Titan Târaka, the Earth trembled on its base and lost its breath. The troubled gods made their way to the dwelling of Shiva in order to request his aid.

"Shiva came to the door without having released his seed. He told the gods, 'What must come to pass, will come to pass. Nothing can stop it. What has come to pass has already come. Listen only to what concerns the matter which brings you here. Its solution will depend on him who takes up my sperm'. Having said this, he let his sperm fall onto the ground. Agni, the god of Fire, took the form of a dove and swallowed it with his beak.

"In the meanwhile, Pârvatî drew near, annoyed at having been disturbed at her pleasure. She cursed the gods, and in particular Agni, saying, 'It was not proper for you to swallow the sperm of my master. You are a wretch, a criminal'.

"Each god received a part of every offering cast into the sacrificial fire. Thus, all the gods were impregnated by Shiva's burning sperm, swallowed by Agni, which caused them terrible suffering. Shiva took pity on them and allowed them to vomit up his sperm. They threw up the shining, golden seed which, on falling to the ground, seemed to touch the sky like a mountain of fire. Through the pores of their skin, the sperm then penetrated the bodies of the wives of the seven celestial sages, who were taking their ritual bath. They became pregnant and began to suffer a terrible burning. Their husbands were angry at seeing them in this condition, and repudiated them. They then threw up the sperm on the snowy peak of Mount Himâvat. Unable to withstand the burning sperm, Himâvat, the King of the Mountains, threw it up, and the sperm fell into the Ganges. There, in a bed of rushes, Shiva's sperm was deposited into the sacred waters of the river.

"Very soon, the seed was transformed into a superb infant, shining with splendour and glory. Thus it was that, on the sixth day of the moon in the month of Mârgashirsha (November–December), the son of Shiva was born. The six Pleiades came by chance to bathe in the sacred river. They found the infant and quarreled as to who should have the pleasure of looking after him. In order to stop their quarreling, he gave himself six heads to drink the milk from the breast of each. He is therefore called Shanmukha, "six-faced". The Pleiades brought him to their dwelling and took the greatest care of him . . . Shiva inquired what had become of his infallible sperm and, learning that there was a child with the Pleiades in the forest, he sent his guards to find him . . . Shiva never tired of drinking in the nectar of the beauty of Skanda's face . . . he was overjoyed to clasp him in his arms and kiss his head." (*Shiva Purâna, Rudra Samhitâ*, IV, chap. 3, I, 7.)

Skanda, the god of Beauty, who became the leader of the army of gods, was thus born without the intervention of a female being. He is the expression of the very nature of the god, his most direct revelation. Skanda is in fact a clone, a sort of double Shiva, and their cults have been mingled in India as elsewhere. "The goddess asked what were the child's virtues. Shiva replied, 'I myself have six aspects. These aspects are reunited in this six-faced boy. He is none other than the expression of my power. As for qualities, there is no difference between him and me . . . This carrier of the hunting-spear (Cevvêl) will himself take over the functions of the Creator of the world'." (The Tamil *Kanda purânam*, I, chap. 14, 13–21.)

In the Mediterranean world, Skanda appears as a new Dionysus and his legend is mingled with that of the old Dionysus. As early as the fifth century, Iacchos is considered the son of Dionysus. It is he who directs the mysteries at Eleusis. He shows all the characteristics of Bacchos, leading the procession of Dionysus. "The nativity of Dionysus... covers a... pre-Dionysiac... mythical nucleus,... the heritage of the Phrygian or Asian divinity, from which our god is derived." (H. Jeanmaire, *Dionysos*, p. 331.)

The mixing of the myths of Shiva and Skanda in the cult of Dionysus, together with the fact that this cult is found in a more or less adapted form in Egypt, the Middle East, Crete and the Mediterranean countries, gave rise in the Greek world to different genealogies of the god, reflecting the various aspects of the cult of Shiva and Skanda.

The first and older Dionysus is the son of Zeus and Proserpine, who is also Zeus' daughter (the goddess sprang forth from Shiva). It is he who is credited with the invention of wine and agriculture. Leucothea, the White Lady (the Indian Gauri), replaced Proserpine. It was this Cretan Dionysus whose archaic cult long continued in the islands, where the White Lady of the sea was worshipped.

The second Dionysus corresponds to the Egyptian form of the god, who was born of the god Nile and is called Hapi or Serapis (Osiris-Apis) – a bull-shaped god, connected with the god Priapus and with the *Linga* cult. Osiris-Dionysus is the god of the Phallophoria. His mother is named Flora, which is suitable for a Nature goddess.

A third Dionysus of Asiatic origin, who ruled over Asia, had no mother at all. Like Shiva, he is self-born (*Svayambhu*). Elsewhere, Dionysus appears as the son of Zeus and Semele. It is this Theban Bacchos who is connected with the mysteries of Orpheus. He was conceived by Semele (the Earth) and Zeus, and was hidden in Zeus' thigh to escape the anger of Hera, Zeus' sister and consort. He is born a second time, without a mother, from the thigh of Zeus. He was entrusted to Hermes and sent to Ino and Athamas, to be raised as a girl. Saved once more from the wrath of Hera, Hermes entrusted him to the nymphs of Nysa, in Asia. This is certainly the myth of Skanda. Dionysus was also made out to be the descendant of a certain Nisos, in order to explain the origin of his name.

Diodorus distinguishes "Bacchos, son of Semele", who is Skanda, from an older Dionysus (Shiva), born of Zeus and Persephone. It is the latter who is depicted with horns. The bearded god, corresponding to the first Dionysus, was the inventor of agriculture and taught men to yoke oxen to a plough. The kind of young and beautiful god, who prevailed from about the fourth century, was the son of Semele.

Sabazios, the Phrygian wine-god, was one of the aspects of the older Dionysus. The recognition of the forms taken by the god in other countries led to a distinction between the different types of Bacchos, such as, for example, the Indian Bacchos.

"After discovering wine and teaching man how to grow the vine, Dionysus travelled all over the earth, civilizing many countries... He made a two-year expedition to India: on his return..., he celebrated his first 'triumph', mounted on an Indian elephant. The god was also accompanied by satyrs who diverted him with their dances and drama." (H. Jeanmaire, *Dionysos*, p. 364.) The Satyrs and Korybantes are Shiva's Ganas.

"Zeus Kretagenes [Cretan Zeus] undoubtedly assumed the epithet Diktaios from the Diktaian Cave on Mount Dikto where the birth supposedly occurred. Here too... he was reared and fed [by nymphs with bees' honey and milk from the goat Amaltheia]; and entrusted to the Kouretes (or to the Korybantes, later identified with them) who danced around the baby, beating drums and clashing shields and spears so that its cries should not be heard by Kronos." (R. F. Willetts, *Cretan Cults and Festivals*, p. 216.)

The Homeric hymns evoke the god's birth: "I sing of the boisterous Dionysus with the ivy-bound hair, the noble son of Zeus and glorious Semele, whom the beautiful-haired nymphs received as a nurseling from the hands of the Lord his father, then nourished and raised with care in the valleys of Nysa... He grew up in a perfumed grotto..., then he began to haunt the woods, clothed in ivy and laurel, followed by the nymphs. A great noise possessed the immense forest." (*Hymn to Dionysus*, II.)

Skanda is known by many names referring to his legend. He is Kumâra (the Adolescent), Guha (the Mysterious), Senâpati (Head of Armies), Gangeya (Son of the Ganges), Subrâhmanya (Dear to the Brahmans). He is the "Son of Fire" (Agnibhu or Pâvaki) like Dionysus, who is called Pyrigenes or Pyrisporos (Born or Conceived by Fire). He is also the "Son of the Pleiades" (Kârttikeya), who became stars. In the same way, Zeus metamorphosed the nymphs of Nysa into Pleiades, the stars of the constellation of the Bull (Taurus). The constellation of the Pleiades has only six stars, but the Greeks add a seventh, invisible one.

Electra, in the *Dionysia*, says, "I was once, I too, one of the illustrious Pleiades". (Nonnos, *Dionysia*, song II, 3–31.) It has been suggested that the fact that Shiva's sperm stayed on the snowy mountain Himâvat, identified with Mount Meru, the axis of the world, is not extraneous to the legend of Dionysus' sojourn in the thigh (*meros*) of Jupiter. The god Brahmâ was also born from Shiva's sperm deposited in the belly of Vishnu, like Dionysus in the thigh of Zeus. Skanda is Sharadhâmaja (Born in a reedy marsh); Dionysus is Limnaios ("of the marsh"). The Ionians considered that Dionysus was brought by the waters, or was raised in the marsh near which his sanctuary was situated. In Egypt, it is Horus, the divine child, who is born in the marshes of the Nile delta.

In Dravidian languages, *vêl* means hunting-spear. Skanda is called Cevvêl or Vêlavan. It is difficult not to compare this name with the Cretan Velcanos. According to Hesychius, Velcanos is the "Zeus of the Cretans". On coins from Phaistos, Velcanos is represented as a naked young man, seated on a tree, with his right hand on a cock. The cock is the sacred animal of Skanda-Murugan. A bull appears on the reverse of these coins.

The god of armies

"The sage Vishvamitra, who belonged to the warrior caste, came to visit Skanda, who took him as a preceptor and told him, 'Thanks to me you will from now on be accepted amongst the Vedic sages as a Brahman....'. [This is a reference to the recognition of pre-Aryan sages in the Vedic world.] When the boy (Kumâra) had found his parents again, the gods gave him arms and chariots. Agni gave him a sword. Kumâra took over the leadership of the army of gods. He massacred the hordes of Titans and slew the powerful spirit Târaka." (*Shiva Purâna, Rudra Samhitâ*, IV, chap. 3.)

As the god of Armies, Skanda is called Senânî (Head of Armies), or Senâpati. He is Mahâsena (Possessor of a vast army), and Shaktidhara (Armed with a sword). The young Cretan god is armed with a bow, a hunting-spear and a shield, employed for both hunting and war.

The marriage of Ganesha

"When the two boys were of marriageable age, Shiva and Pârvatî did not know which of the children to marry off first. So they proposed a competition: We shall celebrate the marriage of the one who first returns after having gone around the world. The clever Ganesha walked around his parents and said to them, 'You are the universe'.

He was considered the winner and his wedding was celebrated with Siddhi (Success) and Buddhi (Intelligence), the two daughters of the Lord of the World, Vishvarûpa.

"After many months, Skanda returned, having journeyed around the vast earth with its forests and oceans. He was indignant at having been deceived by his father and adoptive mother and retired to the Mountain of the Heron (Krauncha), where he lives. He has never married." (*Shiva Purâna, Rudra Samhitâ*, IV, chap. 19–20, abridged.)

He is called Kumâra, the Boy; it is said that his only wife is the army (*sena*). His cult is strictly forbidden to women. He is the favourite divinity of homosexuals. In a later tradition of south India and Ceylon, Skanda was given two wives: *Sena* (the army) and Valli, the daughter of the primitive hunters of the mountains, the Väddäs. This is probably an allusion to the prehistoric origin of his cult among the first inhabitants of India.

Only the great goddess Pârvatî, the Lady of the Mountains, has access to Skanda's place of retreat, just as the goddess (today the Virgin Mary) is the only woman residing on Mount Athos. Mount Athos, where there is still an altar for the bull sacrifice near the Great-Lavra monastery, is an ancient sacred place of Dionysus. Access is still forbidden to women. Dionysus also went to a mountain in Phrygia, where the goddess, called the Mother of the Gods, or the Lady of the Mountain, purified him.

"During the month of Kârttika (October–November), when the full moon is near to the constellation of the Pleiades which is dedicated to him, the gods came to visit Skanda. Shiva desired to take up his abode near his son, in the form of a *Linga* called Mallikârjuna, but the son of the Pleiades refused to see his parents and went to live further away." (*Shiva Purâna, Rudra Samhitâ*, IV, chap. 19.)

"In the northwest direction of the *yantra*, the diagram which serves as a plan for the temple, the votary must worship the young god, shining like the rising sun, seated on a peacock, with four arms and magnificent limbs, wearing a crown and making the gesture of giving and protecting. He carries a hunting-spear and is accompanied by a cock." (*Shiva Purâna, Kailâsa Samhitâ*, chap. 7, 20–21.)

"He has a cock on his standard and a peacock as his steed. He is accompanied by a ram." (The Tamil *Kanda purânam*, VI, chap. 24.)

According to the *Kanda purânam*, it was the King of Heaven, Indra, who took the form of a peacock in order to become Skanda's steed.

THE SONS OF THE GODDESS AND OF THE GOD

Guha, the Mysterious

"The sage Vâmadeva, wandering through the world, arrived one day at the Mountain of the Boy (Kumâra shikhara), to the south of Meru, where joyfully lives Shiva's son, the child of the Pleiades, whose steed is a peacock. The sage was wise, with neither ties nor abode, and was naked. Near that place is the lake of Skanda (Skanda saras), as wide as the ocean. The sage went bathing with his disciples, and saw Skanda seated, shining on the mountain. He had four arms and a magnificent body. He carried a magic weapon (*shakti*); a cock perched on his hand. He made gestures of protecting and giving. The sage bowed before him and said, 'I bow before the Mysterious one (Guha), the secret god, wielder of secret knowledge, who knows the hidden meaning of the sacred texts. I bow before him who knows the six ways and the six meanings of the texts'. Skanda then spoke with a voice as majestic as that of the clouds." (*Shiva Purâna, Kailâsa Samhitâ,* chap. II, 10–43.)

Skanda is the god of transcendent Knowledge and knows the secret nature of things. He is therefore called Guha (the Mysterious) or Naigamesha (the Master of sacred tradition). "Skanda knows the meaning hidden in the teachings of the Vedas and other sacred texts. He knows the meaning of all ritual acts. He possesses all gifts. He is the first-born, the master of the world. He is gracious. His body is delicate, like that of Vishnu. He is the noble chief of armies, the mysterious destroyer of sacrifices. He rides the celestial elephant Airâvata; his hair is black and curly, his skin dark; his eyes are red and his ornaments are the moon and the snake. He is surrounded with spirits, ghosts, evil gnomes and magician-spirits (Kûshmândas). He worships Shiva." (*Linga Purâna,* chap. 82, 92–95.)

The Infant God

Skanda is worshipped in the form of a child suckled by the Pleiades, or in his effeminate adolescent form. Dionysus was entrusted by Hermes to the nymphs in order to be raised as a girl. This cult of the infant-god was carried over to Krishna in Vishnuite India. His games and misdeeds are a subject of endless delight in popular religion.

In the cult of Dionysus, "childhood episodes relating to the ancient practices of a *bambino* cult and the ancient cycle of tests for the adolescent, or *Kourus,* have left deep traces. The god who leads the women's bacchanalia, always remains the nurseling of the nymphs and Nereids. The little new-born god was Dionysus, until the day when the nativity *bambino* would be Christ." (H. Jeanmaire, *Dionysos*, p. 413.)

"...Minos, by a regal fiction, [was] always young. For Homer calls him a nine-year king, familiar friend of Zeus... If Minos was also a god, he has to be identified with the young god of Crete who renewed his youth every year." (R. F. Willetts, *Cretan Cults and Festivals*, p. 87.)

Chapter 5

THE COMPANIONS OF THE GOD

Ganas and Korybantes, the Delinquents of Heaven

In the *Rig Veda*, the companions of Rudra-Shiva are the Maruts, the Storm-gods. "They are furious like wild beasts, but play innocently, like children or calves." The Greeks speak of "the demoniac cohort which is the following of Dionysus".

In Shivaite tradition, the god's companions are described as a troupe of freakish, adventurous, delinquent and wild young people, who prowl in the night, shouting in the storm, singing, dancing and ceaselessly playing outrageous tricks on sages and gods. They are called Ganas, the "Vagabonds", corresponding to the Cretan Korybantes and the Celtic Korrigans (fairies' sons). Like the Sileni and Satyrs, some of them have goats' or birds' feet. The Ganas mock the rules of ethics and social order. They personify the joy of living, courage and imagination, which are all youthful values. They live in harmony with nature and oppose the destructive ambition of the city and the deceitful moralism which both hides and expresses it. These delinquents of heaven are always there to restore true values and to assist the "god-mad" who are persecuted and mocked by the powerful. They personify everything which is feared by and displeases bourgeois society, and which is contrary to the good morale of a well-policed city and its palliative concepts.

In Crete, the companions of Dionysus were those supernatural beings, the Korybantes, who were born of Cybele, the Lady of the Mountain. The Greeks identified them with the Dactyls of Mount Ida. The Kouretes (from *Kouros*, boy), the servants of the Mother-goddess, were young men who had been initiated into the god's rites and take part in his orgiastic cult. They were still venerated in Crete during the Greek period. Hesiod connects the satyrs with the Kouretes. According to him, they are dancers, musicians, acrobats, practical jokers and lazy. They press the grape and get drunk. They are perpetually over-excited, jolly fellows in quest of good fortune. They are ecstatic demons for whom eroticism is a form of expression.

99

In their native land of Crete, it was the Kouretes who nursed the infant god. Dionysus is invoked as the Great Kouros, the Murugan or *Kumâra* (the Boy) of Shivaite mythology. According to Nonnos, (*Dionysia*, 13, 137 et seq.), it was the Korybantes and Kouretes who founded Knossos and instituted the cult of Cybele. Demetrios of Skepsis considered that the Kouretes and Korybantes were the same, meaning young men (*Kouroi*), unmarried, chosen for war dances and the rituals of the Mother of the gods. They were probably called Korybantes because of the ecstatic dance they performed involving a forward movement of the head like bulls. "[In ritual practice] the Kouretes are Young Men who have been initiated themselves and will initiate others, will instruct them in tribal duties and tribal dances, will steal them away from their mothers, conceal them, make away with them by some pretended death and finally bring them back as new-born, grown youths, full members of their tribe." (R. F. Willetts, *Cretan Cults and Festivals*, p. 213.)

"The Korybantes, Kouretes, Pans, Sileni, and other elemental spirits were particularly apt to produce mental disorder in those who fell under their sway... In late mythology, the male entourage of Sileni and satyrs, dancers and musicians, is no less essential to the idea of the Dionysiac thyasos than the nymphs and maenads... Heraclitus..., speaking of those inspired by Dionysus, describes them as *nyktipoloi*, night prowlers..., a designation usually applied to spectres, ghosts and all sorts of frightening beings, a swarm of whom, at nightfall, threatened the late traveller with assault." (H. Jeanmaire, *Dionysos*, pp. 132, 271, 276.) *Nishâchâra*, "night prowler", is the name given to the demoniac spirits who are Shiva's followers, as well as to the god himself.

The "Bhaktas" or Bacchants (participants)

The followers of the god have a tendency to identify themselves with his heavenly companions and imitate their behaviour. This is why the Korybantes are sometimes confused with the Kouretes, or, in Indian Shivaism, the Ganas with the *bhaktas*, or bacchants.

The practitioners of the ecstatic or devotional rites which characterize the cult of Shiva are called *bhaktas*, a word which is sometimes translated as "votaries", but which really means "participants". This name is applied to the god as much as to his followers. Bacchos is one of the names of Dionysus and was probably originally the Lydian equivalent of his name. It appears that the Greek words *Bacchos* and bacchai (bacchants) are of foreign origin, being a transposition of the word *bhakta*. "The word *Bacchos* is derived from no known root of the Greek language... The designation of Bacchos is common both to the god and his faithful; the god has taken the name of his votaries." (H. Jeanmaire, *Dionysos*, p. 58.)

In India, the *bhaktas* are followers of the god, some of whom practise the most extreme forms of devotion, – leaving their possessions and family, wandering the roads, dancing ecstatic dances and singing impassioned hymns in which human and divine love are mingled. The great mystic poets of India have often been *bhaktas*. In the state of ecstasy, the *bhakta*'s spirit abandons his body. He can perceive the thoughts of semi-divine beings and wild animals. There is no difference either in concept or practice between the Shivaite *bhaktas* and the Dionysiac bacchants.

In the *Rig Veda* (XI, chap. 2, 18), we already find the type of follower, or companion, of Shiva-Rudra, "with long hair, clothed with the wind [i.e. naked] or wearing dirty garments. Possessed by the gods, he follows the tracks of the nymphs (Apsaras) and celestial spirits (Gandharvas) as well as wild beasts, and understands their thoughts. The poison (*visha*) [i.e., drug] he has drunk in Rudra's cup gives him strength to break whatever resists him". (*Rig Veda*, X, 136, 1–7.) [See Narayana Ayyar, *Origins and Early History of Shivaism in South India*, pp. 15–19.)

"The long-haired sages (*keshin*) are mentioned in the *Atharva Veda* (XI, chap. 2)... such itinerant ascetics were worshippers of Rudra or Shiva rather than of any other god... Shiva alone... is spoken of in later religious literature as the mendicant god (*kapâlin*)... [The god's followers imitate his heavenly companions and practise ecstatic rites.]... The high position attained by such worshippers [of Shiva] must have been understood by the people in the days of the *Atharva Veda*... Their abandonment of the Vedic rites [however] would have been disapproved of by the orthodox people who would therefore have called such men by the name of *Vrâtyas* (heterodox)... To open the eyes of men to the greatness of the true *Vrâtyas*,... a whole chapter of the *Atharva Veda* was dedicated to them" (C. V. Narayana Ayyar, *Origins and Early History of Shivaism in South India*, 16–19.) The Shivaite sects opposed the Vedic norms occasionally with violence. However, some of these sects became assimilated, and joined with the Vedic sects in condemning Shivaite extremists, especially in their wanton and bloody rites, animal or human sacrifices, and the representation of Shiva as a violent and terrifying being who haunts cemeteries. Some of these extremist Shivaite sects, attested by sacred literature, have now completely disappeared. Shivaite sects accepted people of all castes and this rejection of caste has always been a characteristic of the *bhaktas*.

These ascetics, as well as certain laymen who practised ecstatic rites, lived on the fringe of Aryan society. They were sometimes called "strangers", as was also the case of the bacchants.

The *Vaikhânada-smartasûtra* mentions several sects of ascetics and hermits who are recognizable by their unkempt hair and torn garments. Some wear bark loin-cloths, whilst others live naked. They consume small quantities of cow urine and cow-dung, a practice which still continues today. Some of them live near funeral pyres or in cemeteries. They practise Yoga and magical rites. The *Kapâlikas* (wearers of skull necklaces) are represented as leading a dissolute life, mocking the sacred texts, getting drunk, dallying with prostitutes and forsaking the Vedic sacrifices.

In the *Mahâbhârata*, the *vrâtyas* are called "the trash of society, incendiaries, poisoners, pimps, adulterers, abortionists, drug addicts, etc.". (*Mahâbhârata*, V, 35, 46, 1227.) Livy uses practically the same words to describe the activities of Dionysiac sects: incest, rape of young boys, stealing, false-witness, drunkenness, etc. This kind of argument against the *bhaktas* has been employed in all periods of puritanical, conservative society and in Greece served as a pretext for persecuting groups of bacchants. It later was used for persecuting these myhtic sects in the Christian and Islamic world.

Bacchos, like Shiva, is the god of Drunkenness, of Wine and orgiastic Ecstasy. *Baccheia*, "the state of being a bacchant", is the equivalent of *Bhakti*. The ecstatic and mystical way of devotion, the *Bhakti mârga*, is essentially of Shivaite origin.

Bacchos and *Baccheia* are employed in describing those possessed by the Kouretes, the masculine counterpart of the nymphs, as well as the prototypes of the members of Dionysiac confraternities. They practise the rites which make them live like the Korybantes, the joyous vagabonds of heaven who form the entourage of the goddess of the Mountains. The notion of "frenetic madness" (*mania*) is inseparable from that state which is cultivated and plunged into by the bacchant. The followers of the god, maenads, bacchants, and thyai (female participants), all seek to "get out of themselves" (*ekstasis*) and to be possessed by the divinity in a wild delirium.

THE COMPANIONS OF THE GOD

The existence of *Iobacchoi*, or bacchic confraternities, is found among the Ionians as early as the seventh century B.C. "The *Iobacchoi*, or bacchants, during their exercises, uttered the ancient ritual cry, the 'iou-iou'. They survived at Athens for a long time under the form of a confraternity which, in the second century of our era, was the baccheion, or thiasos (association), mainly or solely recruited from men." (H. Jeanmaire, *Dionysos*, p. 236.) They held their monthly meetings in the marshes near the old temple of Dionysus. At Rome, the Luperci were young people who ran naked through the town, striking the passers-by with a goat-skin thong in order to make them fertile.

In the *Linga Purâna*, Shiva takes up the defence of the bhaktas: "No one shall condemn a naked ascetic who is my follower, and who expresses the principle of things, but acts like a child or a madman. None shall mock them, nor call them unpleasant names, if he desire his welfare now and later on. The stupid man who condemns them, condemns the Lord himself." (*Linga Purâna*, I, chap. 33, 3–10.)

"Shiva speaks, 'I, who am the soul of Yoga, by the magic power of Yoga, shall take the form of an ascetic and shall inspire fear among men. I shall enter into a dead body, abandoned in a cemetery . . . and shall live under the name of Lakulisha (the Club-Man). The place of this incarnation shall become a sacred place . . . There my children will be born: the ascetics Kushika, Garga, Mitra and Kaurushya. As worshippers of the phallus, their bodies smeared with ash, they shall practise the rites of *Pashupâta* (animal friendship). Having accomplished the *Maheshvara Yoga*, they shall depart for the heaven of Rudra from which there is no return'." (*Linga Purâna*, I, chap. 24, 126–136.)

". . . Bhandarkar . . . (*Epigraphia Indica*, XXI) . . . fixed the date of Lakulisha, the founder of the *Pashupâta* sect, between 105–130 A.D., but it appears that the sect is much older." (P. Banerjee, *Early Indian Religions*, p. 57 abridged.)

During the sacrifice of the *vrâtyas*, a *mâgadha* (bard) filled the rôle of cantor. On the occasion of a solstitial rite (*mahâvrata*), a prostitute copulated ritually with the bard or with a wandering monk (*Atharva Veda*, XV, chap. 2). The presence of a prostitute is necessary even today for the accomplishment of certain rites, and marriage in particular. "It is necessary to distinguish between the conjugal union, considered as hierogamy, and the orgiastic type of sexual union whose purpose is both universal fecundity and the creation of a 'magical defence'. . . Tantrism has elaborated a whole

103

technique aimed at the sacramental transmutation of sexuality." (M. Eliade, *Histoire des croyances et des idées religieuses*, p. 250.)

The works of Western orientalists are almost exclusively based on the texts of Aryanized Shivaism, which was adapted to the Vedic tradition, and on the teachings of Aryan Brahmans. Even the most open-minded people seem to have had little contact with popular Shivaism, which has remained faithful to ancient traditions. Neither have they attended the immense and bloody sacrifices of he-goats, buffaloes and bulls which are still practised today in several regions of India, or the ecstatic and orgiastic dances, with their consumption of palm-wine and bhang (hashish), which recall the Dionysiac orgies, omophagy (the eating of raw flesh), and human and animal sacrifices. The author has himself attended sacrifices in the Bihar province, where thousands of he-goats were slaughtered, as well as buffalo-sacrifices in the villages of the Himalayas, and ecstatic dances with orgiastic drinking bouts amongst the Shivaite working classes of southern India.

Titans, demons and spirits

Titans and Asuras

Rakshasas (demons), Asuras (Titans) and Pretas (spirits of the dark) make up the train of Shiva. They are the dominant powers of the first ages of the world. Due to the decline of these ancient gods, Shiva himself was obliged to cooperate in their destruction, or to tolerate it, in the perpetual battle which thereafter involved the Titans and gods.

According to the Shivaite concept of the fundamental unity of the world, all forms of existence are related and interconnected. Thus, what happens in one domain also happens in another. For this reason, the conflicts of men are also the conflicts of the gods. In legendary history, the wars of heaven cannot be distinguished from the terrestrial wars which reflect them. During the course of world evolution, the first species are overcome by new species. The immense forests, referred to in the *Rig Veda* when it speaks of "heaven, higher than the vault of trees", have today almost disappeared. In the same way, the gigantic animals of the first ages have vanished, and amongst them the Giants have ceded their place to more modest human races. In the celestial world, the Titans and Asuras who were the ancient gods, lost the war against the "new gods". It is not that the new men or the new gods are better. Quite the contrary. But this evolution follows the transformation of beings throughout the cycle of ages.

The Asuras are the sacred powers of a happy age which existed before the present world. They were followers of Shiva. The war between the Devas, or new gods, and the Asuras reflects the war between the Shivaite people and the Aryan invaders. According to the *Shiva Purâna*, the defeat of the ancient Dravidians was due to the influence of Jainism. This strange atheist religion promised the human individual a sort of immortality through transmigration, and replaced the rites ensuring communication between men and gods, with negative practices, A puritan moralism develops which binds the progress of the individual – his survival and immortality – to forms of abstinence. This concept is found in one form or another, throughout all later religions, and in particular Buddhism and Christianity.

A large part of the Purânas describes the history of the celestial and human world as a conflict between the Asuras and the Devas, which is at the same time the history of man and gods. Similar conflicts take place between animal species, but there is no explicit account of them in surviving texts.

Dionysus' wars are also presented as the chastisement of the Titans. Like Shiva, Dionysus takes part in the destruction of his unfaithful followers. Having defeated them, he is content to frighten and reprimand. He pardons them and leaves them free to depart or to serve with his army. As with the Asuras, it is a question of a "previous race... which according to mythological tradition, was the pre-eminent enemy of the Olympian gods and the new order of Giants which they had set up. This is probably the more ancient layer of tradition, as Titans replace the Giants in the version prevailing amongst the Orphics". (H. Jeanmaire, *Dionysos*, p. 404.)

Like the Purânas, the Vedic texts allude to the conflict between the new gods (Devas) and the Asuras, the more ancient divine family (*Atharva Veda*, VI, chap. 100, 3), depicted as magicians. This conflict is largely related and commented on during the post-Vedic era, in the Brâhmanas, (first millennium B.C.); those works dedicated to the mysteries and to sacrificial rites.

The victory of the Devas over the Asuras was presented as the triumph of Indra, King of the Vedic gods, over the Dasyus, the celestial counterpart of the ancient inhabitants of India who were cast into the deepest darkness (*Atharva Veda*, IX, chap. 2, 17; *Rig Veda*, VII, chap. 99, 4). The new gods took over the sacred powers, which were the magic powers of the Asuras.

According to the Vedic version, the gods' victory became inevitable from the moment when Agni, through whose mouth the gods are fed, abandoned the Asuras as they no longer performed sacrificial rites (*Rig Veda*, X, chap. 124; V, chap. 5). Afterwards, the Devas stole the magic Word (*Vâc*), and Indra – the Aryan "King of heaven" – invited Varuna (the Asuras' sky-god) to come to his kingdom (*Rig Veda*, V, chap. 5). The royalty of Indra is the fruit of usurpation: god the son has dethroned his father (Varuna). Zeus similarly ensured his power by fighting the Titans and his own father.

The *Rig Veda* (X, chap. 99, 3) speaks of Indra as having slain the worshippers of the phallus and conquering by ruse the riches of their hundred-gated cities.

According to a Libyan tradition recounted by Diodorus, Rhea, the wife of Zeus-Ammon and the sister and wife of the Titan Kronos kindled war between Zeus-Ammon and Kronos. The latter was supported by the army of Titans and gave chase to Ammon who found refuge with the Kouretes in Crete. Dionysus-Bacchos came to the rescue of his father, Zeus, with an army of Sileni. He defeated Kronos and the Titans and, after slaying an earth-born monster which devoured all living beings, he undertook the conquest of Egypt, civilizing the country and installing there a son of Kronos and Rhea as rulers. This implies that despite the apparent defeat of the Titans, it is once more the Titanic, or Shivaite, tradition which ensured the supremacy of the Egyptian civilization. Until the Roman conquest Egypt was never subjected to Aryan domination.

The fire of Tripura
The god Shiva himself had to cooperate in the destruction of the wonderful cities of the Asuras, or Titans, who were his worshippers. This is because the Shivaite ethic can admit of no compromise. The destruction of the Dravidian cities by the Aryan barbarians was attributed to the influence of Jainism. Similarly, Zeus' thunderbolt reduced the guilty Titans to ashes.

At the request of the gods, Skanda slew the cruel Asura Taraka, who sowed terror everywhere. Dionysus, in the same way, slew the Monster. The Asuras are, however, generally described as "self-controlled, educated, disciplined, honest, sincere, faithful, courageous, and enemies of the Devas".

"With the aim of reconquering the sovereignty of the world, the three sons of Taraka had for centuries practised the most severe mortifications, until the god Brahmâ – who is the forefather of the Devas as well as of the Asuras – appeared and promised to grant them the gifts which their austerities deserved. The Asuras asked to be freed from sickness, old age and death. Having invoked Shiva the supreme Lord, Brahmâ said, 'Immortality is unobtainable for the gods as it is for the Asuras. All that is born must die'. The Asuras then made another request. 'Build us three flying cities, marvellous, full of riches, and unassailable even by the gods. Let these cities be aligned only once every thousand years and let only Shiva then have the power to destroy them. We respect and worship Shiva. He has no enmity towards us and we thus fear nothing'." (*Shiva Purâna, Rudra Samhitâ*, V, Yuddha Khanda, chap. I, 7–53.)

"Maya,[1] the architect of the Asuras, built three cities, one of gold, the other of silver, and the third of iron. The three towns were situated, one in the sky, the other in the middle air, and the third on the earth. They were filled with many palaces, decorated with jewels, and flying chariots, shining like suns, moved in every direction.

"There were towers and temples of Rudra-Shiva. All the priests were votaries of Shiva. There were camping grounds, beautiful horses and elephants. There were machines for telling the time, playgrounds and places for study.

"The city was filled with very rich and courageous Asuras. They had broad chests and bull-like shoulders. Some were peaceful, others aggressive. Their hair was black and curly. Many of them were heroes in the wars. They took no interest in the rest of the world and lived in their cities, governing themselves according to the precepts of Shiva. Thanks to the god's protection, their desires came true. They enjoyed every sort of pleasure. These Asuras, who were votaries of the cult of the phallus, took advantage of the joys of life and afterwards were rewarded with paradise." (*Shiva Purâna, Rudra Samhitâ*, V, chap. 1, 55–78, and chap. 3, 44.)

After numerous battles in which the gods were shamefully defeated, they obtained Shiva's cooperation in destroying the three marvellous and corrupt cities. Shiva had to destroy them with a single arrow, at that moment when they were aligned. When this moment arrived, "Shiva shot a shaft at them, which shone like innumerable suns. This shaft, of explosive energy and fire, burnt all the Asuras who lived in

[1] Maya is the equivalent of Daidalos, the divine architect who built the labyrinth for Minos.

the city. The Asuras, who were votaries of Shiva, lamented and called for his aid, but, with the agreement of Shiva, they were reduced to ashes, even while they were calling on him. Even as the universe will burn up at the end of the ages, so all things and all living beings, women, men, and chariots, were reduced to ash by the fire. Some women were torn from their lovers' embraces and burnt. Others who slept intoxicated or exhausted by love, were also burnt. Some of them, enveloped by the flames, ran hither and thither and fell fainting. Not the smallest thing, movable or immovable, escaped the terrible fire of Tripura." (*Shiva Purâna, Rudra Samhitâ,* V, chap. 10, 27–39.)

Hesiod relates the similar destruction of the Titans by Zeus-Shiva. "Zeus . . . cast his lightning without respite and the squadrons of thunder bolts flew from his vigorous hand, accompanied by thunder and lightning, making the divine flame spin and hurling down blows. All around, the soil, the source of life, crackled with fire; and, in prey to the flame, the immense woods cried with a loud voice. The whole earth boiled, and the ocean waves, and the unfruitful sea. A burning breath enveloped the Titans, sons of the soil, whilst the flame arose, immense, toward the divine sky, and, despite their strength, they felt their eyes blinding, as the flash of the thunderbolt and the lightning blazed. A marvellous heat penetrated the abyss. The sight to the eyes, the sound to the ears, were equal to those which earth and heaven would make on crashing together." (Hesiod, *The Theogony,* pp. 690–700.)

The memory of the three cities of the Asuras is found even in the Celtic world, in the three kingdoms of Merlin.

Rakshasas, demons and ghosts

Besides Ganas and Asuras, Shiva's train includes all kinds of spirits, demons, elves, nymphs, ogresses, phantoms, snakes, and all the spirits which rule the aerial or terrestrial world – over the forests, springs, storms, and also over the mysterious infernal regions. Dionysus, apart from the Korybantes, is surrounded with Pans, Sileni, nymphs, and various spirits. As with the Korybantes and Kouretes, it is not always easy to distinguish the supernatural beings from their human equivalents. Some of the spirits from the mysterious world of prehistoric forests have birds' or hinds' feet, horses' tails, or serpents' bodies.

Ghosts (*Pretas*) are also counted amongst the servants of Shiva, the god of Death. They are the spirits of human beings who died a violent death, the elements of whose subtle bodies remain intact for a longer or shorter time.

The Rakshasas play an important rôle. They belong to the Asura family, but are cruel and ferocious. They are fallen angels who have become evil, and are called scalders, devourers, and burners. Their long fangs call to mind the vampires. Originally, the word *rakshasa* meant "guardian". They later became the demons of Christian tradition and it is they who preside over the tortures in Hell.

Heroes and demigods

In Shivaite Tantrism, "hero" (*vîra*) is the name given to initiates who through practising Yoga, have acquired the strength to dominate, both the physical world and the subtle world of spirits. Thus they are able to vanquish the gods and to conquer heaven. These are the men who have become demigods. In Aryanized Shivaism, both Hindu and Achaean, a divine origin is often attributed to heroes or supermen, who accomplish wonderful deeds and are finally received amongst the gods. After their death, they become the object of a cult. Krishna and Râma are considered partial incarnations, or *avatâras*, or Vishnu, the god whose function is to protect the world. Indeed, the Greek word hero means "protector". Both Hercules and Achilles have a divine ancestor. The same concept is found with the Semitic Gilgamesh or Celtic Cuchulain, who was the son of the god Lug and author of a thousand exploits.

"The deification of certain dead persons in Crete paved the way for mystery religions, at the same time explaining more clearly the traditions concerning privileged heroes, survivors during the Greek era of pre-Hellenic civilization. The deification of Hercules on the famous pyre on Oeta, that of Achilles on the isle of Leuca, the version given by the Odyssey of the carrying of Menelaus to the Happy Isles, the immortalization of Peleas..., are relics... of a past belief." (Charles Picard, *Les Religions préhelléniques*, p. 172–173.)

Women could also attain the rank of hero, such as Arundhati, who was placed in the heavens as the pole star, or the Pleiades, the foster-mothers of Skanda-Dionysus, who became stars. Plato mentions Alcestis who, moved by love, did not fear to die and returned victoriously from Hades. He also compared the words êros (hero) and Eros (love), since heroes are characterized even more by their generosity, detachment and love, than by their courage.

Râma and Krishna, non-Aryan dark-skinned princes, are the favourite divinities of popular religion in India. Râma (Charming), who has become the Prince Charming of Western fairy-tales, performed wonderful deeds in order to find his beloved. Krishna, who was transferred from his mother's womb to that of a shepherdess to avoid the massacre of all new-born children commanded by the cruel king Asura Kamsa, is worshipped as the infant-god – the *bambino* – and often replaces the infant Skanda. In just such a way did the cult of the infant Jesus replace the cult of infant Dionysus. Krishna became the lover of sixteen thousand shepherdesses in the forest of Vrinda, and especially of his sister Râdhâ. Then, after performing numerous heroic deeds and killing the cruel Kamsa, he re-established peace on Earth. He became the charioteer of Arjuna in the "Great War" of Mahâbhârata, which recalls the conflicts of the Aryans and Dravidians.

Animals as well as half-man half-animal beings can also become heroes. Such is the case of the Minotaur, and also of the incarnations of Vishnu, who as the man-lion, slays and devours the demon Hiranya-Kashipu to save the pious Prahlad. Other examples are the wild boar who raises the earth swamped by the waters, and the fish which guides the ark to a safe place.

In the *Râmâyana*, Shiva – incarnate in the form of the monkey Hanuman – himself takes part in destroying the powerful Rakshasa Râvana, who was one of his followers. The *Shiva Purâna*, briefly summarizing the sources which inspired the long Râmâyana poem, recounts that:

"In due time, Shiva became incarnate in the form of a monkey called Hanuman, renowned for his strength and his deeds. From his earliest youth, Hanuman, the most powerful of monkeys, was extremely audacious. One morning, he took the sun for a fruit and wished to devour it, but desisted at the request of the gods... He went to see Sugrîva, who had been exiled to the forest by his brother Bali, the king of the monkeys. It was there that he became allied with Râma, who also lived in exile with his brother Lakshmana, and lamented because [the demon] Râvana had carried off his wife Sîtâ. Râma slew the powerful king of the monkeys, Bali, who was evil. At the request of Râma, Hanuman, strong and cunning, went with an army of monkeys to search for Sîtâ. Learning that she was to be found in the city of Lanka (Ceylon), he crossed the sea in a single bound, which none had done before him, and reached Lanka. There, after many exploits, he gave Sîtâ the sign of recognition entrusted to him by Râma... and consoled Sîtâ. On the way, he destroyed the gardens of Râvana and slew many Rakshasas. He even slew the son of Râvana... The heroic monkey sowed disaster wherever he went. Finally, he was captured. Râvana had his tail wrapped in oil-soaked cloth and set on fire. Hanuman took advantage of this to spread fire throughout the town... after which, he leaped into the sea, thus quenching his tail, and attained the other shore. Without any sign of fatigue or suffering, he gave Râma the jewel which Sîtâ wore on her forehead. With the aid of his army of monkeys, he transported pieces of mountain and built a bridge on the sea.

"Râma put up a phallic image of Shiva and venerated it so as to obtain victory. He then crossed the sea and besieged Lanka with the army of monkeys. The hero Hanuman commanded Râma's army and slew many Rakshasas. He healed Lakshmana, wounded by a javelin, with bull's sperm.

"He destroyed Râvana, his family and his servants, and then returned with Râma and Lakshmana to their hermitage... He forced all the Rakshasas to submit to Râma and performed many great deeds. He established the cult of Râma in the world. He was the incarnation of Shiva, who is the resort of all his followers. He saved the life of Lakshmana and humiliated the Titans. He is called the Messenger of Râma in the world. He protects those who worship him." (*Shiva Purâna, Shatarudra Samhitâ*, chap. 20.)

Chapter 6

ANIMAL AND VEGETABLE FORMS OF THE GOD AND GODDESS

The Zoomorphic forms of the god and goddess

In the cosmic universe, the principles which are revealed in gods, spirits and men also appear in the animal, vegetable and mineral world. There exists a hierarchy amongst animals and plants, revealing differences both of nature and degree. For this reason, while there are some unclean animals, or pernicious and poisonous plants, there are also plants and animals which are beneficent and sacred. Due to their nature and to the symbols they represent, certain animals are always associated with certain gods. Each divine aspect is connected with an animal species, such as the elephant of Indra (the king of heaven), the ram of Agni (the god of Fire), the mouse of Ganesha, the vulture of Vishnu, etc.

The principles represented by Shiva and the goddess correspond to the nature of the bull, the snake and the panther (occasionally replaced by the tiger or lion) and in the case of Skanda, the ram, the cock and peacock. These same animals are also worshipped in Crete. In India, as in the Minoan world, a few fantastic hybrids, such as the griffon, are also found.

"Dionysus is not a man: he is an animal and at the same time, a god, thus manifesting the extremes of the opposing characteristics in man himself." (Giorgio Colli, *La Sapienza greca*, p. 15.) The different types of men are also related to certain animals.

The bull

"Some evil spirits, born of Vishnu and the daughters of the Titans, sowed terror in the heavens and on the earth . . . Shiva took the form of a bull and exterminated them." (*Shiva Purâna, Shatarudra Samhitâ,* chap. 23.) In times of danger, Baal, too, reverts to his primitive form as the cosmic bull.

The bull is the vehicle of Shiva. The bull is Shiva, and in the animal kingdom, is the manifestation of the principle represented by Shiva-Dionysus. Apis, the bull, is identified with Osiris. The bull is the sacred animal of the Minoan era, the ancient Cretan god worshipped since the dawn of civilization. "Son of the Earth, the expression of the welcoming, receptive and passive chthonian powers and, at the same time . . . the symbol of the seed-producing active principle, the bull was the sacred animal in all cattle-rearing civilizations." (Paolo Santarcangeli, *Le Livre des Labyrinthes*, p. 234.)

The bull is associated with the idea of supreme godhead, or great divinity. According to Jean-Clarence Lambert (*Labyrinthes et dédales du monde*, p. 10), the Sanskrit work *Go* (bull) is one of the etymologies for the English word *God*, Scandinavian *Gud*, and German *Gott*. In Anatolia, during the seventh millennium, as in Minoan Crete, the male god has the form of a bull, or is associated with the bull. During the period indicated by the Purânas for the spreading of Shivaism (the seventh millennium B.C.), the first representations are found at Çatal Höyük in Anatolia of the god in the form of a boy or adolescent, or even as a bearded adult, mounted on his sacred animal, which was the bull. Bull-heads are also found fixed on walls.

An image of Shiva found at Mohenjo Daro (second millennium B.C.) shows the ityphallic god seated in a Yoga position. His head is crowned with bull horns. Many horned masks and representations of humped bulls are also found. The unicorn-bull is also depicted at Monhenjo Daro. Ktesias and Aristotle attributed the origin of the unicorn to India. "We worship him who unites the strong and the weak, who causes trouble and is never troubled, Nandi, the bull, with his wide hump and his single shining horn." (*Linga Purâna*, I, 21–25.)

"There is no true break between the ill-shapen statuettes of a male deity seated on a bull – examples of which have been found at Çatal Höyük – the representations of the storm-god of the Hittite era, and the statues of Jupiter Dolichenus worshipped by the soldiers of the Roman legions; nor is there between the leopard goddess of Çatal Höyük, the Hittite goddess Hepat, and the Cybele of the classical period." (Maurice Vieyra, *Les Religions de l'Anatolie antique*, p. 258.) On coins found at Gortyna, in Crete, the goddess also appears mounted on a bull. Coins from Phaistos show the goddess as Europa welcoming the bull. Near the village of Doliche, a divinity was worshipped on the top of a mountain, who after many transformations, became Jupiter, protector of the Roman armies. He was depicted standing on a bull, holding the double axe in his hand.

Humped bulls and other Shivaite emblems from the Chalcolithic period were found by Sir A. Stein in Gedrosia (Quetta region, in present-day Pakistan). Furthermore, images of an ithypallic Shiva, standing on the horns of a bull, were found in the Kazbek treasure, from the Caucasus mountains. He holds a double axe, the symbol of the labyrinth.

"To the Canaanites of Ugarit, [the most important deities were] Bull-El... and Baal. This god can be identified with the Phoenician Hadad, the Syrian-Hittite Teshub and the Egyptian Seth... different names for a god of heights, storms and rains. The voice of Baal is heard in the clouds,... he carries a thunder-bolt. He has the strength of a bull, and horns rise from the front of his helmet. Baal... meets monsters with a human body and the head of a bull." (R. F. Willetts, *Cretan Cults and Festivals*, p. 162.)

The struggle of the new Hebrew monotheism against the Baal cult reflects the deep penetration of Shivaite concepts in the Semitic world. The persistence of ecstatic dances was even attested at the time of Samuel (about 1020 B.C.).

The bulls, Apis and Mnevis, the living incarnations of Osiris, played a fundamental rôle in the religion of the Egyptians, who were from a linguistic point of view, Semites. According to Cicero and John Lydus, a second Dionysus (corresponding to Skanda, Shiva's son) was born of the god of the Nile (which, in the case of the Hindus, was the Ganges), who was Hapi or Serapis, a god in bull form. The Pharaoh was called "the Bull who makes the mother fertile".

The mythical figure of Minos is always associated with the bull. According to the legend handed down by the Greeks, Zeus in bull-shape appeared to Europa, the daughter of Agenor, on the shore at Tyre. He swam with her to Crete and there coupled with her. From this union were born three sons, Minos, Sarpeon and Rhadamanthos. Minos was adopted by the King of the country and later succeeded him. Pasiphae, daughter of the sun and wife of Minos, gave him several children. Then, being enamoured of a bull, she gave birth to Asterios (the star), called the Minotaur (bull-Minos). He had the head of a bull and the body of a man. Minos shut him away under guard in the labyrinth built by Daedalos. Coins from Gortyna show the marriage of Zagreus and Europa and also Europa's approaches to the bull. In India, we find the description of Shiva taking the form of a bull in order to fecundate the goddess. At Çatal Höyük, images are found of the goddess giving birth to a bull. The image of the

114

Minotaur is identical to that of Nandi (joyous), the bull of Shiva. Nandi, the man-bull, is figured on many seals from Mohenjo Daro, which are identical to those found at Sumer, representing Eabani, or Enkidu, who was created by the goddess Aruru to fight against Gilgamesh. Nandi is depicted in the form of the Minotaur in all Shivaite temples, even today.

Bull-Dionysus was invoked in Elis. He appeared coming from the sea, dancing in bull-form. According to the Shivaite myth, it is Nandi, the bull, who taught men dancing and music. Athenaeas remarks (XI, para. 5, 476a) that Dionysus is often referred to by poets as a bull. Though not only a bull-god, he willingly reveals himself in this shape. In Crete as in Egypt, the cow was the symbol of the Moon and the Bull that of the Sun, and thus of fertility. At Olympia, Dionysus, identified with Cretan Zeus, was worshipped in the shape of a bull or a snake. Dionysus and Poseidon are often depicted on Greek vases, mounted on two bulls, one white and the other black. "[Among the Celts,] the bull [represented] the male principle of fertility distributing his sexual favours and energy among female devotees and initiates . . . One example . . . is the cult of the Celtic horned god Cernunnos." (P. Rawson, *Primitive Erotic Art*, p. 54.)

Popular legends have been created about the birth of the bull. In the *Kanda purânam* (VI, chap. 13, 303), the goddess of Fortune, Lakshmi, for fear of being drowned in the flood, took the form of a bull and became the mount of Shiva.

Shiva is always shown riding on a bull or accompanied by one. In the temple of Shiva, where the *Linga* is worshipped, the bull is represented either standing or lying down, facing the sanctuary. The faithful touch his testicles in order to obtain virile power and divine protection. The bull wandering in search of adventure personifies the erotic impulse. Only Shiva, who dominates Eros, may ride the bull. Bulls are let free in order to obtain favours from the god. In India, the entire bovine species is sacred. In Phrygia, as elsewhere during Antiquity, it was a criminal offence to kill an ox. The cow and the ox were sacred. Bull festivals, bull cults, as well as bull sacrifices, are everywhere the remnants of Shivaite rites.

In Minoan Crete, bull-fighting games were part of the cult. The sacred corridas were celebrated in the tiered courtyards of the palace. The Knossos paintings show acrobats vaulting over the bull. The bull personifies rectitude and justice, the virtues of the strong. In the Hellenic world, children were in some way dedicated to the bull.

Spartiate children of different ages ate and slept together, forming a community called "the herd" (*agela*), under the surveillance of a young man, the "chief bull" (*bouagoi*). During the Thiodaisia festival, associated with the young people's leaving the *agela* and with their collective marriage (according to Strabo), the god who was worshipped was the Minoan bull-god, later called the Cretan Zeus (Kretagenes). In the thiasoi, or Dionysiac associations, like those of Torre Nova (second century A.D.), the rôles of *boukolos* (cowman) and *archiboukolos* demonstrate a return to the cult of the bull-Dionysus. Just as the Minotaur was slain by Theseus, the divine bull was also finally sacrificed: the god was put to death to redeem mankind. His blood was carefully collected in a vase.

The Kouretes' hymn in honour of Zeus-Diktaios is addressed to the bull about to be sacrificed, which is identified with Dionysus. The meaning of the putting to death of the god will be discussed later on in treating of sacrifices. In Shivaite India, the bull-sacrifice is rarely performed nowadays, but it forms an essential part of the ancient ritual.

The horns and divine royalty

At Mohenjo Daro, Shiva appears in a Yoga position, wearing bull-horns. On a stele dating from the fourteenth century B.C. at Ugarit, the mighty and merciful bull-god is depicted seated on a throne. He is dressed in a long robe and wears a horn-crowned tiara. The symbol of the horns everywhere expresses the god's power. The portraits of kings were decorated with them, to show that their power came from heaven. The bull and the snake, connected with Mesopotamian divinely-ordered royalty, reached Greece through Crete during the Minoan era. The ancestor of the Cretan royal family was the bull-god. The bull thus became the symbol of Minoan royalty.

The Minotaur was perhaps originally Minos himself, conceived in the form of a bull, and the principal mythical figure of ancient Crete. The Macedonian kings also wore horns to show their divine origin. When Moses descended from the mountain, with the spirit of God upon him, his head appeared to be adorned with horns (Exodus, XXXIV, 35). In the Babylonian epopee, Gilgamesh leaves for war against Khumbaba, a giant whose head is adorned with horns. In Egypt, the bull Apis represents the god-king. Reshep, the warrior-god of Asiatic origin identified with Seth, and the brother of Osiris, wears the crown of Upper Egypt adorned with two horns.

Dionysus is represented as a horned god:

"Zeus... found for him another womb wherein to rest, for he hid him in his thigh and fastened it with golden pins... And when the fates had fully formed the horned god, he brought him forth and crowned him with a coronal of snakes..." (Euriphedes, *The Bacchantes*, 95–102.)

The Etruscan royal "ossuaries", in the form of huts, bear horns as decoration on the median line of the roof. At Delos, apart from a cubic stone, there existed an altar called the *Keraton*, made of the horns of oxen and goats and dedicated to the cult of Karneian Apollo, the protector of horned animals. In Brittany, this cult has reappeared in that of Saint Cornelius. "The very word horn is clearly connected with the root KRN, and with that of *crown*, another symbolic expression of the same idea... Both are an 'apex' and placed on the head... Similarly, the Greek word *Keraunos*, thunder-bolt, which usually strikes peaks, high places and tall objects, appears to be derived from the same root." (René Guénon, *Symboles fondamentaux de la science sacrée*, p. 204.) The name Carnac, the centre of megalithic temples, also recalls the root KRN, as does Egyptian Karnak, Indian Konarak, etc.

The significance of the horns spread all over the pre-Celtic, Celtic and Germanic world, reaching as far as central Germany. "Kernunnos or Cornely, the patron of horned beasts, is the builder of megalithic monuments near which are found the *mein gurun* or 'thunder-stones', as the prehistoric axes are popularly called. The cult of Saint Cornely, who was sacrificed for his faith, evokes the image of the sacred bull of Minos together with his attributes, the horns and the double axe." (Gwenc'hlan Le Scouëzec, *La Bretagne mystérieuse*, p. 170.)

The horned devil of popular stories, with his cloven hooves, brandishing a trident, is doubtless of the same origin.

Leopard, lion and panther

At Hacilar in Anatolia, images from as early as the sixth millennium (about 5700) have been found of the goddess riding a leopard. The leopard, lion and panther are the vehicles, symbols and incarnations of the goddess. Pârvatî is shown riding a feline which represents the seductiveness and cruel character of the female principle. In Dionysiac tradition, the leopard is sacred to Dionysus, and the maenads are considered panthers. According to Antoninus Liberalis (whose source is Nicander), Dionysus warned the daughters of Minias not to neglect his rites of initiation (*teletai*). He does this in the guise of a girl, and then reappears successively in the forms of a bull, a lion and a leopard. The chariot on which Dionysus is often depicted is sometimes drawn by panthers. The maenads also play with panthers. Some of the maenads identify themselves with carnivores. They wear a leopard-skin. "Panthers today are wild beasts. However, they were not so originally, but were pretty girls, adorned with vine branches, . . . the dancing nurses of Bacchos during his wanderings." (Oppian, V, 230.)

Under the New Empire in Egypt, Shiva and Pârvatî once again appeared as Reshep and his companion Kadesh, who were considered "Asian" gods. The goddess is shown mounted on a lion and the god has a crown and horns. They can be likened to the ancient forms of the divine couple, Seth, the violent god, and Hathor, the cow-goddess.

Snakes

Snakes are traditionally inhabitants of the subterranean world. They live in the entrails of the Earth and know its secrets. They are secretors of poison and are consequently the antithesis of the sky gods who possess ambrosia, the elixir of immortality. The ancient Dravidians worshipped snakes. The Asuras are often represented as snake-gods. Relegated to the underground world, they are the great people of the Nâgas or serpents, everywhere depicted with a man's body and a snake's tail. Temples contain many such statues and they play a great rôle in Shivaite legends. The snake-cult is also a very important aspect of Cretan religion. Snakes are even occasionally involved in the world of men. In the *Nâgânanda*, "the Serpent's Luck",[1] the poet Harsha recounts the adventures of a young Nâga, saved from the cruel vulture of Vishnu by a heroic prince, thanks to the intervention of the White Goddess, Gauri.

It is the Nâgas who preserve the wonderful knowledge of the ancient sages, and the secrets of magical power. The *Shatapatha Brâhmana* (XIII, 4, 3, 9), (about 1000), recognizes that true knowledge, "the Veda, is in fact the wisdom of the serpent". The Âdityas, or twelve suns, were originally snakes. Snakes are thus the survivors of the more ancient gods.

[1] See: *Le Théâtre de Harsha*, trans A. Daniélou.

ANIMAL AND VEGETABLE FORMS OF THE GOD AND GODDESS

The cult of the snakes or Nâgas was incorporated into the Aryan religion during the period of the sûtras (circa 600 to 400 B.C.). "When Alexander had attacked and captured several Indian cities, he discovered in some of them, besides other animals, a snake which the Indians considered sacred. They kept it in an underground place and worshipped it with devotion. The Indians supplicated Alexander to let no one molest these reptiles, and he consented." (Aelian, *Variae historiae*, chap. 21.)

"The snake-cult is associated... with that of the subterranean powers, which sometimes produce fertility and are thus benevolent. Sometimes they are fearsome, since according to their will, they can ensure or destroy the stability of the world." (Paolo Santarcangeli, *Le Livre des Labyrinthes*, p. 112.) A snake is entwined around the wand of Hermes. Two snakes wind around Mercury's caducaeus and the healing wand of Aesculapius. Aesculapius is accompanied by a snake, which indicates his magical powers and is a reminder that the science of healing came originally from the ancient snake-gods.

The Ureus, or snake which the sovereign wears as a diadem in Egyptian representations, symbolizes the power of healing, often associated with kingship. The Asura sovereigns wear an identical diadem in Hindu temple iconography.

"Dionysiac congregations had preserved and renewed the tradition of familiarity with reptiles and of snake-handling, an ancient practice whose religious character is witnessed by monuments as early as the second Minoan millennium." (H. Jeanmaire, *Dionysos*, p. 403). In India today, a great number of "snake charmers" are not only an attraction for tourists, but form confraternities to whom magical powers are attributed.

Snake-cults are still to be found today in Italy. In the Abruzzi, for the Feast of St. Dominic, snakes are wound around the saint's statue. Handling snakes, the Faithful follow the statue in procession, a custom which is clearly the inheritance of a Dionysiac rite.

The most important of the Minoan house-cults was the snake-cult, particularly in the form of the snake-goddess, the Mistress of the Animals. The old snake-goddess arose beside Zeus, in the person of Hera. In Greece, the snake later became a male god, but remained the centre of the domestic cult. Cretan Zeus, in the form of a snake, is called Meilikhios, the Benevolent.

The snake as an image of the female principle, represents attachment to the things of the earth and distils the poison which prevents man from attaining freedom and therefore is the counterpart of the elixir of immortality (*amrita*).

In the Greek myth related by Athenagoras (XX, chap. 292), Zeus pursues his mother, Rhea, who takes the form of a snake. Zeus takes the same shape and, binding her with what is called "the knot of Heracles", possesses her. In western Asia, Astarte is depicted with serpents ringing her hands and arms. In India, Kâli appears covered with snakes. A snake entwines the *Linga* of Shiva and with its pointed tongue touches the opening. Shiva himself wears snakes as ornaments around his neck and arms.

The primordial Energy, or Shakti, is Shiva's power of realization. It is the principle of the unwinding of revelation. As the origin of the cycles of time, it is represented in the form of a snake. When the universe unfolds, the snake uncoils and, when it retires within itself, it coils up again and serves as a bed for the sleeping Vishnu (the cohesive force), according to a cosmological myth deriving from Yogic experience.

The mystery of the labyrinth

In Crete, when those symbols and rites apparently derived from Shivaism appeared, Shivaism itself was at least two thousand years old. This represents a considerable sum of religious experience and explains the variety of the legends with which the basic concepts have been embellished. Since its remotest origins, Shivaism has been inseparable from Yoga. We should not take vague exterior similarities as a basis for the study of these symbols, rites and mysteries. Instead, looking at the profound and unrivalled knowledge of the human being, as represented by Yoga, together with its concepts of the terrestrial world and the cosmos, as established by analogy with the structure of the human being, we see many aspects of the symbolism of ancient religions becoming clear and comprehensible. It is necessary to get used to the idea that symbols represent, and often disguise, a very high level of knowledge from an extremely ancient period, and are not childish and so-called primitive superstitions. If, in order to understand the system of the labyrinth, we envisage it as a symbolic and ritual representation of Yoga experience, its meaning is evident.

The aim of the whole Yoga technique is to awaken the female principle, the snake goddess, or Shakti, coiled "in spiral form" (*Kundalini*) within "the basic centre" – the *Mûlâdhara* – at the base of the spine. It should be noted that in the human being, the goddess is considered an energetic principle residing in the basic centre, not in the female organ, and has nothing to do either with fertility or procreation.

The *Mûlâdhara* corresponds to the principle of earth, the sphere of the olfactory sense, which is the most material of the five elements. The alimentary and excretory functions are the starting point for the manifestation of life in its most rudimentary forms. This point is the basis for all activities and higher levels of accomplishment. The snake-goddess lives in the Earth and is mother of all living beings. The goddess is thus associated with the most fundamental bodily functions, as opposed to the illusory digressions of the brain.

Among the sensory organs of action, in relation to the five elements or states of matter, the anus is associated with the principle of earth, the penis with the principle of water, the feet with the principle of fire, the hand with the principle of air, and the mouth, as the organ of speech, with the principle of ether. The corresponding perceptive organs are: smell (earth), taste (water), sight (fire), skin (touch, air), and hearing (ether). It is by utilizing our entire body and by taking as a starting point its most fundamental functions that we are able to understand our own nature and can thus begin to seek an understanding of more evolved aspects in order to reach the point of intelligence. Beyond intelligence is the divine and deep reality of things, which is incomprehensible by means of logical thought. This is the essential teaching of Tantric doctrine.

Basic energy is therefore lodged in the "earth", that is, in the basic centre. It is the principle which we may consider as the Earth goddess, from whom everything sprang. With its spiral, the *Kundalini* or coiled-up energy surrounds the procreative principle, which is represented as the phallus of Shiva, a self-born (*svayambhu*) *Linga*. The male principle in the basic centre is also represented as a bull. The second essential vital function is reproduction, connected with the union of the male and female principles. The *Kundalini* image is thus a spiral surrounding a phallus or a bull.

It does not please the gods that man should obtain knowledge and free himself from the illusion of the world of appearances. Everything has been foreseen to lead him astray. It is for this reason that the path of knowledge is crooked (*vakra*). Each time we feel we are getting near to the truth, we get lost and then we have to turn back and change route. The human spirit cannot directly attain to divine reality and, in order to reach it, must follow a tortuous path, along subterranean, unexpected and mysterious ways.

The symbol of the cross represents the extension of the world starting from the centre, from a single starting point. The difficulty of returning to the starting point is portrayed by the gammateon or swastika. The uninitiate who follows one of its branches will lose himself in space and never reach the centre, that is, the truth. At any given moment, it is necessary to know how to change route so as to arrive at the starting point. The swastika is the symbol of Ganesha, the god of mysteries. Ganesha is the guardian of the gate which leads to the coiled snake-goddess and of the bull or phallus which she encircles. In the human body, the strait gate leading to the earth-centre, or snake-goddess, is the anus. It is here that the centre of Ganesha is found, the guardian of gates and mysteries, and servant of the goddess. Beyond, is situated the labyrinth of entrails, those tortuous paths leading to all the vital organs, which are examined by the augur during the sacrifice. The Yogi who succeeds in awakening the coiled-up energy may, with its help, reach one after another of the centres where the higher forms of life and subtle powers dwell. This will make him a "hero" (*vîra*), the master of all the energies latent both in and outside himself, and will allow him to dominate the dark forces of elementary nature in order to obtain intelligence and divine light. To do all this, he must traverse the interior labyrinth, the physical form of which is the intestinal maze in which the different subtle centres are concealed.

The symbolic and ritualistic expression of this interior journey, which is the image of the evolution of creation and life, as well as of the process of initiation and enlightenment lies within the juxtaposed representation of the snake-spiral (image of the goddess) and the labyrinth (the secret abode of the male principle, the bull or phallus). Similarly, in Mother-Earth, the sinuous paths of the caves, penetrating the earth's entrails and sheltering the snake, lead to the mysterious centre where the bull-god is worshipped. The swastika, the symbol of Ganesha, guardian of Mysteries and lord of the Ganas or Korybantes, guards the entrance. There is also a celestial bull and serpent hidden in the depths of the mysterious labyrinths of the starry sphere.

The labyrinth always recalls initiatory mysteries; devious ways leading to enlightenment. "The person who travels through the labyrinth... is finally able to find the 'central place', which is, from the point of view of initiatory realization, his own centre... If we consider the case in which the labyrinth connects with a cave, the latter, which is surrounded by the labyrinth's winding and is its final goal, thus occupies – in this overall pattern – the most interior and central point. This corresponds very well with the idea of a spiritual centre and equally well with the equivalent symbolism of the heart." (René Guénon, *Symboles fondamentaux de la science sacrée*, pp. 216 and 392.)

Entering the cave signifies a return to the entrails of the Earth; to the maternal womb. This subterranean journey evokes as a mystery the great maternal womb and labyrinth in which man was born before beginning life. The myth of the descent into hell also evokes a return to "the womb of Mother Earth".

It is interesting to note that Freud, by a different route, also arrived at the intuition of this aspect of the subtle structure of the human being. "The story of the labyrinth reveals a representation of anal birth; the winding paths are the intestines, Ariadne's thread, the umbilical cord." (S. Freud, *New Introductory Lectures*.)

There is a whole ritual connected with anal penetration through the narrow gate opening on to the labyrinth (in man, the intestine). In Tantric Yoga, the centre of Ganesha – the guardian of gates – is found in the region of the rectum. The male organ, in directly penetrating the area of coiled-up energy (*Kundalini*), may help its brutal awakening and thus provoke a state of enlightenment and sudden perception of realities of a transcendental order. Hence this act may play an important part in initiation. "This probably explains one male initiation ritual, widespread among primitive people but rarely recorded frankly by Western observers..., during which adult male initiates have anal intercourse with novices... Such a custom may well lie behind the homosexual eroticism actively encouraged among the Classical Greeks." (P. Rawson, *Primitive Erotic Art*, p. 48.) The performance of this act is one of the accusations brought against Dionysiac organizations by their detractors, and also against certain initiatory groups in the Christian and Islamic world. It involves a technical process, analogous to the use of certain drugs, which by means of direct action, affects the internal organs connected with the subtle centre.

The coiled Energy is the principle, or Motor, of all human achievement. Human tendencies and achievements all appear as so many impulses coming from this coiled energy, which are in turn so many aspects of the snake-goddess. Concupiscence, hate, fear, anger, sorrow, etc., are all manifestations of the Shakti, and are so many *shaktis*, or powers of a trans-subjective nature. One should not say, "I love, I hate, I am afraid", etc., but rather, "A force is present in me, under the form of love, anger, hate", etc. This Yogic concept explains the existence of the human being's unreasoned impulses. The various *shaktis* are part of the living being, and rule him. Man, like the world, is inhabited by spirits, or powers, to which he is subject. Only the *siddha*, the realized being, can control them. He leaves the world of action (*karma*), and no longer has any use for either rites or virtues. In his own body, he becomes the master of creation, and dominates the power of the snake. The power of these internal impulses may be observed in those persons whom we say have a dual personality. They speak of themselves, saying, "He wants this or that. I can do nothing about it. I cannot contradict him", etc.

Representations of the coiled snake-goddess, or of the labyrinth leading to the god she encircles, are numerous and are found wherever Shivaite doctrine and symbols have spread. This is why, starting from the sixth millennium, more or less complicated representations of the spiral or the labyrinth are found all over the Indo-Occidental world. Legends such as that of the Minotaur are popular myths invented to explain, or rather to disguise, a mystery which is only revealed to the initiate, the *vîra*, or "hero", who conquers the labyrinth.

"The labyrinth... is one of the most constant themes in European cave art, from the Mediterranean to the North Sea. It appears engraved in stone in Europe toward the second millennium B.C. and, from this time, spread over the whole continent... It is seen on the funerary figures of the pre-Indo-Germanic peoples." (P. Santarcangeli, *Le Livre des labyrinthes*, pp. 160–168.)

There are "Mesopotamian and Babylonian representations of labyrinths, which are very similar in design to those much later ones found on Cretan coins... According to cuneiform descriptions, these drawings represent the viscera of sacrificed animals... The spiral-shaped ensemble was the 'palace of the viscera'... All Nordic labyrinths repeat the same form as the Cretan or 'visceral packet' style". (P. Santarcangeli, *op. cit.*, pp. 156 and 205.)

In Antiquity, the Cretan labyrinth was considered an imitation of the Egyptian labyrinth. Its architect, Daedalos (the expert craftsman), who corresponds to Maya, the Asuras' architect, was walled up in it by Minos, but managed to escape with his companion Icaros. It is in the labyrinth that Minos imprisons the Minotaur, who was later killed by Theseus. The conquest of the spiritual and magical world by a "hero", with the aid of Yoga techniques, has become the victory of an Aryan hero over the ancient god of Mysteries. Among other possible etymologies, it has been suggested that the word labyrinth stems from the Greek *labrys*, the sacred "double axe" depicted everywhere, on stones, plaster-work, pottery, seals, as well as on the altar of Knossos. At the same time, it should be noted that *labra* means a cave; and *labirion* a mole's tunnel. The Cretan word for "axe" was *pe-le-ky*. The symbolism of the double axe and the swastika is similar. The outline of the double axe also represents a road which has no end. The symbol of the double axe is found all over pre-Celtic northern Europe. "The Greeks called the palace of Minos the labyrinth, crumbling although it had not entirely vanished... it was still possible to get lost in the confusion of its corridors. On the other hand, Strabo places the labyrinth in a grotto... The version already known *ab antiquo*... situated the labyrinth in the cave of Gortyna... Claudian (third century A.D.) identifies it with the grotto situated at the foot of Mount Ida. It was a cave with many winding passages and cavities, going for miles deep into the mountain, with repeated bifurcations... At the bottom, gushing out of the rock, there was a living spring." (P. Santarcangeli, *op. cit.*, pp. 32 and 114.)

In other areas, caves were used as labyrinths for the performance of mysteries. The vestiges of Shivaism in Malta are more ancient than those of Crete. "At Malta, there is a grotto, the subterranean complex of Hal Saflieni... Three floors, reaching a depth of more than ten metres, a series of halls, caverns, inter-communicating niches, an inextricable confusion of passages, which unwind in a double spiral, first turning to the left and then to the right... The ceilings are decorated with red spirals... Sacred axes, ceramics, statuettes of women and of animals, and many human bones have been found there, as well as the statue of a 'sleeping woman', probably representing a priestess in a state of incubation before giving an oracle, dressed in a costume which is identical to that of the Cretan priestesses." (P. Santarcangeli, *op. cit.*, p. 120.)

In Indian Shivaite tradition, we have the representation of labyrinths, which are analogous to the Cretan labyrinth, with accounts referring to the difficulty of access. According to the Tamil *Kanda purânam*, "An Assura magician named Krauncha (the Heron) took the form of a mountain, with a sort of passage in its middle, whose entrance gave onto one side towards which came a sage called Akattiyan. The latter was astonished at the sudden appearance of the mountain, and, having decided to enter it, followed the path which opened before him. As soon as he had walked a certain way in, the path disappeared. Another opened in a different direction. The sage started along this new path, which also disappeared in a very short time. He then saw a new path in front of him. Suddenly he perceived a great flame on both sides, which went out after a few moments. There was a clap of thunder, and the whole place was plunged into darkness." (The Tamil *Kanda purânam*, II, chap. 24, 5–8.)

The cave of Smnisos, in Crete, is also a sacred cavern. There are phallic-shaped stalagmites, near which offerings were left. This was an extremely ancient holy place, the centre of a cult of Cretan Zeus, who was worshipped here up to the Roman era.

Caverns are the favourite abode of Shiva and the goddess. The cavern of Amarnâtha in Kashmir, with its *Linga* of ice, is one of the principal sacred places of the god.

In the *Shiva Purâna* (*Rudra Samhitâ*, chap. 44–45), Shiva is described as dwelling in a cavern. He says, "In the cavern, I accomplished the rites of the friends of the beasts (*Pashupâtas*)". When Shiva departs into the forest, Pârvatî remains alone and afraid in the cavern. The gods Brahmâ, Vishnu and Indra, the sages, adepts and snakes, change themselves into women, so as to have the right of entry (chap. 45, 1–3). A Titan watches the approach to the cavern, which is guarded by Ganesha, the goddess' courageous servant.

"In the hollow of a grotto was born the divine Echidna with the violent soul. Half her body was that of a young woman with beautiful cheeks and sparkling eyes, and half was an enormous serpent, as terrible as it was big, spotted and cruel, which dwelt in the secret depths of the divine earth, . . . It was the Great Earth which received the child to nourish and keep it in vast Crete . . . She . . . hid it in the hollow of an inaccessible cave in the secret depths of the Earth, on the slopes of Mount Egeon." (Hesiod, *The Theogony*, 295–300 and 478–484.)

The caverns which allow us to penetrate into the womb of Mother Earth have been sacred places since the very beginning of mankind. Caverns are never used as dwellings, although their winding passages may have served as temporary shelters or refuges. The cave-man is a fiction. There have never been cave-apes.

In Tantrism, caves are considered as a sort of vagina in the body of Mother Earth, and as such are worshipped as the female organ. They are the refuge through which we may return to our Mother's womb, and are propitious places for the most sacred rites. "In pre-Hellenic Greece, votive grottos, which were frequented, especially in Crete, from the second or third millennium, are situated at a certain distance from built-up areas, in out-of-the-way places." (H. Jeanmaire, *Dionysos*, p. 180.)

"Although the links between the traditions of the earliest inhabitants of Crete and those of the palaeolithic hunters, which are so intimately associated with cave-cults, must remain conjectural, the caves of Crete have yielded much evidence of their sacred character from neolithic times until the historical period. So much so that it has been inferred that the cave-cult of Minoan divinities was the chief characteristic of popular region . . . The Cretan archaeological record confirms the Greek tradition that caves were . . . the earliest shrines . . ." (R. F. Willetts, *Cretan Cults and Festivals*, p. 141.)

Dionysus was born in a grotto, which symbol was incorporated in the legend of Jesus. The Proto-Gospel of James (XVIII, I et. seq.), Justin Martyr and Origen were the first to have located the Nativity in a cave. At the end of each eight-year period, Minos retired to the cave of the Oracle on Mount Ida, where he communicated with is father, Zagreus.

The Hindu temple is conceived as representing a mountain. The dark sanctuary represents a cave, the cave of mysteries. The narrow path which goes around the sanctuary is likened to the labyrinth.

Sacred plants and trees

The cosmic principles revealed in the mineral and animal world, and the world of the gods, are equally expressed in the vegetable world. There is a subtle correspondence or analogy between certain plants or trees, certain gods, certain animals, and certain aspects of the human being. There are noble and vile plants, beneficent and harmful trees, plants which are friends and plants which are enemies of man. Some plants nourish man and transmit to him a vital or intellectual force. Others provoke states of intoxication or ecstasy, and still others, death. Nearly all remedies and poisons come from plants. In the harmony of the world, there exists a vital bond between the vegetable species and all aspects of life itself. From plants we assimilate the vital principles which correspond to the three fundamental tendencies of nature: the power of concentration and intellectual development (*sattva*); the power of organization and action (*rajas*); the power of

127

explosion, which is the force of the passions, of eroticism, birth and death (*tamas*). Man lives in symbiosis with certain plants (wheat, rice), and animals (the cow, and goat). Following the principle of the apparent inversion of values, which is peculiar to Tantrism, the *tamasic* powers – poisons, drugs and passions – are employed as a means of conquering the supernatural world, since by mastering that which normally destroys us we can vanquish death and attain immortality. Shiva is the incarnation of the *tamas*, the destructive and procreative principle of explosion, since it is through destruction that life is born and subsists.

Some plants and trees are, by their very nature, connected with what are called spirits or gods. They embody certain aspects of the divine. Hence there are certain sacred beneficent plants and trees which may serve as a means of contact with the invisible beings, since the effectiveness of plants is not only assimilated in the form of food, drugs and drink derived from them.

Since plants are in direct non-intellectual contact with the life which surrounds them and with the world of spirits through which it is animated, they can serve as intermediaries for communicating with the spirits themselves. Plants can immediately perceive our feelings and deepest thoughts and transmit them to the subtle powers which they embody, whose benevolence or hostility plays an important rôle in the development of our lives.

"The sacred tree, as the seat of natural power, the source of blessings and the cult-object of very different peoples, is common, or nearly so, to all races. It has kept its magical or symbolic value in the religious systems of the most varied societies . . . It was in the form, if not of a tree-god or tree-spirit, at least of a *daimon* whose vitality was in some way connected with that of the vegetable species, that the Athenians conceived of Dionysus, in whose honour the rites were celebrated by women . . . The complex of representation and religious emotion centred on Dionysus appears to be deeply influenced by the persistent idea of an equivalence, or even identity, between the potential of life, its exaltation and renewal which the presence of this *daimon* means for the followers of his cult, and the virtues which emanate from the essences of the vegetable world." (H. Jeanmaire, *Dionysos*, pp. 12–15.)

"At the beginning of the Minoan period . . . trees played a central rôle. Iconographic documents show various persons touching leaves, or adoring the vegetation goddess, or performing ritual dances. Some scenes underline the extravagant, or ecstatic, character of the rite . . . , a mystical solidarity between man and plant." (M. Eliade, *Histoire des croyances et des idées religieuses*, p. 146.)

Even today, sacred trees are found in all parts of India, to which the faithful attach small pieces of cloth as ex-votos. Stone or bronze images of the god are placed near their roots and are worshipped daily. Certain flowers, such as the marigold, which has an orange colour, are used to make garlands to adorn the *Linga* during the ceremonies. These flowers are picked with great care, as flowers whose scent has been smelled by anyone cannot be offered to the gods.

"The tomb of Ariadne, the goddess of Vegetation and of Trees, was at Argos, in the temple of Dionysus. . . There are also traces of old Minoan rites in Greece, under the disguise of Zeus-Hyakinthos, father of the virgins who die to assure life. The importance should be noted of the cult of bulbous plants, whose annual resurrection had already been remarked." (Charles Picard, *Les Religions préhelléniques*, pp. 147 and 188.)

"In later times in Greece, it was the minor divinities of local cults, and especially nymphs, whose life was identified with that of trees and springs." (H. Jeanmaire, *Dionysos*, p. 19.)

The sacred plants of Shiva are mainly the Pippala (*ficus religiosa*), called "the lord of trees" (*Vriksha-nâtha*), the herb *dharba* or *kusha*, the plant called *Rudraksha* ("the eye of Rudra"), whose seeds are used to make Shivaite rosaries, the vine, Indian hemp, etc. The laurel, the vine and the ivy were the sacred plants of Dionysus. The pine of Athis was the object of Roman devotion and the oak was the sacred tree of the Celts. "Oak is my name," says Taliesin, the Druid bard, who also speaks of "the three ends of man and oak". The gathering of the mistletoe was an occasion for important rites.

"The veneration connected with the sacred tree is also given to its off-shoots or equivalents. The young trunk is uprooted to make the maypole and the green branches are made into votive objects. . . Amongst the Greeks, green branches and shrubs played an important part in a great number of ceremonies, and especially in those which boys and girls took part. At Athens, on various occasions, young people or children carried in procession a maypole made of laurel and olive branches. . . At Sparta and in Sicily, the laurel branch was called Corythalia, and this emblem was used in processions for the rites of puberty or marriage. . . Religious processions regularly involved the participation of *thallophoroi*, or branch-bearers. . . The strewing of flowers (stibade) was essential for the performance of certain rites." (H. Jeanmaire, *Dionysos*, pp. 13–14.) The Christian feast of Palm Sunday and the flower-strewing of Corpus Christi are the continuation of these rites.

At Thebes, Dionysus was represented in the form of a laurel-crowned pole, the lower part of which was enveloped by a saffron-coloured robe. In India, a sacred tree is planted at cross-roads, or in places where certain festivals take place. The tree is worshipped with dancing, rites and offerings. The thyrsus, held and waved by bacchants and bacchantes in performing their dances, is the stem of a reed, at the end of which is attached a bunch of ivy, vine leaves or occasionally, a pine-cone.

Chapter 7

SACRED PLACES

Sacred places

There are places where the visible and invisible worlds are very close
to each other. In a certain way, these points on the globe correspond
to the *chakras*, or subtle centres of the human body. Anyone who is
aware of the mystery of the world can perceive the unusual nature of
these places where invisible presences are felt. They are a sort of door,
through which it is a little easier to pass from one world to another.
They are the ways by which it is possible for the clairvoyant to tumble
suddenly into another world, and for others to feel nearer to what is
called the supernatural; the mysterious world of gods and spirits. All
religions recognize places where miracles are possible. Often there is
nothing apparent to mark these places which are nearer heaven, but
their magical character has been felt by man since time began. Their
position is defined by means of a particular science, known as sacred
geography. Sometimes new places are found, or forgotten ones
rediscovered. Whether in Kâshî (Benares), Mecca, or Lourdes, the
nature and magnetism of these places are always similar. Occasionally,
certain organic elements of the Earth's body can be discovered there.
Benares, the holy city of Shiva, is the place where the rivers of the
three worlds cross each other on the same axis. They are the Milky
Way, the Ganges, and an enormous underground river descending
from the Himalayas towards the south.

At Mecca, the Makeshvara of the ancient Indian geographers, the
Black Stone, which is the emblem of Shiva mentioned in the Purânas,
is still venerated. The Celts inherited ancient sacred places from
previous peoples. The origin of the oracle near the Castalian Spring at
Delphi goes back long before the Mycenaean era. Outside of Crete,
there were many such sacred places in the Mediterranean world.
Naxos was called Dionysias, or Dia, the Divine, and was especially
sacred to Dionysus, while the wines of Naxos were famous.

Sacred places are often indicated by the existence of ancient
sanctuaries: Amarnâtha, Gangotri, Jageshvara, Mathura, Hardwar,

Kanchipuram, Konarak, as also Delphi, Malta, Filitosa (Corsica), Carnac, Nice, Stonehenge, Gortyna, Olympus, Athos, Ida, Kailâsa, Mecca, Sinai, etc. These are privileged places where it is almost impossible not to feel a special atmosphere, which is out of time, or in another dimension of space. Great importance is attached to receiving sacraments, or dying in these places, which are often thought to be the gates of Heaven.

Many Christian churches as well as mosques have been built on the site of ancient sanctuaries. Trying to explain their sacred character with the aid of new myths is fruitless.

Forests, rivers, lakes and springs
Apart from the great magical sites which are the nerve centres of the Earth and also the object of sacred geographical research; mountains, lakes, grottoes, springs and forests are the favourite haunts of Shiva. These are places where nature has not been debased by man, or the Earth wounded by agriculture or defiled by habitations.

Wherever we find sacred mountains, grottoes, woods or springs, a Dionysiac origin can generally be traced. Nature is the temple of Shiva. For this reason, Shivaite initiatory rites are performed in the forest, on the banks of rivers or sacred pools, never in temples or the dwelling places of men.

Springs are inhabited by nymphs and spirits, whereas rivers are goddesses and the Ganges' source comes from the hair of Shiva.

Such stories could be treated as mere frivolity. However, sitting at the side of a spring and invoking its spirit, one can feel its beneficent and pacifying influence.

The Grande Troménie ceremonies at Locronan in Brittany, end with a sacrifice (a mass) in a sanctuary on the top of a mount, after walking in procession around it. This is undubitably the continuation of a Dionysiac rite. Along the route, altars have been built in honour of all the saints (or gods) of the region.

Kailâsa, the paradise of Shiva
The Hindu temple represents a mountain, and the phallic aspect of mountains is evoked in the bell-towers and minarets of the sanctuaries.

Mountains are magical places which should be approached with dread. They are places where the gods dwell and where sages retire to receive divine inspiration. It was on a mountain that Moses spoke with God. Shiva also dwells on a mountain and his wife is the Lady of

132

the Mountain. In the same way, Dionysus is worshipped on Mount Ida and Diktynna is the goddess of Mount Dikte. For the Greeks, Mount Olympus was the dwelling-place of the gods, although they had previously dwelt on Mount Athos, the ancient Akte. Athos, the son of Poseidon, tore up the mountainous block from where it stood in Thrace, and flung it where it now is. Athos has always been the sacred mountain of Dionysus. Near the Great-Lavra monastery, once the site of an ancient city mentioned by Herodotus, an altar for bull-sacrifice can still be seen.

Skanda, whose cult is forbidden to women, retired to a mountain. This tradition has been preserved on Mount Athos, which was the ancient retreat of Dionysiac hermits. According to a legend which has been transposed into Christian terms, it was the Virgin who blessed the mountain, broke in pieces the images of the ancient gods, declared it to be her garden, and forbade it to other women. The Essenians, amongst others, inherited this aspect of the Skanda cult, and refused all contact with women.

In speaking of the goddess, we discussed the magnetic power of mountain tops. Mountains are the dwelling places of the gods. Sanctuaries may be built there, but the habitations of men may never be built near to the summit. Their arid aspect deceives the eye. Like Olympus, Ida or Athos; Kailâsa in Tibet appears to be only a snowy peak where storms rage. For the "Seeing person", however, it has a completely different aspect.

"Kailâsa, the mountain on which the paradise of Shiva is situated, is covered with marvellous gardens. The court of the god is composed of all kinds of animals, nymphs and spirits, as well as his faithful companions. It is a place of delight, where everything which leads to happiness is found. There lives Shiva, in the form of a naked Yogi." (*Shiva Purâna*, *Rudra Samhitâ*, chap. 18, 44.)

"Kailâsa is the blessed and splendid mountain where Shiva dwells. There live also the Kinnaras (with goats' feet), the Apsaras (nymphs), the Siddhas (the elect), and other heavenly spirits. The mountain is of a great height, its sparkling peaks sown with many-coloured precious stones and other ores. All sorts of trees and creepers are found, hinds, fallow-deer, gazelle, and thousands of birds. The nymphs play there with their lovers in the springs and pools, in grottoes and on the peaks. The trees have silver hues. There are many animals there, tigers and others, but they are not ferocious. There nature is shining and inspires wonder and admiration. The Ganges, which springs from the mountain, purifies and sanctifies all things... Not far off lies Alakâ, the city of Kubera (the guardian of the treasure), and the garden of perfumes` (*Saugandhika*), with every variety of tree. Their murmuring makes divine music. Around the mountain run the rivers Nandâ and Alakanandâ, a sole glance at which effaces every fault. The nymphs go down to drink their waters. Worn out by their amorous games, they come here to refresh themselves. Further off is the Pippala, the fig-tree under which Shiva practises Yoga. There are no nests in it. It gives deep shade. It is magnificent and sacred." (*Shiva Purâna*, *Rudra Samhitâ*, chap. 40, 22–36.)

In the world of men, Shiva appears as a half-mad beggar, but when the gods visit Kailâsa, he reveals his glorious aspect.

"The moon takes the place of his crown; his third eye is the adornment of his forehead and the snakes become his jewel-encrusted earrings. The snakes encircling the other parts of his body become ornaments studded with jewels. The ash with which his body is smeared becomes a precious ointment. The elephant skin appears as delicate silk. His beauty is indescribable. He seems to possess all riches." (*Shiva Purâna*, *Rudra Samhitâ*, chap. 39, 38–42.)

We find analogous descriptions of the paradise of Dionysus. "The limbs of the son of Semele were delicate and voluptuous, his beauty singled him out amongst all others. He was very given to the pleasures of Aphrodite. He was accompanied by a crowd of women armed with spears... he wore panther skins... A half-clothed ephebe, [he sits] in an abandoned pose. The members of his thiasos, a medley of satyrs and maenads, disperse all over the countryside..., some in whirling and violent dances..., in the frenzy of their leaps, whilst others... enjoy their repose and play various musical instruments." (H. Jeanmaire, *Dionysos*, pp. 365 and 277.) According to the Homeric hymns, "The satyrs entice the nymphs to make love with them in grotto-retreats. Pan pursues nymphs and young shepherd-boys. He teaches the panpipe to the beautiful Daphnis." Cretan Zagreus was worshipped on Mount Ida for more than four thousand years, until the Romans came. The word *Ida* means forest, as is the case with the names of other mountains. The Shivaite mountain-paradise is also found amongst the Greeks. "Olympos itself must be considered... as a generic term for 'mountain'. In one passage of the Odyssey, the celestial Olympos is described in legendary terms more reminiscent of the Minoan fields of the Blest than the mountain centre of storm, rain and lightning." (R. F. Willetts, *Cretan Cults and Festivals*, p. 118.)

Kailâsa is sometimes identified with Mount Meru, the axial mountain which is the centre of the world, and which is situated in Tibet, the "ceiling of the world". Four rivers run from this mountain (Sîtâ to the east, Alakanandâ to the south, Vannu to the west, Bhâddha to the north) and water the four regions of the Earth: the Rose-apple-tree (Jambu) continent to the south; that of the Jasmine (Kadamba) to the west; of the Fig-tree (Vâta) to the north; and of the Mango-tree (Amra) to the east.

"In Genesis, the Garden of Eden, with its river which divided into four branches and brought life to the four corners of the Earth . . ., recalls Mesopotamian imagery . . . Like all paradises, Eden is situated in the middle of the Earth, whence the four-branched river springs." (M. Eliade, *Histoire des croyances et des idées religieuses*, p. 179.)

Nysa, the Sacred Mountain

In Dionysiac tradition, the place of the god's childhood and education is called Nysa. *Nisah* is an epithet of Shiva, and means supreme. *Nisam* is bliss, *nisâ*, joy. Nysa, the Happy Mountain, is the equivalent of Kailâsa, the Earthly Paradise.

The infant-god is Skanda, the second Dionysus. Most descriptions of Nysa are related to his legend. The name Dionysus itself probably means the god of Nysa, or of the Nysai nymphs. (see A. J. Festugière, *Etudes de religion grecque et hellénistique*, p. 14.) "Nysa is well-known as Dionysus' nurse (and also fatherland) . . . Nysa is clearly the feminine form of the word *nysos*, which very probably comes into the composition of the god's name, inexplicable in Greek . . . Nysos may be the equivalent, in a Thracian or Phrygian dialect, of the Greek *kouros* (young man)." (H. Jeanmaire, *Dionysos*, p. 7.) If this etymology is correct, it would be a direct translation of the name Murugan or Kumâra (Skanda), the Boy.

The Greeks believed that they had found the Mountain of Nysa almost everywhere. Compilers could list up to ten Nysas, from the Caucasus to Arabia, and from India to the Libyan West. "There is a certain Nysa, a high mountain, where the forests blossom, much further than Phoenicia." (Homeric hymns.) A Nysaean grotto is also mentioned.

Diodorus of Sicily (I, 27), who like Herodotus, identifies Egyptian

Osiris with the Greek Dionysus, places the tombs of Isis and Osiris at Nysa, in Arabia. Dionysus was thus raised at Nysa, a town of happy Arabia, and it was there that he discovered the vine. However, Diodorus also cites a Libyan tradition referring to a western Nysa. On the other hand, Herodotus localizes "Nysa the Holy" in the cinnamon country; in perfumed Ethiopia.

"Nysa is situated on an island, enveloped by the River Triton, which is precipitous on all sides leaving a very narrow entrance on one side only. This opening is known as the Nysaean Gates. Beyond, there is a charming space with soft meadows and beautifully watered gardens. There are fruit-trees of all kinds, the wild vine grows abundantly and mostly climbs all over the trees. The whole country is well-ventilated and extremely healthy." (Dionysus the Lybian, quoted by Diodorus, III, 68.)

Not far from present-day Peshawar, near to the Indus, the soldiers of Alexander discovered the hill of Nysa and rushed there to embrace their brothers in Dionysus.

According to Diodorus, Bacchos gathered together an army composed of the noble inhabitants of Nysa who were called Sileni, because they were the descendants of Silennis, the first king of Nysa, "who had a tail behind, which is why his descendants continue to wear this remarkable piece of false hair". The Nysaeans' dances were dedicated to Bacchos. Philostratus, in his Life of Apollonius of Tyana, recounts that in Pamphylia a panther had been captured, wearing a golden collar with an inscription in the Armenian language: "King Arsaces to the god of Nysa".

According to Diodorus, "Since the god has left proofs of his good deeds and manifestations in many places in the universe, it is not at all surprising that each should believe there is a particular familiarity with his own town or country". Indeed, the name of Nysa is found in the formation of many different place-names which have preserved Dionysiac traditions, carnivals and Spring festivals.

Dionysus was the mythical founder of the town of Nicea, the modern Iznik, which was a flourishing city where sumptuous festivals were celebrated in his honour every five years. Devastated by an earthquake in 123, it was rebuilt by the Emperor Hadrian. In 362, the Emperor Julian re-established the Dionysiac cult there.

The town of Nice also appears to have been a Dionysiac holy place. The cult of Diktynna (the Mountain-mother) was probably imported to Marseilles by the Greeks. According to Strabo, Pliny and Stephen of Byzantium, Nice belonged to the Marseillais. The capital of Vediantii Liguria was at Cemelenum (modern Cimiez), three kilometres north of the acropolis of Nikaia (today, Colline du Château). This had been a sacred place since prehistoric times.

"Nice cannot have been a settlement, nor a trading centre. What was then the purpose of its foundation?" asks the author of the *Histoire de Nice et du pays niçois*.

The name Nikaia, the ancient name for Nice, is in appearance purely Greek. It is supposed to derive from Nike, "Victory", although Nice was never the site of a battle. Nevertheless, "it is impossible to find a true explanation of the name Nikaia through Greek alone... N. Lamboglia noted that similar names had been found in Italy in places which had nothing Greek about them, such as Nizza in the Monferrato area and Val di Nizza near Vogherese. F. Benoit adds Languedocian toponyms like Nissan and Nissargue. It is probable that there was a common indigenous root, a place-name which the Greeks took over and to which the 'gave a new garb'." (*Histoire de Nice et du pays niçois*, p. 12–13.) Nissa, (modern Nish) in Jugoslavia should also be cited, as well as many other places. Antibes (Antipolis), "the City opposite", which faces the acropolis of Nice from the other side of the gulf, dates from the fifth century B.C. The cult of the goddess of Ida was widespread in this area, as indicated by several Roman inscriptions. Many details of the Nice carnival (*carnevale*, "meat-days", recalling sacrifices), such as the ass led in procession, the pelting of those taking part with "haricot beans", the freedom of morals, the floats, are all clear vestiges of Dionysiac festivals. The "*abbés*" of the festival call to mind the thiasoi. They numbered eleven and were chosen from amongst the four castes represented in the town to organize the festivities. Two were elected by the nobles and three from each of the other groups: merchants, artisans and fishermen. They were called the "abbés of the fools" (*abbates stultorum*). The mixing of castes is one of the characteristics of the Shiva-Dionysus cult. In modern times, the carnival was only mentioned offically starting from 1294, when Charles II of Anjou honoured it with his presence.

Crossroads

Rudra wanders from place to place. Offerings must therefore be left for him along the roads and especially at intersections, since "crossroads are well-known as the places he most willingly frequents". (*Shatapatha Brâhmana*, II, 6, 2, 7.)

137

In his *Gorgias* and *Phaedo*, Plato alludes to crossroads, and the Pythagorean "Y" is connected with the same symbolism. Hermes signifies "the god of the Pile of stone": he is the spirit of boundary stones and pillars, which indicate the road. The Celts built piles of stone or shrines at crossroads, in which spirits lived. During certain festivals, fires are lighted there, as is still the practice in India. The Blacks, who brought rites of Dionysiac origin with them to Brazil, still choose crossroads for performing their macumba rites.

The *Hatha Yoga Pradîpikâ* (III, 109) speaks of a widow, seated at the confluence of two rivers, who must be stripped by force and possessed, since she leads to the supreme place. The widow is the coiled energy (*Kundalini*), or Shakti, which must be mastered by the Yogi; the rivers are Ida and Pingala, the two arteries of the subtle body which lead to the thousand-petaled lotus at the top of the cranium. Shiva dwells in the form of a self-born phallus in the middle of the coiled energy, at the crossroads.

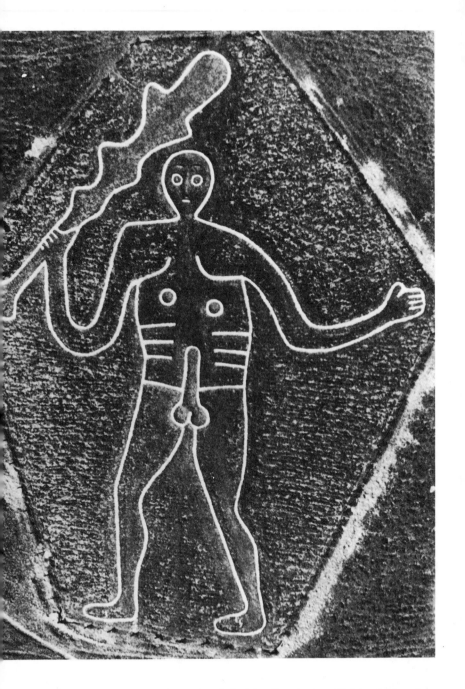

Cerne Abbas Giant. Dorset. (Rawson, *Primitive Erotic Art*, Weidenfeld and Nicolson)

2. Phallus with face and serpent. Maryport, Cumberland. (Photo: C. M.
Dixon, Rawson, *Primitive Erotic Art*, Weidenfeld and Nicolson)

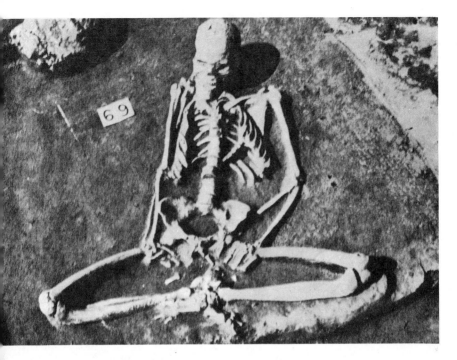

Burial in yoga position. Lepensk Vir, Yugoslavia, between 6500 and 5500 B.C. (Author's collection)

Cernunnos, Lord of the Animals. The Gunderstrup Caldron, Jutland, 1st century B.C. (Photo: National Museum, Copenhagen)

5. Ice (Linga) Cave. Amarnath, Kashmir. (Photo: Yves Barbeau)

Naudikeshvara, the Indian Minotaur. Khandariya temple, Khajuraho, 10th century. (Author's collection)

7. Phallus with face, Filitosa, Corsica, 2nd millennium B.C.

8. Bull's head. Kato Zabros,
   Eastern Crete, 1450 B.C.
   Candia Museum,
   Heraklion. (Photo:
   Leonard von Watt)

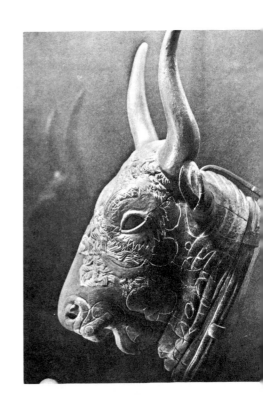

Cover:
   Shiva in yoga position.
   Vaital Deul temple,
   Bhuvaneshwar, Orissa, 9th
   century. (Author's
   collection)

Chapter 8

MAN IN THE WORLD

The paths of knowledge

All civilizations and cultures are the fruit of the accumulation of
man's knowledge and experience, handed down from generation to
generation. Shivaism, whose sources go back to the furthest prehistory, represents an immense sum of experience. The descriptions
of the human being's subtle structures, which are the basis of Yoga
techniques, reveal a level of knowledge compared to which the
stutterings of modern psycho-physiology appear rudimentary.

None of the concepts concerning the nature of the world – nor the
methods of realization of the human being as expressed in Shivaism –
originally belonged to the barbarian world of the Aryans. The Aryans
gradually assimilated a few aspects of the knowledge of the conquered
peoples, both in the Indian and in the Hellenic world. Apart from the
older parts of the Vedas, all later Hindu texts bear the mark of the
philosophical ideas and ritual techniques of ancient Shivaism, more
or less adapted in order to be integrated into a theoretically Vedic
world. Greek thought bears the same relation to its Minoan or
Pelasgian heritage.

In the Purânas, the philosophical and moral teaching of Shivaism is
attributed to Skanda. He therefore corresponds to what the Greeks
called the Second Dionysus, not because a less ancient doctrine is
involved, but due to the period in which it was accepted in the Greek
or Indian world.

According to the evolution of the cycles, man's pride rises against
his instinct, creating artificial mental constructs which oppose his
perception of the subtle world. Subsequently, the disastrous *grandeur*
of the human species develops on a material level, until Shiva – the
Prime Cause and source of life – appears and teaches men the three
ways of knowledge and realization, which are Sânkhya (cosmology),
Yoga (the mastery of the subtle man), and Tantra (initiatory and
magical rites and practices). Sânkhya explains the structure of the
world and the system of creation, the parallelism and interdependence

139

of the various aspects of matter, life and species, and the fundamental oneness of macrocosm and microcosm of the universe and the living being. The ancient Sânkhya is the Shivaite Sânkhya, which is a much greater system than that bearing the same name in classical Hindu philosophy. Yoga is a technique which by means of introspection, man learns to know himself. He is able to silence the digressions of his thought, to pass beyond the limits of his senses and go back to the deep sources of life. Contact is made with the invisible powers hidden within himself, as in all aspects of the created, which constitute the deepest nature of the living being. The body, including the mental and intellectual faculties, is only its support; a sort of clothing. Tantra is the link between Sânkhya and Yoga. It teaches the initiatory and magical methods through which man can enter into direct contact with the secret nature of things of the invisible and mysterious world of gods and spirits. Of these methods, inebriety, eroticism, music and ecstatic dancing are the easiest means of shaking off mental or "rational" control. To free oneself and go beyond the barriers of conscious will allows the first direct perception of the subtle forces surrounding us.

The techniques of love-play and worship of the principle of life allow man to realize the true nature of pleasure and to perceive in the living being a state of tension which is the very principle of creation and nature of the divine being. The act of love may thus be used as a means to perfection and subtle knowledge, of returning to the beginning and of direct contact with God.

Physical drunkenness, induced by wine or other intoxicants, may equally facilitate and prepare man for mystical ecstasy by freeing him momentarily from his inhibitions, material worries, attachments and ties.

Dionysiac orgiasm exactly corresponds to Tantra. Through the power of initiation, man is able to attain self-consciousness and master the reality of what he has perceived in orgiasm. It is this that constitutes enlightenment. Through orgiasm, man first feels the reality of certain forces within and without himself. Only then will he be able to grasp the principles involved and comprehend the nature of the world and of the divine.

The nature of the world
Shivaite cosmology envisages twenty-four basic elements or "autonomous principles" (*tattvas*) which make the apparition and development

of the world possible. There are five conditions or preliminaries which determine the possibility of creation: 1) a prime cause called Shiva. In this case, the word Shiva derives from the root *shi*, which denotes sleep. Shiva is "he in whom all sleeps", sleep being the image of the latent state of creation; 2) an energy or power of manifesting, called Shakti; 3) a possibility of localization or extension, the principle of time and space; 4) absolute sovereignty, which means the non-existence of anything else; 5) consciousness, or the faculty of conceiving and knowing. From these five principles spring the first constituents of manifestation: 1) Mâyâ, appearance or perceptibility: 2) Kâla, the "dimension" or unit of measurement or of rhythm, determining relative time and space; 3) causality, or connection, by which an action (*karma*) obtains a result; 4) divisibility (*kalâ*), the essential element for all multiplication or reproduction; 5) memory, or the accumulation of experience or knowledge (*vidyâ*); 6) attraction (*râga*); 7) the plan (*avyakta*), which is the not-yet-manifested state of manifestation; and 8–9–10) three tendencies (*gunas*), which are centrifugal, centripetal and orbiting (*tamas, sattva, rajas*) and which determine the structures of the matter, as well as all the impulses, of subtle or living beings. These three tendencies, symbolized by three colours, represent the three aspects of divinity manifested in the world. Shiva, the centrifugal or creative tendency, is black; Vishnu, the centripetal or conservative tendency, is white; Brahmâ, the orbiting or active tendency, is red. The three tendencies together form Nature (Prakriti), described as a three-coloured goat (Ajâ, the not-born). "A red, black and white goat gives birth to many little ones which resemble her." (*Taittirîya Upanishad*. 10, 10, 1.)

The oracle of Minos mentions a calf which changed colour every four hours, being white, then red, then black. These are also the colours of Io, as a cow, and of the sacred bulls of Augeias. This is clearly a case of the same colour symbolism, which is used in many different ways and particularly in ritual drawings. In a traditional society, the significance of these colours is obvious to all.

Then come the constituents of living beings, the cosmic being (macrocosm) as well as the human being (microcosm), which are: 11) *manas*, or "thought", which discusses; 12) *buddhi*, or intellect, which chooses; 13) *chit*, or "consciousness", which records; and 14) *ahamkara*, or notion of individuality, the sense of the ego, the sensation of being an autonomous centre. Together, these four faculties form the internal or transmigrant being (*antahkarana*), to which are added:

15–19) the five elements (ether, air, fire, earth and water), which are the spheres of perception of the five senses; and 20–24) the senses themselves (hearing, touch, sight, taste, smell), with the five perceptive organs and the five related organs of action.

From the point of view of the creative principle, the world may be seen as illusory, a sort of energetic ectoplasm which may be reabsorbed by its source. "Just as the spider secretes and reabsorbs its thread, as the earth grows plants, as man grows hair on head and body, so the Immutable emanates the universe in which we are living . . . From the Immutable come all the different kinds of creatures, which return and lose themselves in him." (*Mundaka Upanishad*, I, 1, 7 and II, 1, 1.)

In this sense, the universe is called Mâyâ, meaning illusion or appearance. However, "from the point of view of finite consciousness, and thus of man, . . . the world is an indisputable reality which he can in no way disregard. Man is part of creation, outside of which he exists in no way, whether physical, mental or spiritual". (J. Evola, *Le Yoga trantrique*, p. 36.)

From man's point of view, Mâyâ, the raw material of the universe, is therefore considered real and eternal. It is ephemeral from Shiva's point of view only. The same ambiguity exists in all aspects of the created world. The questions man asks himself about the world are in reality, unanswerable. Shivaism recommends experience rather than intellectual speculation.

In the *Shiva Purâna*, the sage Sûta interrogates Skanda. "'Is the Prime Cause of the universe male, female, or an intermediate being, or a mixture of the two, or something else? Has the soul, the *atman*, a shape? Can it be identified with the body, or with the senses, the mind the intellect, and the ego?' Skanda replies, 'The speculations of philosophers, beginning with stories concerning the result of actions, the *karma*, and the principles of existence, have given rise to interminable controversies. The wise man considers these matters with prudence. This is the beginning of wisdom. Part of the body comes from the father, part from the mother. In the same way, in all beings there is an element of Shiva and an element of Shakti'." (*Shiva Purâna, Kailâsa Samhitâ*, chap. 16, 8–33.)

Having expounded the principles of Shivaite cosmology and the rites of initiation, Skanda explains the rules of conduct which lead to wisdom.

The five aspects of Shiva

The number "5" is a symbol of Shiva, since it plays an essential rôle in all manifestations of life (see the commentary on the *Shiva Purâna*, *Vidyeshvara Samhitâ*, chap. I).

Shiva is thus represented with five faces, corresponding to the five main aspects of the perceptible world from which sprang the five elements, the name given to the five aspects of creation as perceived by our five senses. All the structures of the world are made of five states of matter. The living being disposes of five senses in order to perceive these structures, which are the expression of the very nature of the Creator. The number "5" plays a basic rôle in the genetic code of all living beings. For this reason, we have five fingers and five senses, and the leaves of the trees have five veins.

The first aspect is called Ishâna (the Lord). It corresponds to the "ether" element whose characteristic is space, and which allows the manifestation of the vibratory principles determining the measurement of time. Ether is considered the sphere of the sense of hearing. The corresponding state of being is subtle knowledge (Kshetrajña).

The second aspect is Tat-purusha (the identifiable Being). It corresponds to the "air" element of the gaseous principle, the sphere of the tactile sense. The corresponding state of being is basic Nature (Prakriti), the first state of matter.

The third aspect is called Aghora (the Non-Terrible), or Agni (fire). It corresponds to the male element, fire. Heat is the principle of the organization of matter. It belongs to the sphere of the sense of sight. Its corresponding state of being is the intellect (*buddhi*).

The fourth aspect is called Vâmadeva (God of the Left). It corresponds to the female element, "water", the sphere of the sense of taste. Its corresponding state of being is the "notion of self" (*ahamkara*). From the union of fire (vertical) and water (horizontal), represented symbolically by the cross or the overlapping triangles of the "seal of Solomon", is born the fifth aspect called Sadyojata (Born spontaneously). It corresponds to the element "earth", the apparently solid element of which the stars and bodies of living beings are formed. Its sphere is the sense of smell. The corresponding state of being is the mind (*manas*), or thinking organ. The agitations of the brain are thus considered as a sort of chemical reaction of a material order, and are an obstacle to true knowledge, which is immediate and intuitive. The first aim of Yoga technique is to silence the digressions of thought to allow an opening towards the higher aspects of the being.

The number "5" is found in all aspects of the world and of life, which are themselves material structures. The pentagon is the symbol of Shiva. This number was sacred in Egypt, as well as in all later initiatory organizations. Hence the importance of the pentatonic in music, or the "golden segment" in architecture, both of which are based on the properties of the pentagon and allow "living" proportions to be created. The crescent moon, as represented in Islam, is the five-day moon which Shiva wears on his forehead and which represents the cup of *soma*, the elixir of life.

The various aspects of the god play an important part in the rites, cult-forms and practice of Shivaism. In worshipping the god's image, Ishâna (ether) is invoked in his crown, Tatpurusha (air) in his face, Aghora (fire) in his heart, Vâmadeva (water) in his sexual organ, Sadyojata (earth) in his feet. This symbolism is important, as it helps us to understand rites and myths wherever Shivaism has had an influence. Examples include the association of the crown with sovereignty, or the representation of the spirits of the air as winged faces, of male spirits with fire, and nymphs with waters, etc.

Shiva is worshipped on the fifth day of the lunar month (*Shiva-panchami*). It is a day of prayer and also of rejoicing. But, since Shiva is also the destroying principle, it is not a suitable day for human enterprises. No work must be begun on the fifth day of the moon. "Avoid [when working] the fifth days of the month. They are arduous and baneful." (Hesiod, *Works and Days*, 807.)

The Lord of Yoga

The Yogic methods come down to us from prehistoric Shivaism. Shiva is the Lord of Yoga. The methods of Yoga involve a hitherto unrivalled knowledge of the structures of the human being, of the bonds uniting physical and mental, and of man's latent powers and the techniques for developing and utilizing them in order to obtain knowledge of both the physical and the supernatural world. It was through Yoga that the scientists of ancient India learned to go beyond the limits of the senses to escape the dimensions of space and perceive the structures both of the infinitely small and of the infinitely great. Yoga was used to describe distant objects and continents, make contact with invisible worlds, develop man's aptitudes, control his vital mechanisms and utilize his vital energies for material as well as spiritual achievements, to pass through the barriers of life so as finally

144

to obtain identification with the divine. "The basis of Yoga is the analogical-magical correspondence of macrocosm and microcosm. All the powers which are manifested and operating in the world are present and active in the body." (J. Evola, *Le Yoga tantrique*, p. 215.) "Further than the farthest, it is very near in the body. For those who are enlightened, it is there in the hollow of the heart." (*Mundaka Upanishad*, III, 1, 7.)

By means of introspection, the Yogi discovers in his own body the existence of certain centres connected with the subtle functions. These centres are called wheels (*chakras*) or Lotuses (*padma*). From these centres run the subtle arteries (*nâdis*) connecting them with the centres of perception, thought and consciousness situated in the brain.

All the *nâdis* depart from a centre, the *Mûlâdhara* or root. This centre corresponds to the material aspect of creation, the "earth" or female principle, which is the final step and materialization of divine manifestation. Therefore it is the first step of the return to the beginning. From this is derived the notion of the Earth-goddess, the mother of the gods, who is also found in the Mesopotamian and Minoan forms of Shivaism. The subtle body is inverted in relation to the physical body.

Yogic experience thus starts from the apparently most material level of the human being and rises gradually to the more subtle levels until reaching the source of things and beings. Yoga is always an ascending process. If the base is not the starting point, the experience lacks solid foundations and the Yogi is certain to stop en route and fall back. All Yogic experience must begin with an awareness of the basic centre, the *Mûlâdhara*. There reposes the sleeping energy coiled in the form of a serpent. If it can be awakened and controlled, this energy is the instrument of all achievement. The serpent is thus the symbol of the potentialities of realization.

The essence of the Yoga method consists in calming the mental agitation which distracts man from physical reality, and in utilizing his vital automatisms and instinctive powers to reintegrate him with his natural environment in the entirety of creation. Those methods which free man's instinctive powers are the only ones which can put him into contact with the vegetable, animal and supernatural world.

The "Chakras"
The energetic centres of the human body are perceived by the Yogi's

introspection as precise structures in well-defined areas of the body.

"Between the anus and the virile organ is the basic centre, or *Mûlâdhara*, which is like a matrix or *yoni* (female organ). It opens towards the west (behind). There lies the 'root' in bulb-form and it is there that the fundamental energy or *Kundalini* is found, coiled around itself three-and-a-half times. Like a snake, it surrounds the starting point of the three main arteries, holding its tail in its mouth just in front of the central artery opening (*sushumna*)." (*Shiva Samhitâ*, chap. 5, 75–76.)

The *Mûlâdhara* is of a yellow colour. In its middle there is a square, the symbol of the earth element, which is the perceptive sphere of smell and is connected with an active organ, the anus, and a perceptive organ, the nose. This centre controls the excretory energy (*apâna*). Here is found the self-born primordial phallus, the *Svayambhu linga*, which is the source of generative power and is represented by the syllable LAM, as well as of creative desire, represented by the syllable KLIM, the *mantra* of desire. The tendencies associated with this centre are the desire to possess and sleep.

The second centre is the *Svâdhishthâna* (the self-supporting). It corresponds to the prostatic plexus situated at the root of the genital organs. It is white in colour and at its centre there is a half-moon which is the cup of nectar or sperm, the symbol of the water element. *Svâdhishtâna* corresponds to the perceptive sphere of taste, with the tongue as its perceptive organ and the penis as its organ of action. This centre controls the tendency of dispersion of vital force, or procreation. Here is the seat of the power of concentration, conservation, and perpetuation, called Vishnu, represented by the syllable VAM. The tendencies associated with this centre are desire, fatigue, aversion and thirst.

The third centre is called *Manipura* (the jewel-city). It corresponds to the epigastric plexus, situated near the navel. Its colour is red and in its centre is a swastika-triangle, the image of the labyrinth. The labyrinth is the symbol of the element fire, and corresponds to the sphere of sight, whose perceptive organ is the eye and active organ the foot. This centre controls the assimilatory functions and the area of the buttocks. The force of assimilation is represented by the fire *mantra* RAM. The tendencies associated with this centre are anger, fear, surprise, violence, pride and hunger.

The fourth centre is *Anânhata* (the spontaneous sound), which corresponds to the cardiac plexus, situated in the dorsal region at heart level. It is grey in colour and at its centre is the starred hexagon (the seal of Solomon), the symbol of the element air, the perceptive sphere of touch, whose perceptive organ is the skin and whose active organ is the hand. This centre controls the blood system. Here is found the principle of movement represented by the *mantra* YAM.

The fifth centre is *Vishuddha* (the purified), corresponding to the larynx plexus, situated on the spine at throat level. Bright white in colour, in its middle is found a circle, the symbol of the ether element, whose characteristic is space. It corresponds to the perceptive sphere of hearing, and its perceptive organ is the ear and active organ the mouth. The notion of space is represented by the *mantra* HAM. In this centre dewlls the Hermaphrodite (*Ardhanarîshvara*), whose vehicle is half-lion, half-bull. The tendencies associated with this centre are affection, sadness, respect, devotion, contentment and regret.

The sixth centre is the *Ajña chakra* (the control centre), corresponding to the cavernous plexus and to the third eye situated in the orbital arch. Fire-coloured, at its centre is a female triangle (downward-pointing) and the phallus, the symbol of the beyond (*itara-linga*). Here, the intellectual and mental faculties (*antahkarana*) are found assembled. This centre controls the cerebellum and medulla. Extra-sensory perceptions are its sphere of action. The *mantra* AUM symbolizes the power of the thunder-bolt by which Shiva destroys the worlds with the glance of his third eye. At the top of the cranium is the opening towards the principle, the lotus with the thousand petals, the high way by which the realized Yogi leaves the world of appearances.

The physical body forms a triangle of fire (upward-pointing), in which the mouth kills (devours), the anus frees (rejects), and the sexual organ creates.

All traditions recognize the importance of the Mûlâdhara, the basic centre which is often associated with the coccyx. The name of the coccyx in Aramaeic is *luz*. In his *De occulta philosophia*, Agrippa reports that there is "a tiny bone, called *Luz* by the Jews, which is not subject to corruption, cannot be destroyed by fire, and always remains undamaged, from which, they say, our human body will grow again like a plant from its seed, on its resurrection from the dead . . . Its virtues are not tried by reasoning, but by experience".

"The reason why the principles of Tantrism, the *Tantrashastra*, are not understood is due to the fact that they become intelligible only through experience, the *Sâdhara* . . . To really worship a divinity, one must 'become' that divinity." (see Woodroffe, *Shakti and Shakta*, 2nd Ed. pp. 14 and 19.)

Tantrism or Orgiasm

Tantrism is the name of the practical methods, rites and techniques which allow Yogic experience to be linked to the universal principles expressed in Sânkhya cosmology. These techniques are realistic and are based on experience. Tantrism exploits and utilizes the physical, subtle and spiritual possibilities of the human being, through taking into account the interdependence of all aspects of living beings and their correspondence to the diverse aspects of the cosmic being. The body is the basis, or instrument of all realization. No life, thought or spirituality can exist independently of a living body. In the same way, we can conceive of cosmic thought or cosmic existence insofar as the universe is a divine body. There is no divine "person" who is independent of the material universe, no human person who does not reflect in all his functions an aspect of the divine nature.

For man, the purpose of the Tantric method is to awaken, utilize and control – starting from the energy coiled at the basic centre – the potential energies connected with all bodily functions. These digestive, excretory and reproductive functions of the human animal are the very basis of life. However, there are also potential energies connected with latent powers, subtle perceptions which are not conditioned by time and space, as well as magical, supernatural and spiritual powers which are not directly controlled by thought or will.

The Tantric method reproduces in man the very history of evolution. It starts from the basic mechanisms of the living being in order to rise to the higher functions – the intellectual and mental mechanisms – and the spiritual openings of the human being, so as to control and go beyond them. All attempted experiences are illusory if they do not take into account the nature of the living being in its entirety. This is especially so at the end of the evolutionary cycle, the Kali Yuga, when the apparent development of certain mental faculties really corresponds to an overall decrease in intuitive perception and vital force. What in fact occurs is a decadence announcing the death of the species.

The divine is found outside the apparent limits of the living being, on both sides of the created world. In order to pass through the barriers imprisoning us and free ourselves, so as to draw near to the divine, we can take one or the other road. The Shivaite way is the

Tantric way, the Tamasic (descending) way, which utilizes the physical functions and the apparently negative, destructive, sensual aspects of the human animal as a starting point. The Sattvic (ascending) way employs asceticism, virtue and the intellect as instruments. The Sattvic way is considered ineffectual in the Kali Yuga. In any case, since it is associated with the principle of concentration, that is with the Vishnu or Apollonian aspect, it can only lead to the realization of the divinity incarnate in the world. The ultimate way of liberation is always Shivaitic, as for all the higher degrees of initiation. This has important implications for what may be called the moral aspect of virtues, actions, and rites.

"The Vajrayâna (the way of the thunderbolt in Shivaite Tantrism) emphasizes the relativity of moral values and rightly proclaims that the passions lose their impure character (*klishta*) when they become absolute through the elemental powers of fire, water, earth, wind, etc. They 'wash by burning' and thus allow openings beyond the conditioned consciousness." (J. Evola, *Le Yoga tantrique*, p. 99.)

Before envisaging liberation into the world beyond, the first effect of the techniques used by Tantrism is the realization of freedom in this world. They ensure to the "hero", or superman, the powers and invulnerability by which means he can dominate the elements. For example, the transmutation of poisons into medicines, changing water into wine, or removing himself from one place to another.

Tantrism is opposed to Vedanta, since it rejects the concept of the world as an illusion, or Mâyâ, from man's point of view. On the contrary, it recognizes the world's reality as a form of power, or Shakti.

"In examining the ethics of the way of the Left Hand and the disciplines which tend to destroy ties, or *pâshas*, we find such a deep anomie, a 'beyond good and evil', that the Westerners who have propagated the superman theory appear as amateurs. . . Tantrism has foreseen fundamental problems which are perfectly suited to our times. It has prognosticated the phase of the last age, the Kali Yuga, whose essential characteristics as an era of dissolution are undoubtedly recognizable in the very numerous phenomena arising during the progress of this present age. . . It has sought new forms and new ways which, even in the 'dark age', would be effectual in realizing the ideal of past ages, so that man can awaken to the dimension of transcendency." (J. Evola, *Le Yoga tantrique*, pp. 287–288.)

Tantric concepts and practices are also found in Dionysism. These concepts and practices have, more often than not, been misunderstood in a world steeped in the strictly negative moral theories of Christianity. As Marcel Détienne says, "Passing beyond the sacrifice, which the Orphics and Pythagoreans practised from above, Dionysism accomplished from below... The followers of Dionysus... made themselves savage and behaved like ferocious beasts. Dionysism provides an escape from the human condition from below, by breaking into bestiality, while Orphism proposes the same escape, from the side of the gods". (*Dionysos mis à mort*, pp. 149 and 198.)

In the Dionysiac world, Orgiasm refers to practices which correspond to those of Tantrism. These are generally group ceremonies during which bloody sacrifices, ecstatic and prophetic dances, and erotic rites are performed. Like Shiva in India, Dionysus in Greece is presented under the double aspect of a god of Nature and a god of orgiastic practices, presiding over the *frenzy* of the *bhaktas* – the bacchants and bacchantes – which the Greeks called *mania*.

Dionysus-Baccheios is the inspirer of *mania*, as revealed in the state of trance of the maenads and followers of the god, who himself takes part in the orgiasm, since he is essentially the bacchant, *bhakta*, or participant. Shiva is termed libidinous and mad, just as for Homer, Dionysus is *mainomenos*, the madman, rejected by the "well-doers" of the city. The later Celtic ballad of Merlin also says, "They call me Merlin the Madman and cast stones to chase me away".

Dionysism throws itself wholeheartedly into savagery in seeking to possess and contact the supernatural. Plato attributes considerable importance to orgiastic madness, or *mania*, considered as a source of divine inspiration and as an expression of divine "participation" in the world of men. According to Philo, "Those who are possessed by Dionysiac and Korybantic frenzy, in their ecstasy reach the object desired". (*De vita contemplativa*, 12.) In *Phaedrus*, Plato develops a theory of knowledge based on this participation (*bhakti*) and on amorous *mania* as a source of such knowledge. He envisages four types of *mania*, which he places in a symbolic relationship with Aphrodite (and Eros), the Muses (and dancing), Apollo (Vishnu), and Dionysus. He distinguishes the erotic mania connected with love from the one related to inebriety and ecstatic dancing, which are more directly linked with Dionysus. Similar distinctions exist in India between ecstatic practices placed under the aegis of Shiva, Skanda, or Ganesha (Hermes), and those relating to the goddess or Krishna, or in other words, to Vishnu-Apollo.

Collective dancing leading to *mania*, or orgiasm, is called *kîrtana* (song of glory) in India, and dithyramb by the Greeks. Ethnologists and religious historians have often tried to give collective orgiastic ceremonies an agrarian, seasonal, or other meaning. In reality, it is one aspect of the uncondititioning of the human being, who is thus enabled to regain for a moment his deepest and most repressed nature, which is his true nature, still close to the divine. This return to man's vital elemental instincts forms an essential part of the Tantric method.

"Repressed desire engenders pestilence", writes Ananda Coomaraswany in *The Dance of Shiva*. Promiscuity, the momentary disappearance of all constraint and the evocation and orgiastic reactivation of primordial chaos, all favour certain forms of ecstasy. One may return to the origin of life, the creative principle, the divine.

"The sacralization and ritualization of life was a characteristic of the Hindu civilization in general, as of all other traditional civilizations. Christianity was able to say, 'Eat and drink to the glory of God', since the pre-Christian West also knew sacred meals, and even the Roman *epulae* had a religious and symbolic element up to a relatively late period... It is only when, apart from food, women and intoxicating drinks are admitted, that difficulties may arise – but only from the point of view of the religion which has prevailed in the West, in which the dominant sexaphobic complex considers the sexual act impure and not susceptible of being made sacred. This attitude may, however, be considered abnormal, since the sacralization of sex, the notion of a sexual *sacrum*, was achieved by many traditional civilizations." (J. Evola, *Le Yoga tantrique*, p. 179.)

Orgy-meals found their greatest development in opulent Greek and Roman society. A festive meal followed the great Olympian feasts at Daphne... "To this all-male meal were invited those of less than twenty years of age. Men and adolescents reclined on the same couch, the younger one in front, next to the table. The man made him drink, caressed him and made him, if I may say so, his mistress." (A. J. Festugière, *Etudes de religion grecque et hellénistique*, note p. 246.) At Rome, every sort of pleasure was sought during these nocturnal orgies at which adolescents were initiated.

One of the characteristics of orgiastic-type associations, is the abolition of all social barriers. This principle exists in all Shivaite rites. Organizations performing dances and rites of an orgiastic nature are open to all, and are associations of an essentially popular type, frequented by people of high caste in search of an experience which will break social as well as moral taboos. According to Livy, to take nothing as being illicit was considered by the bacchants as the very expression of devotion. In the Greek world, the thiasoi were cultural organizations whose purpose was to regularize Dionysiac orgies, and were mainly composed of the less-favoured elements, women and poor people. Puritan bourgeois society looked with great mistrust on these associations which were accused of the most varied crimes. The practitioners of the Osiris cult in Egypt were similar to those of the Dionysus cult in Greece. "Cadmos... had learned, in his fatherland, the mysteries of divine knowledge, Egyptian wisdom... And when the evoe resounded, he showed the mysteries of the Egyptian Dionysus, Osiris the Wanderer, whose nocturnal cult and rites of initiation he had learned; and in secret he made a magic hymn re-echo, with the accents of sacred frenzy." (Nonnos, *Dionysia*, IV, 270–273.)

Shivaite orgiasm has been widely practised by Tibetan Buddhism, and in more ancient times, in Middle-Eastern cults, particularly among the Canaanites, Babylonians and Hebrews. Certain passages of the Old Testament refer to people, events and concepts known to the Purânas; the *bhakta* tradition is also mentioned. "The coexistence of contradictory 'attributes', and the irrationality of some of his actions, keep Yahweh aloof from any 'ideal of perfection' on the human scale. From this point of view, Yahweh resembles certain Hindu divinities, Shiva, for example, or Kâlî-Durgâ, but with a considerable difference. These Indian deities are placed beyond morals and, since their mode of being is taken as a model, their followers do not hesitate to imitate them... In the seventh century B.C., the Israelities began to practise the holocaust ('Olah), which they interpreted as on oblation offered to Yahweh. They also took over a number of Canaanite practices relating to agriculture and even certain orgiastic rituals. The assimilation process was further intensified under the monarchy, when sacred prostitution of both sexes is spoken of." (M. Eliade, *Histoire des croyances et des idées religieuses*, pp. 194 and 197.)

According to G. Hoelscher's study on Biblical tradition (*Die Propheten*), "The traditions relating to the *Nebî'îm* (prophets) present these persons and the companies of 'sons of the prophets' which they seem to have formed, as groups of energumens devoted to exercises and a kind of religious gymnastics which usually tended to provoke collective ecstasy and strange manifestations accompanied by a state of trance... Hebrew has a word meaning 'to make *nabi*' which corresponds to the Greek translated as 'to be bacchant'." (H. Jeanmaire, *Dionysos*, p. 102.)

Samuel sent his young son Saul to inquire of the sooth-sayer the fate of the she-asses. "After that thou shalt come to the hill of God... and thou shalt meet a company of *Nebî'îm* coming down from the high place with a psaltery (*nebel*), and a tabret (*taph*), and a pipe (*halil*), and a harp (*kinnor*)... and they shall make *nabi*. And the Spirit of the Lord will come upon thee and thou shalt make *nabi* with them and shalt be turned into another man... And when they came thither to the hill, behold, a company of *Nebî'îm* met him and the Spirit of the Lord came upon him and he made *nabi* among them." (I Sam. 10, 5.)

Samuel became the sheikh of the *Nebî'îm* and director of their spiritual exercises. David took refuge in the "lodges" of Ramah, near Samuel. Saul sent his emissaries to seize him. "And when they saw the company (*lahgah*) of the *Nebî'îm* making *nabi*, and Samuel standing as appointed over them, the Spirit of God was upon the messengers of Saul, and they also made *nabi*." Saul then sent other messengers, and yet others, whom the frenzied contagion also seized. The king then went in person to the lodges of Ramah. "And the Spirit of the Lord was on him also and he went on and made *nabi* until he came to Nâioth in Ramah. And he stripped off his clothes, and made *nabi* before Samuel in like manner and lay down naked all that day and all that night. Wherefore they say, Is Saul also among the Prophets?" (I Sam. 19, 18–24.) (as quoted in Jeanmaire, *Dionysos*, p. 103.)

The expression "to make *nabi*" so completely denotes the idea of frenzied delirium and possession that, in the same account, Saul desires to kill David in an access of fury. "The evil spirit from God came upon Saul, and he made *nabi*." (I Sam. 18, 10.)

Certain aspects of the ecstatic cults of Shiva-Dionysus have been preserved in more or less secret form in later religions. "In the Islamic world..., in the ecstatic dance..., the possessed person and the possessing spirit may be of the same or different sex... He or she who dances is always the possessing spirit and is spoken of according to the gender corresponding to the sex of the possessing spirit. The spirits are named *Bori* in the Sudanese language, or *Zar* (*Sar*) in Egypt and Abyssinia." (H. Jeanmaire, *Dionysos*, pp. 120–121.) Female *Bori* ceremonies with the bloody sacrifice of a ram could be seen until recently in Egypt.

The Ankle Bracelet, the ancient Tamil epic poem of the third century, describes a scene of possession identical to those which can be observed today. "Devandi appeared to go into a trance – the flowers in her hair fell to the ground; her contracted eyebrows began to throb; her lips drawn against her white teeth showed a strange contraction. Her voice changed timbre and her pretty face became covered with pearls of sweat. Her large eyes grew red. She flung her arms about in a threatening gesture. Suddenly, her legs moved; she stood upright. None could recognize her. She seemed in a state of stupor. Her dry tongue uttered inspired words... I am Shâttan, the Magician, speaking through the body of a Brahmin woman." (*The Ankle Bracelet*, trans. A. Daniélou, p. 198.)

Dionysus-Bacchus: God of drunkenness and wine

All religions in which mysticism and contact with the supernatural play an important part, attribute a sacred character to an intoxicating drink or other intoxicant. The tradition of sacred drinks and ritual libations is found in all ancient civilizations. Wine is still today a part of the Christian ritual. Dionysus had the power of turning water into wine. According to Plato, this miraculous power became current practice in the ritual exercises performed by the bacchants and maenads in a state of trance. This power is also attributed to Jesus, as are many of Dionysus' other miracles.

Drunkenness induced by wine and hallucinatory drinks is a part of the technique of ecstasy. They help man to free himself from material cares and are a preparation for perceiving higher realities. "Drinking and drinking again, falling down and rising to drink. This is how to attain liberation." (*Kûlârnava Tantra*, VII, 99.) According to the *Tantra Râja* (VIII), "Those who have known supreme liberation and those who become or strive to become adepts always make use of wine". The *Mahânirvâna Tantra* (XI, 105–108), explains that intoxicating drink is consumed in order to liberate oneself, and that those who do so, in dominating their mental faculties and in following the law of Shiva, are to be likened to immortals on earth.

The invention of wine and its diffusion among men are an essential theme of Dionysiac legend. It appears that the vine is a plant of Indian origin and was imported into the Mediterranean area together with the Bacchus cult well before the Aryan invasions. Megasthenes mentions the importance of the Indian vineyards. Wine became the

154

sacred drink of the Mediterranean peoples and Cretan gardeners cultivated the vine.

"The vine has been cultivated in the Aegean area since Minoan times... It is attested to in Egypt at a very early period... Skylax (fourth century B.C.) mentions the famous wines which Phoenician merchants went to buy along the African coast, particularly in Libya and Tunisia (in the Sousse area)." (H. Jeanmaire, *Dionysos*, pp. 23, 351.)

According to Apolloderus (III, V, 1), it was Dionysus who discovered wine. As the god of ecstasy and deliverance, he is also the god of Wine, and his cult is associated with the vine. It is under this aspect that he is generally called Bacchus. "Liber, the Latin Dionysus, is present in most viticultural operations as their patron, since he is also a technician... He is invoked together with Libera..., due to the sexual symbolism which in Latium was attached to this divine couple, and was readily evoked by the pressing operation." (G. Dumezil, *Fêtes romaines d'été et d'automne*, p. 107.) According to Diodorus of Sicily, the legend of Dionysus torn to pieces and boiled by the Titans is a symbol of wine production. The vine-dressers tear and crush the grape and make the wine "boil". The vine, like Dionysus, is reborn each year.

Honey liquor (mead) is also an intoxicant, and plays an important part in the rituals of Hindus, Minoans, and Greeks. However, it appears that in India, the sacred intoxicating drink *soma* was often made from plants other than the vine. Some modern authors have suggested that a type of mushroom was used. This ancient sacred drink was likely to resemble a drink what today is called *bhang*, made from the crushed leaves of Indian hemp. Every Shivaite has to consume *bhang* at least once a year. This drink, which intensifies perceptivity, induces visions and above all leads to extreme mental concentration. It is widely used by Yogis. Details concerning its preparation are to be found as early as the Vedic period. The description of the way in which *soma* was prepared, and its immediate use without fermentation, can only apply to *bhang* and is identical to the method employed today.

Apart from *bhang*, which is recommended for the purpose of para-psychological experience, grave-wine, palm-wine and fig-liquor all play a considerable part in the life of the Indian people and in Shivaite rites. Dionysus-Bacchus himself appears as the very personification of inebriety.

GODS OF LOVE AND ECSTASY

The climate of Shivaite and Dionysiac life is not purely ritual. It is a seeking after joy and pleasure, and the self-realization of the individual. Wine and other intoxicating drinks are a part of this joy of living, which is one of the basic goals of all kinds of existence, since happiness (*ânanda*) is the nature of the divine state itself. Everything which is pleasure and joy draws us nearer to God. All Dionysiac or Shivaite festivals are an explosion of happiness. Physical drunkenness, like eroticism, is an image of, and often a preparation for, mystical drunkenness. "My life is a success when I have a pretty girl near me, and perfumed wine on my lips... All the Messengers of Wisdom are busy getting drunk in the flower garden, in the company of their lovers." (Harsha, *Le Bonheur du Serpent*, Act III.) The same is true for the festivals of Bacchus.

"There are ritual systems associated with the sacrifice of *soma*, as for example the Mahâvrata (Great Observance) which involves music, dancing, dramatic gestures, obscene dialogues and scenes (one of the priests balances on a swing, a sexual union takes place, etc.)... The revelation of a full and blessed existence in communion with the gods has continued to obsess Indian spirituality long after the disappearance of the original drink. The attainment of such an existence has therefore been sought by other means: ascesis, or orgiastic excess, meditation, the techniques of Yoga, and mystical devotion." (M. Eliade, *Histoire des croyances et des idées religieuses*, pp. 225–230.)

"Those who have not known the sacred orgies and those who have taken part in them will not have the same fate after death in the regions of darkness." (Homeric Hymns, *Hymns to Demeter*, 480–483.)

"In Tantrism, wine is called 'causal water' (*Kâranavâri*), or the 'elixir of wisdom' (*Jñânâmrita*). According to the *Kulârnava Tantra*, the form of the Brahman is enclosed in the body and can be revealed by wine, which is why it is used by Yogis... In Dionysism, wine had the same meaning, so that the expression 'sacred orgy' is in current usage in the ancient literature of the mysteries; the same idea is found in Persian mysticism, in which wine and drunkenness involved a ritual and symbolic meaning. Pursuing this theme, one reaches the tradition of the Templars... [The French proverb,] 'drunk like a Templar' may have a secret operative meaning, very different from the grosser meaning which has prevailed." (J. Evola, *Le Yoga tantrique*, p. 184.)

Eroticism: the sacralization of sexual acts

Eroticism

"Divine love is reached through carnal love" (Saint Bernard). Shiva is the principle of erotic pleasure, not of fecundity. Wandering in the forest, he spreads his sperm by masturbatory practices and inspires desire and erotic madness. His son, Skanda, is born without the intervention of a female element. All the beauty and all the joy in the world is manifested by means of an erotic explosion. Flowers cast their pollen to the wind. Fecundation is but an accident in the manifestation of erotic joy. Eros recognizes no difference of sex or object. An inner impulse leaps towards beauty and harmony. The creation of the world is an erotic act, an act of love, and everything which exists bears this sign and this message. In living beings, everything is organized in accordance with this expression of pleasure, joy, beauty and happiness, which is the nature of the divine and the secret of all that exists.

Eroticism is the bond of attraction uniting two opposite and complementary poles. The lesser eros is oriented towards procreation, producing children and material goods. Free or pure eroticism, oriented towards universal beauty in all its forms, is a reflection of the divine, and is the way that leads to God. This is the higher, sublime eros. Only the love of "the woman who does not belong to you" (*parakîya*) is true love. Relations with "her who belongs to you" (*svakîya*) are a part of man's social duties, and have no ritual value. In Tantric rites, the rule which allows a man to use his own wife is only valid for the lower, preparatory degrees: for the *vîra* or "hero", she is left aside. "Metaphysically, the physical, animal act of generation is only a vain substitute for spiritual generation. The continuation of the species, ensured by the use of sex as a generative power, represents a kind of ephemeral terrestrial eternity, a facsimile of continuity." (J. Evola, *Le Yoga tantrique*, p. 222.)

"The experience of absolute light . . ., when attained through *maithuna*, or sexual union, is capable of penetrating right to the heart of organic life, and of discovering there, too, in the very essence of the *semen virile*, the divine light, that primordial brilliance which created the world . . . The light experienced in *maithuna* is the Clear Light of Gnosis, and of Nirvanic consciousness." (M. Eliade, *Méphistophélès et l'Androgyne*, pp. 46–49.)

"The sexual act may be a process of mystical identification, in the same way as other primitive ecstasy-inducing methods. Its use is therefore quite normal, from the moment a social group desires to ally itself with the natural powers..., represented by the sacred protagonists. Such is the meaning of the divine marriage (*Hieros gamos*) publicly celebrated during the course of so many pagan ceremonies." (André Varagnac, *Civilisation traditionelle*, p. 241.)

The sexual union of a monk with a prostitute takes place in certain Tantric rites, as does the offering of sperm, associated with the man-fish; or anal penetration, associated with the man-bird. Couplings between men – or women and animals – also have a symbolic and ritual significance, of which numerous representations can be seen on Hindu temples. The union of Pasiphae and the bull, which gave birth to the Minotaur, as well as all the representations of half-man, half-animal beings, found in Egypt, in India and in the Mediterranean world, all involve the same concept.

"The Homeric hymn identifies the sexual instinct with the unifying element of the three modes of existence: animal, human and divine... It is the religious justification of sexuality... Incited by Aphrodite, even sexual excess and outrage must be recognized as being of divine origin." (M. Eliade, *Histoire des croyances et des idées religieuses*, p. 296.)

"Respiration and sexuality are considered to be the only two ways still open to man in the Kali Yuga. It is on them that the *sâdhana* (the method) is based. In Yoga..., *prânâyâma* or respiration is all important. The use of women, sex and sexual magic plays a significant rôle in another sector of Tantrism, in which obscure practices from the ancient pre-Indo-European substratum have been taken over, transformed, completed and brought up to an initiatory level... In the *Siddhântâchâra* (behaviour in accordance with esoteric principles) and *Kaulâchâra* (rules of behaviour of the 'companions')..., which are essentially a part of the way of the Left Hand, the emphasis is shifted and passes from the freeing to the freedom of the god-man, of him who has overcome the human function and is placed beyond all law." (J. Evola, *Le Yoga tantrique*, p. 21.)

Samarasa (identification through sensation), meaning identification with the divine being through enjoyment, is accomplished by means of sexual rites. Every sexual act can become a sacrament, and is known as the *vaira-padma-samskara*, "the sacrament of the thunder bolt and the lotus". In the secret language of the Tantras, *Vajra* (thunder bolt) and *padma* (lotus) respectively represent the male organ and the receptacle (*arghya*), or female organ. In the same way, the *bindu*, the limit point between non-existence and existence, represents the sperm and the *mudrâ* (seal), or female secretion.

"In the rite, the man is identified with the first principle, the woman with the other, and their union reproduces that of the divine couple. These two principles are Shivaitic and male on the one side and Shaktic and female on the other. In the revealed and conditioned world they appear separately in a duality of which the male and female organs are only a particular expression, reuniting for the instant of sexual orgasm, thus evoking 'androgynous Shiva', the Ardhanarîshvara, and the oneness of the Beginning... This interpretation of sexual union... would suspend the law of duality and induce an ecstatic opening... The law of duality being suspended... in the simultaneity of pleasure, orgasm and ecstasy uniting the two beings..., a state of identity... can be induced... which prefigures... absolute... 'unconditioned'... enlightenment... The *Kûlârnava Tantra* goes as far as to say that supreme union can only be attained by means of sexual union." (J. Evola, *Le Yoga tantrique*, pp. 191–192.)

In Tantric rituals, the sexual organ of a very young woman is venerated. According to the *Mahâmudrâtilaka*, "Young women of over twenty have no occult power". In order to experience interior enlightenment through ceremonial sexual union with a young girl personifying Shakti, the divine love-game must be imitated in which the union does not climax in a seminal emission. Woman has a double personality. The Virgin and the Mother are different beings, each having a distinct rôle, both symbolically and in the rites.

In the Yoga of the Right Hand, development of sexual power is also essential, but in this case it mainly used to awaken the coiled energy and to make it rise through the various centres up to the brain, while avoiding any ejaculation. "The split *bindu* (here meaning sperm) brings death; retained *bindu* brings life." (*Hatha Yoga Pradîpikâ*, III, 85, 90.) The adept who is "near to the divine" (*divya*), in whom the ascendant force (*sattva*) predominates, no longer practises the sexual rites of the *vira* or "hero", who unites with a *shakti* (a realizing energy) in the person of a woman. Instead, he strives to awaken in his own body the Shakti with which he must unite in order to attain his goal. The realized man (*divya*) can say, "What need have I of an exterior woman? I have a woman within myself (*Kundalini*)".

Whatever form they take, rites of a sexual nature are called "weddings of Shiva", since the god takes under his protection all those who are outside the norm. The entire range of erotic variations is described and Yogic-type procedures utilized in order to intensify and exploit sensual pleasure. In a special rite, prostatic orgasm linked with anal penetration plays an important rôle. This is connected with the cult of Ganesha, the son of the goddess and guardian of gates, whose centre – according to Yoga – is in the prostatic plexus.

"A relationship seems to have been recognized between the *Kundalini* and the sexual organ . . . The secret sexual practices probably involve a momentary awakening of this power . . . It can be said that . . . Tantric symbolism representing the Shakti in man at the level of 'earth' in the *Mûlâdhara*, in the form of a snake coiled around the phallus of Shiva and closing the orifice, has a deep significance." (J. Evola, *Le Yoga tantrique*, p. 222.)

We possess only a few references to the erotic rites practised by Dionysiac groups and the initiatory societies of the West. However, these allusions are sufficient for us to realize that they correspond almost exactly, both in theory and in practice, to those described in detail in the Purânas and Tantras.

The birth of Eros (Kâma)

The following description is a good illustration of the transposition of a cosmological abstraction – the birth of the world – into popular imagery. It refers to a secondary manifestation of the same principle in the order of creation and is also characteristic of all mythology. "At the time of creation, when the god Brahmâ [who represents creative force, born of the union of Shiva and Shakti] made the world appear, he first engendered Aurora (Sandhyâ) who appeared in the from of a young girl of surprising beauty.

"Brahmâ spoke, 'On seeing her, I had in involuntary erection. My heart was disturbed with conflicting desires. All my sons were in the same state. A marvellous being called Eros (kâma) was born of my thought. His complexion was golden, his chest strong and solid, his nose well-formed; his thighs, buttocks and calves were rounded and muscular. His black hair was curly, his eyebrows thick and expressive. His face was like the full moon. His hairy chest was as wide as a door. Draped in a blue robe, he appeared as majestic as the celestial elephant Airâvata. His hands, eyes, face, legs and fingers were red. His waist was slim, his teeth perfect. He gave off the odour of an elephant in rut. His eyes were like lotus petals, and he was perfumed

160

like their stamens. His neck was a conch. His emblem was a fish. He was big, mounted on a crocodile, and armed with a bow and five arrows of flowers. His amorous glances seduced everyone. He winked at all around him. His breath was like a perfumed breeze. The feeling of love came from his whole person. On seeing him, my sons were overcome with amazement. They became agitated and restless, their minds were confused. Troubled by the ardour of love, they lost their strength of mind'." (*Shiva Purâna, Rudra Samhitâ*, chap. I, 20–32.)

"Brahmâ then said to Kâma, 'In this form and with your five arrows of flowers, you can inspire desire, make yourself master of men and women, and thus perpetuate the work of creation'." (*Shiva Purâna, ibid.*, chap. II, 37.)

"'Each of Kâma's five arrows had its proper activity. This is why they are called Joy of Living (Harshana), Attraction (Rocana), Illusion (Mohana), Languor (Shoshana), and Bruiser (Mârana)... Having charmed us all, Eros continued making fun of us until we had all lost control of our senses. Thus it was that we let ourselves go to look at Aurora with lustful eyes...' All the sages were in a state of erotic excitement. Implored by Virtue (Dharma), Shiva burst out laughing and mocked them, making them blush with shame. He said to them, 'Truly, Brahmâ, how can you allow yourself to get to the point of having such feelings for your own daughter? It is not seemly... How is it that your sons are all smitten with the same girl, who, moreover, is their own sister? This Eros must be a fool, and lacking in good manners, to have attacked you with such violence'." (*Shiva Purâna, ibid.*, chap. III, 2–44.)

"The gods, beaten by the Titans, implored Kâma to lend them his aid in bringing Shiva out of his meditation so that he could help them vanquish their enemies. Kâma said to Brahmâ, 'If I must sow disorder in the heart of Shiva himself, my only weapon is a charming girl. Find me some other means of winning him over'. To this request of the god of Love, Brahmâ replied by heaving a deep sigh from which was born Spring (Vasanta), covered with flowers. He was like a red lotus, his eyes like open lotuses, his face shone like the moon appearing at twilight. His nose was comely of form. His legs were curved like a bow, his hair black and curly. He wore earrings and shone like the rising sun. His bearing was majestic like an elephant in rut. His arms were long and strong, his shoulders high, his neck rounded like a conch. His chest was wide, his face round and fine. His appearance was attractive, his complexion dark. He had a strange beauty, capable of charming all beings and of stimulating the feelings of love.

"As soon as Spring appeared, a perfumed breeze began to blow. The trees were covered with flowers. The cuckoos sang and the lotus opened in the pools. Brahmâ then said to Kâma, 'You now have a faithful companion. He resembles you and will be of great service to you'." (*Shiva Purâna, Rudra Samhitâ, Sati Khanda*, chap. 8, 34–41.)

"The sage Brihaspati persuaded Kâma and his companion Spring to go to Shiva, who was lost in his Yoga meditation, and to persuade him to unite with the Lady of the Mountain (Pârvati). The Lord looked at him with derision and scorn and, with a flash of lightning from his third eye, reduced Kâma to ashes. Moved by the tears of the wife of Eros, Desire (Rati), the Lord told her, 'Your husband has lost his visible body, but, in the moment of pleasure, he will do everything he should do'." (*Linga Purâna*, 101, 39–46.)

"If the goddess of the Mountain, the most lovely of creatures, is accepted by me as a lover, Eros will rise again . . . All the gods, sages and ascetics will give themselves without shame to sensual pleasures and abandon the way of asceticism and Yoga . . . Desire leads to anger, anger to error, and error destroys the fruits of austerity." (*Shiva Purâna, Rudreshvara Samhitâ, Pârvatî Khanda*, chap. 24, 18–28.)

The world, however, deprived of the charms of Eros, would not have been able to survive. "Shiva, the trident-bearing god, looked with compassion on the daughters of heaven who implored him. With a single one of his glances, which are more effective than ambrosia, he raise Kâma from his ashes, his charming body adorned with splendid rainment." (*Shiva Purâna, ibid.*, chap. 51, 13–14.)

In Orphic cosmology, Eros, like Kâma, has no mother, since he is antecedent to sexual union. He represents the original oneness to which all "separated" things aspire. The apparent world is the result of the separation of two contrary principles which exist only by and for each other, and aspire only to find each other. Eros is both the principle of existence and that of annihilation or death. Nothing exists without him; through him all things cease to exist. He represents the very nature of Shiva, the principle of life and death.

In Crete, and later on in Dorian society in Sparta, erotic desire played an important part in the organization of society. It is revealed mostly in the form of paederastic love, an expression of desire without a procreative ulterior motive. This form of eros was the source of civic virtue. It was, in fact, by means of an erotic attachment that the elder could lead the younger in the way of wisdom, virtue and courage. "Juvenile delinquency" does not exist in places where paederastic love is the rule. The Greeks perfectly understood the social and educational rôle of this aspect of eros. Thebes won its greatest victories due to the "sacred battalion" formed of couples of lover and beloved.

"The love affairs of the young Cretans... [included] a mock 'marriage' by capture – of an older with a younger boy... The boy's friends... seized him... [and] handed him over to the abductor... He was... taken away into the country... and after feasting and hunting with them for two months they returned to the city... The young initiate then sacrificed an ox to Zeus... It was considered a disgrace... to fail to obtain lovers... The abducted boys... had the positions of highest honour in dances and races [and] were allowed to dress in better clothes... presented by their lovers." (R. F. Willetts, *Cretan Cults and Festivals*, p. 116.)

After this "marriage" episode, the youths were integrated into the warrior group. The elder then offered the younger the three ritual gifts: the warrior's arms, a drinking cup, and a bull for sacrifice. According to Plato, the myth of Ganymede had its origin... at the court of Minos and thus Minos, not Zeus, was the ravisher. In subsequent literature, Eros becomes an *enfant terrible*, charged with the organization of love affairs.

There is probably a relationship between the legends of Kâma and Vasanta and that of Hyakinthos. "The origins of Hyakinthos are markedly prehistoric... Apollo who loved Hyakinthos... accidentally killed him with a discus... The Minoan origin of Hyakinthos is confirmed by the form of his name... [which] also denotes... the wild hyacinth or iris. Thus Hyakinthos was an annually dying and reborn god of vegetation, akin not only to Adonis, Attis and Osiris, but to his Cretan counterpart, Zeus Kretagenes. Like Cretan Zeus, Hyakinthos was not reared by his mother... His nurse... [was the] mistress of animals, pre-Greek Artemis." (R. F. Willetts, *Cretan Cults and Festivals*. p. 222.)

Homosexuality was, and still is very widespread, but in India its ritual rôle was emphasized rather than its sentimental or social rôle. The condemnation of homosexual practices by the British government in India has, in this field as well as in others, been prejudicial to the harmony of life.

Sacrifice: the sacralization of the alimentary function

Sacrifice

The Creator is a cruel god who made a world in which nothing can
live but by destroying life through the killing of other living beings
Thus, no being can exist except by devouring other forms of life
whether vegetable or animal, and this is one of the fundamental
aspects of created nature. Life in the world, both animal and human,
is nothing but an interminable slaughter. To exist means to eat and to
be eaten. Man is what he eats. All living beings feed on other beings
and themselves become food for other beings in an ecological cycle.
This is why the Creator himself defines his nature as devouring and
devoured. "I am the food, food, food, and I am the eater, eater.
eater... from food are born living beings. Those who are on the
Earth live only by food and become themselves food in the end.'
(*Taittirîya Upanishad*, III, 2 and 10, 6.)

"The whole universe is really only food and eater." (*Brihat Aranyaka
Upanishad*, 14, 6.) "Living beings feed on living beings (*Jîva jîvasya
bhakshaka*)", as it is written in the Purânas. In the *Anushâsana Parva*
of the *Mâhâbhârata* (chap. 213), Shiva explains to his companion,
"There is no one in the world who does not kill. He who walks kills
innumerable insects with his feet. Even when sleeping, lives can be
destroyed. All creatures kill one another... It is not possible for
anyone to live without killing... Only those die who are destined to
die. Every living being is slain by Fate; death only comes afterwards.
Nothing escapes Fate".

The basic principle of Shivaism is to accept the world as it is, and
not as we should like it to be. It is only when we accept the reality of
the world that we can try to understand its nature, thus drawing
nearer to the Creator and taking our place in the harmony of creation.
Since nothing can exist without feeding on the life of other beings, we
ourselves must take responsibility before the gods who have ordained
it so. In order to make the gods party to our actions, we must
overcome the instinctive stage and ritualize the act of killing in the
same way as the act of love. In order to share with the gods the
responsibility for the fratricidal act by which we are forced to devour
other living beings so as to survive, we must offer them victims in
sacrifice. The gods must be offered the first-fruits of the harvest, the
first mouthful of all nourishment, and before them we must kill the
animal which we will devour.

MAN IN THE WORLD

It is only when we are fully conscious of the value of our actions, consciously accomplishing the will of the god who has ordained that life should only exist by death and by slaughter, that we can then limit its effects and play the part which has devolved on us in the harmony of the world. Only then can we avoid stepping out of our rôle, and avoid the hecatombs which take place when man tries to ignore his own real nature and that of the divine.

Today, in certain popular Shivaite sects, a man only eats the flesh of animals he himself has ritually sacrificed, taking the gods as witnesses of the cruelty of a world in which life is not possible except by destroying life. By so doing he plays with honesty his role in the harmony of the world, without either sentimentalism or hypocrisy. One should not eat the flesh of living beings without killing them oneself, i.e., taking a conscious part in their slaughter and making the gods a party to it, since the world which they have created and uphold is itself a perpetual sacrifice. This is the meaning of the sacrificial rite. By saying that the gods are thirsty for the blood of victims, we identify them with a world which is the expression of their own nature, and draw near to them by sanctifying the act of killing. Every religion is founded on the notion of sacrifice and the consumption of the sacrificed victim. Whether the victim is animal, vegetable or human, our body is only its cemetary. The body will itself serve in its totality – both physical and mental – as food for other living beings.

Sacrifice has little to do with the discreet massacres of domestic animals which take place in the city. Sacrifice should be public, with a full consciousness of its value and its cruelty. Slaughter and the hunting of an animal for food, is one of man's basic instincts and means of survival which can lead to exaltation, or a sort of trance. This is also one of the mystical ways of identification with the destructive aspect of the deity. The frantic course of the maenads, and the fury with which they tore and devoured their victims alive, is a form of mystical ecstasy.

This exaltation is also found in the great Shivaite sacrifices, still performed today, during which thousands of goats or buffalo are sacrificed; the earth and the participants are bathed in blood, in an atmosphere of religious exaltation. Killing is a sacred act, like the giving of life. Useless murder upsets the balance of nature whose protector is Shiva. "Violence must be avoided always and everywhere. The violent do not attack the man who abstains from violence in thought, word and deed. They pursue those who attack others...

165

Those who care for the welfare of living beings, in thought, word and deed, and who follow the path of benevolence to all creatures, are admitted to the paradise of Rudra... However, violence must be done to the flowers so as to offer them to Shiva, and violence also to the animals for sacrifice." (*Linga Purâna*, I, chap. 78, 8–16.)

According to the most ancient sources, it appears that sacrifices were offered to Skanda, the young warrior-god, rather than to Shiva himself, who is the protector of animals.

According to Shrîdayânanda (*Balidâna Pûjâkâ pradhâna anka, Kalyâna, Shakti anka*, p. 161), "there are four kinds of sacrifice: the first is the sacrifice of oneself; in giving one's own life. This offering reaches the god and the sacrificed one is united with him to whom the sacrifice is offered. The second is the sacrifice of the passions. Amongst these, desire corresponds to the kid, anger to the ram, and illusion to the buffalo. The third sacrifice is offering to the gods the first-fruits of all things which constitute our food: grain, sweet foods, roots, wine, etc. The fourth is the sacrifice of living beings."

Agni, the god of Fire

"Fire only exists by destroying the fuel which makes it live, by consuming the oblation. The whole universe, both sentient and insentient, is nothing but fire and oblation." (*Mahâbhârata, Shanti Parva*, 338, 52.) The sun only shines by destroying its own substance. Fire is the symbol of the universal sacrifice, the image of destruction in its purest form. It represents a sort of limit between two states of being, that of the created world and that of the gods. The gods are beyond the fire and feed on the smoke of the oblations. Any offering to the gods is thrown into the mouth of Agni, the god of Fire. It was Agni who received Shiva's sperm, which gave birth to Skanda when the god offered his own substance in sacrifice.

The acids which burn and transform food in the stomach are considered an aspect of fire, and in this form, Agni is present in man's body. Eating the flesh of the victim is equivalent to the fire-offering rite, so long as the eater is conscious of the gods' presence in himself and so long as the act of eating is a rite. Omophagy, or the devouring of the raw victim, has the value of a sacrifice only when performed in a state of trance, that is, when the eater is possessed and inhabited by a god.

The nature of fire differs according to how it is produced. The sacrificial fire must be made with flint, "thunder-stones", or by rubbing together two pieces of consecrated wood, which is the *need-fire* of Celtic countries. In India, the fire for all *yajñas* (sacrifices) must be made in this way. Indian tradition preserves the memory of the Ribhus, the sages who were the first to domesticate fire and who thus created the "hearth", which is the symbol of sedentary civilization. The keeping alive of the fire lit at the time of marriage continues to be an essential rite of home life. If the fire dies, the element of stability has left the house. If the sacrificial fire goes out, it signifies that the gods refuse the oblation. It is clear that the making of fire was problematic for the ancient world. Even today, nomads carefully carry their fire from one camp to another.

The victim

Only the best of anything may be offered to the gods. The noblest animal, the closest to the god, is the one which must be sacrificed. Often, it is the image of the god himself, and its being put to death evokes the divine sacrifice. All animals or vegetables offered in sacrifice are identified with the god in whose name the sacrifice is accomplished. It is the god himself who is sacrificed in his revealed form. "The spirit of vegetation at harvest time is incarnate in the body of an animal which becomes its abode. In the Dionysiac rites, the sacrificed animal is one of this kind, that is, the god himself." (see: Sir James Frazer, *The Golden Bough*, pp. 160–168.)

The animals usually sacrificed are the bull (the vehicle of Shiva-Dionysus), or the buffalo (the mount of the god of death), the he-goat or ram (vehicle of the Fire-god), and sometimes the cock (the sacred animal of Skanda). At the *bouphonia*, an ox was sacrificed to Dionysus and at other ceremonies, a he-goat. In India, the common sacrificial animals are the buffalo and the he-goat, whereas bull-sacrifice is rarely performed nowadays. The *Grihya-sûtras* mention a sacrifice called *shûla-gava* (spitted bull), during which a bull is sacrificed to appease Rudra (*Ashvalâyana Grihya-sûtra*, IV, 9).

In a ritual witnessed by Pausanias the victim was a bull, seized by men whose bodies were covered with fat and oil. It was a sort of corrida, a hunting rite, preceding the sacrifice, and is clearly inherited from the Minoan "games". The tradition of the corrida continues even today, although its ritual meaning is no longer apparent.

The sacrifice of a bull by cutting its throat is represented on a clay coffin found at Haghi Triada. The bull lies on a table, immobilized by a red rope and the blood pouring from the slit throat is collected in a

167

vessel. The bull was a Celtic sacred animal and putting it to death was a symbol of the end of the world. The Etruscans also performed bull-sacrifices, as well as divination by means of its entrails.

The royal rite of horse-sacrifice (*ashvamedha*), practised by the Aryan nomads, played an important rôle in India, but is not of Shivaite origin. Survivals of this rite are found combined with Dionysiac rites in various parts of the world. The Greeks practised horse-sacrifice, but did not consume the flesh of the victim. Dionysiac influence on the Aryan world is even found among the Kumandin, a Siberian people, where the horse-sacrifice was accompanied by dances performed by masked men wearing great wooden phalli. There is a clear analogy and relationship between the Irish inauguration rites (involving sexual union with a brood mare which was then sacrificed) and the ancient horse-sacrifice of the Aryans of India.

Human sacrifice
Human sacrifice is the highest form, and was practised in all parts of the world. Skanda, the god of War, requires human sacrifices; Dionysus delivered Pentheus to the fury of the maenads. The gods desired man to be a hunter and warrior, and it is by sacrificing victims to them that we can avoid the hecatombs they instigate to limit man's encroachment on other species.

Human sacrifice (*purushamedha*) is mentioned in the ritual texts attached to the Vedas, such as the *Shatapatha Brâhmana* (13, 6, 1–2), and numerous others. A seal from Harappa depicts a man with a curved knife approaching a seated victim who has wild hair and uplifted arms.

In the Kazbek treasure discovered in the Caucasus, there is a representation of two naked ithyphallic men, one of whom is about to behead the other, while another ithyphallic man plays the lyre.

The Minotaur, Lord of the Labyrinth, also required human sacrifice. The Athenians had to send Minos a yearly tribute of seven boys and seven girls. They were only freed from this tribute when Theseus slew the Minotaur. The Etruscans also practised human sacrifice. Among the Phoenicians, the goddess Anat was charged with reviving the gods through the sacrifice of human blood. In Greece, at Chios, Tenedos and Lesbos, Dionysus was hungry for human flesh; the victim hacked to pieces in his honour was a man. Animal sacrifice is often only a substitute for human sacrifice. "Where ancient myth speaks of child sacrifice, the corresponding rite is often the putting to death of a young bull. Symbolically, this is the sacrifice of the god of whom the bull is the manifestation, as is the child which represents the *bambino*, or infant-Dionysus, in human sacrifice." (H. Jeanmaire, *Dionysos*, p. 386.)

Only the best may be offered to the gods, the best male of the herd. The victim must be innocent and without blemish, otherwise the sacrifice is not valid. Thus, the victim cannot be an enemy or a criminal.

Killing for vengeance remains an odious and evil act. Sacrifice is neither punishment nor vengeance and must give no one the satisfaction of getting rid of a trouble-maker. It must be shocking to be efficacious. The death penalty, deriving from the social laws of the city and the protection of material goods, is not a sacrifice, and the gods turn their eyes away from those who practise it.

"Yogis must never by put to death, nor women, even the most guilty, whether dirty or badly dressed, beautiful or ugly... The immolation of women in sacrifice is forbidden: the victim must be male. In human sacrifice, the victim is always a boy." (*Linga Purâna*, I. chap. 78, 8–19.) A sacrifice such as that of Iphigenia is thus completely contrary to Dionysiac tradition. However, the *Shiva Toshini* (commentary on the *Linga Purâna*, I, 78, 15) considers that the prohibition against sacrificing women does not apply to female animals. In India, human sacrifice is severely prohibited by modern law, and is nowadays very rare and kept very secret. There were two or three in the town of Benares, Shiva's holy city, during the time when the author lived there. It is still occasionally practised in Kerala, Bengal and certain regions of the Himalayas.

Omophagy, the consumption of raw flesh

The participants must consume the flesh of the sacrificed animal. Ancient Shivaite or Dionysiac ritual does not allow the cooking of the flesh of the animal victim, which had to be captured after a chase, torn apart and eaten raw. The pursuit and devouring of the living victim are essential conditions for inducing the ecstatic frenzy which makes the sacrifice a mystic experience and not merely a rite. This is borne out by the fragment of Euripides' *Cretans*, cited by Porphyry:

"Son of powerful Zan
And of Europa, the Phoenician,
You reign over Crete of the hundred cities...
I have led a pure life and blameless

Since I was initiated to the Zeus of Mount Ida
And since, sanctified, I received the name of bacchant.
A companion of Zagreus who wanders in the night,
I have participated in the raw-flesh feasts
And waved the torches of the Mother of the Mountains,
The torches of Kouretes."

According to the Latin author Firmicus, it was to commemorate the death and sufferings of a king's son who had been treasonably assassinated, that the Cretans tore a live bull apart with their teeth, in memory of the Titans devouring the child's flesh.

The ancient gods, the Asuras and Rakshasas, were eaters of raw flesh. They belong to the natural world in which beasts, men and gods merge and are interchangeable, where man is both beast and god at the same time. The Dionysiac rite takes its followers back to a primitive stage, which is the antithesis of the city cults in which the victim is eaten cooked. Here we find a very ancient contrast between the two concepts of food and its associated rites. When Dionysus is himself the victim of the Titans who put him to death and boil and roast him, his being cooked implies that Dionysus, as the god of Nature, is the victim of the gods of the city.

Anthropophagy

Sacrifice is closely tied to the sacralization of the alimentary function and to the fact that life feeds on life. Whether the offering is vegetable, animal, human, or divine, it has to be consumed. It is in such a communion that identification with the divine being is to be found. Sacred meals were known in the pre-Christian West, as in India, and it is during these meals that the eating of the animal, human or divine victim takes place. Sacrifice is one of the ties uniting man to other species, to other living beings and to the gods.

In the last analysis, it is always the god who devours himself, since one of his revealed forms devours another. In Shivaism, human sacrifice, which is the culmination of animal sacrifice, was practised in the rites of both Skanda and the goddess. Today, it is rare. It inevitably involves consuming a fragment of the victim's flesh. In the Dionysiac world, the *mania* or exaltation of the maenads leads them to devour the animal or human victim, after a wild chase. "[Pentheus] came tumbling to the ground with lamentations long and loud... His mother first, a priestess for the nonce, began the bloody deed and fell upon him... with foaming mouth and wildly rolling eyes, bereft of reason; for the god possessed her. . . [Agave] tore [his] shoulder from its socket, not of her own strength, but the god made it an easy task to her hands; and Ino set to work on the other side, rending the flesh with Autonoe and all the eager host of Bacchanals; and one united cry arose. . . One would make an arm her prey, another a foot. . . and his ribs were stripped of flesh by their rending nails. . ." (Euripides, *The Bacchantes*, 1100–1136.)

Remnants of the Dionysiac sacrifice are found in all later religions, even if under a symbolic form. There are animals which are considered particular manifestations of the god, such as the lamb, kid, ram, or bull, and which may be substituted for him as victim. In the Christian Eucharist, vegetable elements (bread and wine) are substituted for the consumption of the divine and human victim. "He who eats my flesh and drinks my blood lives in me and I in him." (John 6, 57.) This feast is symbolically repeated by Christians during the sacrifice of the mass.

The idea that man becomes what he eats is the basis of the various diets which, in India, differ according to profession. The qualities of the living beings which are eaten are themselves assimilated, hence the anthropophagous concept, which was very widespread in many parts of the ancient world, and still is today in certain African countries. One chooses as food those men who are considered to possess the qualities one wishes to obtain.

According to Herodotus (IV, 64), the Scyths beheaded their enemies and drank the blood of the first man they killed. The Massagetes, a Scythian tribe from the north of Persia, ate their dead kinsmen. "To become the object of a banquet" was considered good luck by those who had to die, and even the best of fates. "Patrophagous cannibalism was widely practised in all the tropical areas of the globe, in India, as in Persia. Herodotus (I, 216; IV, 26; IV, 34), Pliny (*Naturalis Historia*, VII, II, 1), and Strabo (IV, 5, 4, and IV, 1, 5) refer to the cannibalism of the Massagetes, Carmani, Issedonians, Derbisci, Caucasians and Caspians, the Persian peoples, and also the Padei and Kalati of India. More recent information indicates such practices in Burma and Tibet. In all of these countries, it was customary for a man to prefer the tomb of living bodies to that of the dark earth. The fate of being devoured by his dearest friends and by the new generation was, without doubt, considered desirable." (Giulio Cogni, in *Indologica taurinensia*, vols. II–IV, p. 156.)

The alternative to human sacrifice is the sacrifice of seed. In certain Tantric rites, drink containing the sperm of a respected master is consumed by his disciples. Sperm represents the genetic heritage handed down from generation to generation. "The energy fluid is identified by many Neolithic peoples with ancestral power... Among other peoples (e.g. in Tibet) potions containing the semen of seniors may be drunk by novices." (P. Rawson, *Primitive Erotic Art*, p. 48.) "The Gnostics administered *semen virile* as their sacrament." (Payne Knight, *Culte de Priape*, p. 162.) In the Greek rite of *panspermia*, various types of seed, vegetable, animal, or human, were placed in stone hollows around the altar.

The divine sacrifice

Shivaism considers the world in its entirety as the expression of divine nature, and in some way, the body of god. The fact that life only exists through death implies that the god devours himself, that he dies and rises again from his ashes. He is both the sacrificed victim and the beneficiary of the sacrifice.

This aspect of the nature of the world is represented in various ways in the myths of divine sacrifice and resurrection. It appears in the feigned death which the initiate has to undergo. Initiation implies a ritual death, followed by an awakening to a fuller life. It is the corporal and mystic union of the initiate with the deity of whom the sacrificed animal is an incarnation.

The Orphic myth of the death of Dionysus is not itself directly a part of Shivaite or Dionysiac tradition. It is analogous to the Osiris legend, and is probably inspired by it. It is representative of later illustrations of the notion of divine sacrifice.

The myth of the death and resurrection of Dionysus has preoccupied Christians, either in that it served as a basis for their own myth, or because it was considered a premonition of it. "Justin, in the middle of the second century, speaks twice of Dionysus who was torn apart before ascending to heaven. Justin saw in this story, as well as in the use of wine in the Dionysiac ritual, the work of devils who wished to deceive the world as to the meaning of the prophecies announcing Christianity... Christian authors abstain from saying that the death of the infant Dionysus was not definitive and that he rose again." (H. Jeanmaire, *Dionysos*, p. 381.)

Hunting

Shiva is the god of hunting; Dionysus-Zagreus is "the Great Hunter".

Hunting is indispensable for the survival of primitive man and is part of his nature, just as all other acts which are essential to life. As an element of universal harmony, it can be ritualized and become a means of realizing the divine order. The rites and symbols connected with hunting are seen in the most ancient prehistoric representations.

Hunting territory, for both animals and men, is the first manifestation of property, and property is one of the basic elements of society. Hunting rites and sexual rites are closely bound together. "Forbidden to girls and traversed by the boys before attaining warrior and adult status, the *hunting territory* is not only the negation of agricultural land and the enclosed space of the house, but is also a symbol of the ground outside marriage, welcoming forms of sexuality which are deviational, or simply strange, to the city... Due to his hatred of women, the young man goes away to course the hare in the mountains and returns no more; in order to escape the marriage awaiting her, the young girl decides to go away and hunt wild beasts on the high peaks of the mountains. In male love affairs, the gifts of the erastes to the eromenes are... hunting produce... It is during the hunting season... that the adolescent reared according to custom shares the intimacy of his lover, before being integrated into the warrior community." (Marcel Detienne, *Dionysos mis à mort*, p. 76.)

War sacrifice and genocide

Man is not only a hunter, but also a warrior. As a social animal, organized in a "herd" or group like other animals, he defends his living space against other groups, tribes and peoples. According to mythology, the gods themselves are mostly warrior-gods, in constant battle with the Titans for the possession of the celestial worlds. The warrior aspect is a part of man's nature and is thus a part of the plan of creation. Fighting and killing are sometimes an ineluctable duty, a sacred act, as the hero-god Krishna expresses it in the *Bhagavat Gîtâ*, when Arjuna hesitates to fight against and massacre his own cousins.

Man is a slayer of men, and Shiva is represented wearing a necklace of skulls, carrying a severed head in his hand. Prayers are addressed to him to exterminate the enemies of the gods and of the human society to which one belongs. The myths of Shiva and Dionysus are full of episodes of war, in which the god destroys the hordes of Titans and directs the battle against the forces of evil or the enemies of his faithful. Heroes are deified, and monuments and temples raised to them. They have a right to a cult, whether they be Achilles,

173

Alexander, Napoleon, or the Unknown Soldier. Temples are not raised to pacific sovereigns. In the *Rig Veda*, Rudra-Shiva appears armed with lightning and thunder (*Rig Veda*, II, 3, 3.) "His voice sounds in the clash of the drums, in the midst of the battle." (*Rig Veda*, II, 33, 11.) He carries a bow and arrows (*Rig Veda*, II, 10, 14, 42). His faithful pray to him to spare them and their cattle, and to pour his wrath on others. The war-axe is one of Shiva's symbols, while the labyrinth is the palace of the double axe, the emblem of the Minoans. Skanda is the god of War, the leader of the army of the gods. The first-fruits of war, the enterprise in which man has to kill man, must be offered to the god. This is one of the fundamentals of human sacrifice. We transfer to God the responsibility for the act of killing and do not try to delude ourselves as to the value of our actions.

The severed head is the sign of the conqueror. By taking the head of any enemy, the conqueror at the same time takes from him his physical and sexual powers. Among the tribes of "head-hunters" in east India – the survivors of ancient prehistoric peoples – marriage is not possible until the warrior is in a position to wear several severed heads. In the same way, we know that severed human heads, which were universally venerated by the Celts, were symbols of divinity, knowledge and fertility. The Celts were head-hunters; heads were exposed on stakes around their homes and fortresses, or else were placed on pillars in their sacred groves and temples.

The warrior instinct may find expression between peoples or nations, and also among the various component groups of society itself.

Since cruelty is one of the basic constituents of the world, it also belongs to the nature of all living beings and is found – more or less disguised – in all men. Apart from food requirements, it is found in the form of the defence of vital territory, among both animals and humans. It is also used to ensure the supremacy and "purity" of a species, race, religion, or culture, and is thus one of the causes of genocide.

Each human group instinctively seeks to asset itself at the expense of others, whether "foreigners", or elements who are considered "different" or are discriminated against. Any group may be subject to this collective instinct of cruelty. It may be the people of a nearby country, or of a foreign race (Negroes, Indians), a social class or a religious or political conviction (non-Muslims amongst the Arabs,

Protestants at the time of Saint Bartholomew, Tziganes, Jews, communists, the bourgeoisie, aristocrats, etc.). The taste for violence and slaughter is latent in all societies. It is an instinct which cannot be ignored in any of its forms. The Jews were discriminated against, just as McCarthy discriminated against communists and homosexuals. Many people who protest against anti-Semitism are more than tolerant toward groups of *virtuous* delinquents who hunt out homosexuals, beat them up, rob them and murder them. Even judges show a remarkable indulgence towards such delinquents. We witness the persecutions, tortures and assassinations of aristocrats and the propertied classes in the so-called socialist countries, or of socialists in countries with an authoritarian régime. These "purges" are often considered legitimate by the partisans of whichever régime is in power. As a proverb says, "Give your dog a bad name and hang it".

It is not possible to fight effectively against one of these instinctive forms, such as the need for cruelty, while accepting others. The weakness of the fight against anti-Semitism, which is only a fixation of this instinct is a certain time and place, consists in precisely this kind of ambivalence.

One of the purposes of bloody sacrifice is to channel this instinct, face it, and take the gods as witness of their own and our cruelty, thus immunizing ourselves against its more pernicious forms.

Sacrifice, which satisfies our subconscious need for cruelty, together with a social system in which all races, creeds, social orders and deviances find their place, thus avoids the domination or persecution of one group by others. This is perhaps the only way of establishing the equilibrium and development of a just and human society.

Vegetarianism

Vegetarianism has no place in ancient Shivaism, since it goes counter to the natural order, and since the violence done to the vegetable kingdom is not essentially different to that done to the animal kingdom. The destruction of vegetable species and forests can have far more serious ecological consequences for life on earth than the destruction of animal species. Vegetarianism is, however, practised by certain relatively modern Shivaite sects.

Vegetarianism derives from Jainism and was later incorporated into Vedism and Shivaism, following the Buddhist reform which took its inspiration from Jainism and was opposed to the rites of sacrifice. Buddhism did not survive in India, but caused a kind of syncretism producing modern Hinduism as practised by the governing classes. This did not, however, influence either traditional Jainism or Shivaism in its popular forms or in those practised by initiates.

Some of the Indian sages who established themselves in Greece or Egypt were Hindus. However, many others were Jainas who followed the rules of their sect by living naked or wearing white clothes. Jaina influence can be clearly seen in the development of Orphism. Without being vegetarians, the Pythagoreans, like certain Hindus, refused to touch beef or mutton.

In Hinduism, vegetarianism is only required of a small minority, the Brahmans and merchant-class. As a principle, it is contrary to the rules of life in the warrior, princely and working classes. In feasts at which people of different castes take part, Brahman cooks are employed and the food is always vegetarian.

Survival and reincarnation

The gods die and are born again, but ancient Shivaism believes only in a relative and temporary survival for the individual, and not in transmigration. The concept of the human being's progress through multiple lives came from Jainism.

"Metaphysically, the doctrine of reincarnation is without consistence. It is simply a way of indicating the necessity for a privileged and natural qualification." (J. Evola, *Le Yoga tantrique*, p. 110.) It is an attempt to explain the basic injustice of why some men are born vigorous, handsome, intelligent and rich, and others, sick, deformed, stupid and poor. These differences are thus attributed to actions committed in past lives, which is Jaina doctrine. Shivaism does not attach the same importance to the individual, and believes in his survival only in a temporary and collective way. Human individuality, like that of all kinds of being, is formed by a knot or point in which various elements are bound together, taken from universal matter, consciousness and intellect, and surrounding a fragment of the universal, indivisible soul. This may be likened to the space enclosed by an urn, itself not distinct from universal space. At death, the vase breaks, the knot is untied, and each of the elements constituting the human being returns to the common pool to be used again in other beings. "The fifteen constituents of the body return to their source, and all the divinities of the senses to their respective gods. Man's actions and his soul, formed of intelligence, become one with the Supreme Immortal. Like the rivers which flow down and lose themselves in the sea, leaving behind even their name and form, so the enlightened soul, freed from name and form, dissolves in the universal Man made of light, who is higher than the highest." (*Mundaka Upanishad*, III, 2, 7–8.) The knot may be slow in becoming completely untied. In this case, there is a temporary survival, a particularly distressing state, in which ghosts may appear. The possible temporary survival of individuality after death explains why tombs are built for the dead containing everything necessary for a longer or shorter period. Certain rites may tend to prolong this intermediate state, so that the living may benefit longer from the occult presence and influence of the dead person. This, however, could be a cruel act towards the dead person himself.

Shiva's paradise is not peopled with shadows, but solely with heavenly spirits. The tendency of Tantra teaching is to make the adept a superman, a *vîra* (hero) or *siddha* (a realized being) in this life, rather than just another shadow in an overpeopled paradise. No one dreams of survival for each flower, but of a continuity for each species of flower which thus becomes more and more perfect. It is just the same for human races. The individual is the end-product of his line of forefathers and he himself continues in his descendants. It is for this reason that it is each man's duty to father a son, except when, through practising Tantrism, he seeks to free himself from the earthly ties. "The sages who, having rid themselves of desire, adore this being, no longer have to pass through human seed." (*Mundaka Upanishad*, III, 2, 1.) Every race, each animal or human species, functions as an entity which progresses through time, and their qualities and virtues are handed down and accumulated. The mixing of races, and the degeneration which results from it, is always a regression, a dissipation of the ancestral heritage and a risk of diminishing the same for his descendants. This is a thing no responsible man has the right to do.

The allusions to entering into Shiva's paradise refer to those men who have totally mastered the ties of the natural world, broken all barriers, and who have, in effect, ceased to be men and have become spirits or gods, commanding the forces of nature and altering the course of the stars. Heaven can only be conquered by force; it is not to be gained by virtue. Few are chosen.

However, the heavenly worlds – even though their duration is immense compared to earthly life – are themselves mortal. The heavens and the gods will cease to exist when the universe is reabsorbed, when matter, time and space are reduced to nothing. The notion of the duration of time is only relative and is determined by our own vital rhythms. It ceases with life, and time can then no longer be measured. It melts into a timeless eternity in which to speak of survival makes no sense. When time can no more be measured, there is no longer any difference between the span of a life and that of a universe. It is during this present life that we must realize our eternity. There is no reason to postulate the boredom of an interminable survival in which progress is no longer possible.

Chapter 9

RITES AND PRACTICES

Rites

Communication between the different states of being, that is between men, spirits and gods, can only be achieved by means of special techniques called rites. These rites utilize the breaks, or invisible points of connection, through which communication with other worlds is possible. The points are indicated by signs, forms, and certain arrangements of elements, which may be called symbols.

By arranging the various elements in a particular way (transistors printed circuits and power equipment), we become conscious of messages transmitted on Hertzian waves which are present all around us even though unperceived. Following this principle, the utilization of a series of elements comprising form, sound and energy, allows us to communicate with those states of being which are usually imperceptible to our senses. This rôle could be called the vehicle or medium of the rites.

Rites generally utilize three main components: geometric or numerical elements called *yantras*; sound and rhythmic elements called *mantras*; and symbolic acts called *tantras*, including certain gestures (*mudras*). *Yantras* are diagrams endowed with occult power. They are based on numerical combinations and geometrical diagrams creating harmonies in which certain prime numbers play an essential part. Prime numbers and some incommensurable numbers play a special rôle in all the structures of the universe, of which they are in some way the basic material. *Tantras* are practices of a ritual nature involving apparently gratuitous acts and, occasionally, certain sexual acts, which are the means of establishing contact between the various worlds or states of being, and also of realizing the transmitting magical powers.

Mudras are signs, gestures and postures of a symbolic character which put the human being into a state of receptivity.

Mantras are vocal formulas of a magical nature, which are recited according to certain rhythmic cycles. (See: commentary on the *Shiva*

179

Purâna, Vidyeshvara Samhitâ, chap. 10, 47.)

The adept must discover in the surrounding world and within himself the points of contact or connection with other worlds. He must know how to recognise in the mineral, vegetable and animal world, on the Earth's surface and in his own body, the forms and points through which he himself and the world are penetrated by those fundamental energies in which the thought, nature and activity of the Creator are revealed. Once these points have been identified, the narrow doors between two worlds, the mechanism of diagrams, sounds, formulas, rhythms, actions and gestures allows an entry to be forced and communication to be established.

In describing rites, we must limit ourselves to those of Indian Shivaism, as these are the only ones whose living tradition has been preserved and about which we possess elements of experience and written documents. It is on this basis that we can understand and interpret the rites of the Dionysiac, Orphic, or Druidic mysteries, whose tradition has been lost.

Shiva worship

Before all else, "The faithful must worship the Lord (Ishâna) in the ten directions of space, in the eight heavenly bodies and in the ten sensory organs". (*Linga Purâna*, I, chap. 76, 67–73.)

The votary must therefore first of all become aware of the universal forces in his own body, which are manifest in the ten organs: ears, eyes, nose, skin, and tongue, on one side; and feet, hands, mouth, sexual organ and anus, on the other.

Shivaite rites are fundamentally linked with the phallus-cult, the phallus being the clearest image of the creative principle. However, for the "hero", or *vira*, the self-realized adept, it is the whole body whose several parts are the expression, or symbols of the various aspects of the divine being. The human body thus appears as a "sign", or *Linga*. It becomes in some way sexualized, imbued with the presence of the principle of life, which is Shiva.

The lower part of the body is likened to Brahmâ (the orbital tendency), the middle part to Vishnu (the ascending and centripetal tendency), and the shoulders and face to Shiva (the descending and centrifugal tendency). These three tendencies correspond to the three colours, red (Brahmâ), blue-black (Vishnu), and white (Shiva), which also play a part in the rites. "In the body of Shiva's votary, the part below the navel is Brahmâ, the part from the navel to armpit is

180

Vishnu, while the head corresponds to the phallus of Shiva." (*Shiva Purâna, Vidyeshvara Samhitâ*, chap. 17, 143–146.) In the Indian, as in the Greek or Celtic world, images of the god are often found in the form of an erect phallus with a face.

With the stone *Linga*, the square base is likened to Brahmâ; the octagonal middle part surrounded by the *arghia* – the female receptacle or emblem – is likened to the goddess or Vishnu; the visible part of the erect phallus is Shiva.

"During the Kali Yuga, phallus-worship is the most efficacious type of worship in the world. No symbol can compare with it. The sexual organ brings pleasure in this world and liberation in the next. It protects us from accidents. In worshipping the phallus, man identifies himself with Shiva. There is nothing so sacred in the four Vedas as the worship of the *Linga*. This is the conclusion of all traditions." (*Shiva Purâna, Vidyeshvara Samhitâ*, chap. 21, 25–32.)

"The votary may accomplish the sixteen rites of *Linga* worship, on the erect sexual organ of a man, saint, or image of a god, or on a natural object which has this shape (*svayambhu*), or which has been shaped in stone or metal and duly consecrated." (*Shiva Purâna, Vidyeshvara Samhitâ*, chap. 11, 30.)

Some Yogis worship their own sexual organ, that is, the god's presence in themselves. "The rite of *Nârâchâstra Prayoga* (the casting of the dart) [meaning the erection of one's own sexual organ] is carried out by using the thumb and index finger. The votary rhythmically (*japa*) repeats the *mantra, Nanas Shivâya*, and covers his organ with his hand while repeating the *tatpurusha mantra*, which is the fourth 'basic formula' (*bîja mantra*). This is called 'the Hand of Shiva' (*Shiva-hasta*)." (*Linga Purâna*, II, chap. 24, 2.)

"The men who worship their own phallus must then make an offering of the food with which they feed themselves." (*Shiva Purâna, Vidyeshvara Samhitâ*, chap. 18, 55.) One's own thumb may also be worshipped as a *Linga* image. However, the god is usually represented in the form of an upright stone.

The setting-up of a "Linga"

In the sanctuaries of Dionysus, phalli of metal, wood, or stone were set up, and were generally of a large size. The Purânas explain the rites which accompanied the setting up of phallic emblems, menhirs, etc. Thus the *Linga Purâna* (II, chap. 47):

"This is the way to set up the god in the form of a *Linga*, for the purpose of obtaining virtue, pleasure, riches and liberation:

"The *Linga* should be made of stone. It may also be made of gold, encrusted with precious stones, of silver, or leather. It must have a pedestal with a drain for water. The top of the *Linga* must be sufficiently wide. The votary must clean the *Linga* well before setting it in place. The pedestal represents the goddess, the *Linga* the Great God himself. Brahmâ resides at its base, Vishnu (the female principle) in the middle. Rudra, the protector of animals, the Lord of the World, is at the summit. The lord of the Ganas is worshipped by all the gods. The *Linga* should preferably be of a large size. It must be set up in the midst of an area of consecrated ground. It must be wrapped in cloth with sacred *dharba* grass.

"Eight urns, dedicated to the guardians of the directions of space, shall be placed around the *Linga*, with a bunch of sacred grass placed inside each. Unspoilt grain shall be put into the urns, which shall be decorated with multi-coloured ribbons. Swastikas and other symbols of good omen shall be drawn on these urns. The thunder-bolt (erotic couplings) and other symbols shall also be depicted on them. The urns, covered with cloth, shall be placed around the *Linga*, while repeating the *mantra* of Ishâna (the god's benevolent aspect). A dais erected above the image shall be infused with the smoke of incense and lamps. Hangings bearing the emblems of the guardians of the directions of space and their vehicles, such as the elephant, the buffalo, etc., shall be displayed. Garlands of *dharba* grass, woven in decorative forms, shall be hung all around.

"The votary shall bathe the *Linga* with water and surround it with lights and incense for five days, or else three days, or even for one night. During this period, he shall pass his time reading the holy books, dancing, singing, playing the vînâ and other instruments, accompanied by the ringing of small bells. Meditating on the swastika, he shall then move the *Linga* and place it in the consecrated place, where the pedestal has been set up in the form of a vulva decorated with gold. A five-flamed lamp shall be placed beside it. The pedestal shall be covered over with a white cloth. The god's image shall be planted in the centre. The *Linga* must face east. A pierced urn leaving a small trickle of water shall be hung above it in order to refresh it. [At Delos, a phallus set up on a pedestal in the form of a receptacle could also be seen.]

"The god shall be set up on his pedestal while the *mantras*, 'Namah Shivâya' and 'Namohamsa Shivâya' are recited, together with the

ymn to Rudra, the *Rudrâdhyaya*, after the *Linga* has been well
washed. The offering should not exceed one thousand gold pieces."
Linga Purâna, I, chap. 47, 6–45.)

Initiation

Certain ritual techniques allow us to operate on the latent energies
present in the human being and thus to transform him into a vehicle
for the transmission of certain powers, raising him to a higher level in
the hierarchy of beings and making him a sort of demigod or
superman, and thus closer to the world of spirits. This is the rôle of
initiation. The transformation process of the human being is long and
difficult, and this is why initiation is only carried out by degrees.

The *pashu* (animal-man) first becomes a *sâdhaka* (apprentice), and
then a *vîra* (hero) or adept, signifying a being who can dominate and
go beyond the appearances of the material world. The next degree is
that of *siddha* (self-realized man), which, among the Tantrikas, is also
called the *kaula* stage (member of the group), a word which corresponds
to the title of "companion" in Masonic initiation, in which the degree
of "apprentice" is also found. The *kaula* has attained the "state of
truth". It is only then that the barriers between human and divine
disappear and that the adept may be considered as *divya* (deified). In
the language of the Greco-Roman mysteries, the adept or initiate was
called a "hero". The higher degrees of initiation were probably kept
secret. Such a transformation concerns the entire human being. It is
the body itself which is transfigured, just as, according to the
Christian concept, it is the entire man, body and spirit, who will rise
transfigured from the dead.

Initiation is the passing from one state of being to another. It is a
sort of death, an "active death", from which a new person is born.
Thus, a burial rite is always part of the rites of initiation, and has even
survived in the ordination ceremonies of Catholic priests.

Representations of scenes of Dionysiac initiation are frequently
found in the decoration of Roman and Pompeian villas of the first
century A.D. No description of the rites has reached us. On the other
hand, such descriptions are found in detail in Shivaite texts, which
may be useful in interpreting the various references made to Dionysiac,
Orphic and Mithraic initiation rites, as well as those of several later
traditions, such as the Gnostics and Templars.

Only an initiate can transmit powers to a new initiate. This is the
essential condition for the validity of initiatory transmission, and the

reason why the tradition, once broken, cannot be re-established. Initiation is the real transmission of a *shakti*, or power, and this transmission takes the form of enlightenment. The continuity of transmission from one initiate to another is compared to that of one flame lighting another. Initiates form a group of men who are set apart from others. In Tantrism, these groups are called *kula* (families), whence the name of *kaula* (members of the family, or "companions") which is given to the adepts. The *kula* corresponds to the Dionysiac thiasos.

"The physical body of the initiator is an image of Shiva, and services rendered to him are equivalent to worshipping the god. Service signifies bodily, mental and verbal submission..., the gift of all one possesses, including one's body, to one's preceptor. The disciple must serve him his food, not taking his own until after his master's permission... The preceptor's tongue is like a sexual organ which pours the vital juice of the *mantras* into the receptacle of the apprentice's ears. Each of the preceptor's members, from his head to his feet, is, in effect, a sexual organ, or *Linga*. In order to please him, the disciple must massage his feet, present him his sandals, bathe him, offer him food and money, as well as do any other thing which may satisfy him." (*Shiva Purâna, Vidyeshvara Samhitâ*, chap. 18, 86–94.)

Initiation rites

The rites of initiation are explained in great detail in the Shivaite Purânas and Tantras.

"The disciple must venerate his preceptor without reserve. According to his means, he may offer his master elephants, horses, chariots, jewels, land, houses, ornaments, clothes, and various kinds of grain..

"After having verified his abilities, the preceptor shall make the disciple take a bath. The disciple shall stay with him and serve him for a first trial period lasting a year. Choosing a favourable day according to the stars, the preceptor shall then lead the disciple to a sacred place to perform the first rites of initiation. This place may be on the seashore, the bank of a river, a cattle-shed, temple, or purified place in the house of the master himself." (*Linga Purâna*, I, chap. 85–86.)

It is always the natural world – forests and mountains – which is the temple of Shiva. Sanctuaries are only monuments in the god's honour. They are not places where the faithful foregather, nor where the rites concerning everyday life are practised, such as initiations, marriages, funerals, etc. Initiatory rites take place preferably in the forest or on the banks of streams and pools.

"The soil of the chosen spot must be carefully examined for its smell, colour, and taste. A dais must be built there, in the centre of which a lotus-shaped diagram is drawn, using red and white powder and five diamonds. The initiate shall assiduously worship this diagram, according to the formulas he has received, . . . and shall set up a *Linga* on it. The initiator shall invoke the various deities and the different aspects of Shiva and shall then command the apprentice to meditate on the god . . . He shall then lead the apprentice to a spot to the south of the diagram, where he must sleep on a bed of *dharba* grass. In the morning, an offertory rite (*homa*) shall be performed using clarified butter, while repeating one hundred and eight times the Aghora mantra (AUM *Hamsah*. . .), which drives away fear and by which one can be cleansed from ill-omened dreams." (*Linga Purâna*, II, chap. 21, 1–58.)

The ritual bath then follows.

In the Eleusinian mysteries, the ritual bath preceded what was considered to be the most mysterious part of the initiation. According to Plutarch, it was preceded by a ten-day abstinence from all sexual relations. The same rule applies in India.

"When the disciple has taken his ritual bath fasting, he must make a careful toilet and put on a clean piece of cloth (seamless) draped around his lower body and a shawl on his shoulders." (*Linga Purâna*, II, chap. 21, 39.) "Not far from the altar where the *yantra* was consecrated, the preceptor takes his seat on a cushion of *dharba* grass. The disciple sits facing north, the preceptor facing east . . . The preceptor shall lightly touch the novice's eyes, and then bind them with a silk bandage, while repeating certain formulas." (*Shiva Purâna, Vâyavîya Samhitâ*, II, chap. 16, 31–32.)

"The novice is then led into the initiation area which has been carefully marked out on the ground. The entrance on the west side is best for disciples of all castes, but especially for those of the royal caste, the Kshatriyas . . . The novice shall then walk around the phallic image three times and, according to his means, shall offer the god a handful of flowers mixed with gold, or gold only if there are no flowers, while reciting the hymn to Rudra (*Rudrâdhyaya*). He shall then meditate on Shiva, repeating only the *prânava*, the syllable AUM." (*Linga Purâna*, II, chap. 21, 40–42.)

The same applies to the Dionysiac rite. "The initiate's head is veiled and he allows himself to be guided by the officiant... A basket filled with fruit and symbolic objects, among which one in the shape of a phallus, is placed on the initiate's head. The setting... is a garden where there is a tree: an idol of Dionysus is present. It is, however, a Dionysus with Priapic characteristics, of which the foremost is ithyphallicism." (H. Jeanmaire, *Dionysos*, p. 459.)

"The bandage binding the disciple's eyes is then taken off and the *yantra* is shown to him. He is made to sit facing south on a seat of *dharba* grass... Following this, the rite of consecration of the principles of the five elements takes place... The preceptor places his hand on the novice's head, while the latter repeats the *mantra* he used in casting flowers over the god. He asperges him with water consecrated to Shiva and places ashes on his head, repeating the Aghora [1]*mantra*; he then venerates the novice with perfumes and other ingredients." (*Linga Purâna*, II, chap. 21, 45.)

"With an offertory rite (*homa*), the preceptor releases the disciple from his caste and makes him part of the group of Rudra's companions... With one hand only, the preceptor must touch all parts of the disciple's body. The latter prostrates himself in front of his master who henceforth for him represents the god... The preceptor then enters into the disciple's body by means of the rite of the confluent breath (*prâna-nirgama*). The preceptor breathes the disciple's breath, which penetrates his veins and heart. After having breathed into his veins, while repeating the *mantra* and making the gesture of annihilation (*samhâra mudra*), he refills him by breathing in, thus uniting their two souls. For a moment, he holds their united breath, which is called the 'urn' (*kumbhaka*), and then, breathing out, he places the breath in the disciple's heart... He then touches him and gives him a sacred cord... To the sound of music and singing, he pours the water of baptism over the disciple." (*Shiva Purâna, Vâyavîya Samhitâ*, II, chap. 16, 39–56.)

After this, the novice must perform various expiatory rites: the rite of fire, the rite of the gate, the rites of lightning, seizing, binding, and spreading nectar. These are followed by the rites of adoration.

"The rites of adoration must be accomplished in this order: *samprokshana* (sprinkling), *tâdana* (squeezing), *harana* (taking off), *samyoga* (uniting), and *vikshepa* (rejecting). Then follow the rites of insemination (*arcana*), gestation (*garbhadhârana*), and giving birth (*janana*)...

[1] See p. 194.

"The solar rite of knowledge and of its dissolution must be performed: the first, with the Ishâna *mantra*, accompanied by the magic syllable HRÎM, representing the female organ, or *yoni*... The whole rite ends with the rites of *uddhâra* (arousing), *prokshana* (sprinkling) and *tâdana* (squeezing), with the Aghora *mantra* finishing with the magic sound PHAT... During the whole rite, the preceptor must guide the disciple by holding his wrist. The preceptor then pours holy water over the novice who is from now on a companion of Shiva... The initiation takes place in the presence of Shiva, of fire, and of the preceptor. After his initiation, the disciple must act according to his preceptor's instructions." (*Linga Purâna*, II, chap. 21, 67–75.)

"Having dried the disciple's body, the preceptor takes ash with both his hands and coats the disciple's body with it, while repeating the name of Shiva. He then whispers the Shiva *mantra* into the disciple's ear. Next, in front of the sacred fire, they repeat the initiation formula together. The disciple must thereafter live near his master, serve him in all things, and carry out all his demands. He is henceforth called *samâya* (an integrated one)... His master then gives him a *Linga* of Shiva. He ties a sacred cord to the lock of hair at the top of the head of the disciple, who remains standing, and lets the cord hang as far as his feet. The preceptor then taps the disciple's chest, binds him with the cord, taps his head, makes him sit and gives him consecrated rice to eat... During the night, the disciple must sleep on a bed of herbs, covered with a new (unwashed) and consecrated sheet. In the morning, the disciple must inform his master whether he has dreamt... The sacred cord is then untied and hangs from the lock of hair, as on the day before. The veneration of the *âdhâra* (the centre at the base of the spine) is then performed, after which the rites of penetration in all the various sorts of living beings: gods, animals, birds and men. The rites of new birth then follow... The preceptor purifies the disciple's body from all impurities left by sensual contacts and frees him from three kinds of bond. Drawing to himself the disciple's soul, as he did before, he places it in his own soul... After washing the scissors, the preceptor cuts the disciple's sacred lock and his sacred cord, and burns them in the fire consecrated by Shiva. After this, he returns the disciple's independent individuality to his body... Having made the disciple sit, he obtains permission from Shiva to teach him Shivaite knowledge... He then makes him repeat the triple *mantra*: AUM, HRÎM, SHIVÂYA

NAMAH, HRÎM, AUM." (*Shiva Purâna, Vâyavîya Samhitâ*, I chap. 16–17–18 abridged.)

(The twentieth chapter of the Shiva *Purâna* deals with the initiatio of a disciple to the degree of preceptor.)

In order to be initiated as a *Pashupâta* (friend of Beasts), th disciple, after having received the teachings of his preceptor, mus lead the life of a wandering monk for a certain period. "Havin performed the rites of abultion and sacrifice as well as the other rite of the Sun, the disciple shall observe the rites of Shiva's bath, the as bath, and the worship of the god." (*Linga Purâna*, II, chap. 22, 1 "The fourth day after the full moon, he shall put out the fire an carefully gather the ashes. He shall shave his head and all his bod hair. He shall then take a handful of clay and smear it over his whol body, from head to foot, whilst gazing at the sun. He shall then take bath, after which he shall smear his whole body with ash." (*Shiv Purâna, Kailasa Samhitâ*, chap. 16, 18–26.) "Henceforth, he shall le his hair grow long, or shall shave it completely, or shall leave one loc. only. As a general rule, he must always go naked. However, should h so prefer, he may wear a saffron-coloured robe or clothing made o bark. He shall take a pilgrim's staff and wear a cord for his belt. (*Shiva Purâna, Vâyavîya Samhitâ*, chap. 33.)

He thus departs on his pilgrimage, begging for his food.

The application of ashes

"Ash shall be applied to thirty-two parts of the body, or, if not sixteen, eight, or five parts, while invoking the corresponding deities.

"The head is smeared with ash while invoking Agni, the fire-god the forehead while invoking the deities of the waters; the ears while invoking the Earth or Shiva; the eyes while invoking the Wind o Rudra; the nostrils while invoking the directions of Space; the nec while invoking the Moon; the shoulders while invoking Shakti (th power of realization); the arms while invoking Dhruva (the pole star symbol of Constancy); the elbows while invoking Soma, the intoxicating drink; the wrists while invoking Vishnu, the Preserver; the hip while invoking Anala, the interior Fire; the navel while invoking Prajâpati, the Lord of the Animals; the testicles which invoking Brahmâ, the Creator; the thighs while invoking the Nâgas, th serpents; the knees while invoking the snake-daughters; the calve and heels while invoking the Vasus (deities of riches); the feet while

188

invoking the daughters of the sages, and the back while invoking Ocean.

"Should only eight places be envisaged, they are: the scrotum, the forehead, the ears, the shoulders, the chest and the navel. The presiding deities are called the Seven Sages.

"If the votary cannot smear his whole body with ash, he shall smear some on his forehead while repeating 'Namah Shivâya' (to Shiva); on his sides saying 'Ishâbhyam Namah' (to the divine couple); on his arms saying 'Bîjâbhyam Namah' (to the two types of seed); on his lower body saying 'Pitribhyam Namah' (to the ancestors); on the upper part of his body while invoking the goddess (Umâ) and the lord (Isha) 'Nâmah Umeshâbhyam'; on his back and the back of his head while invoking the terrible aspect of the god, saying 'Namah Bhîmâya'." (Shiva Purâna, Vidyeshvara Samhitâ, chap. 24, 97–116.)

The Titans who seized Zeus also had their bodies smeared with ash or plaster. They are therefore initiates whose troupe accompanies the young god. This principle is also found in the initiation of adults in African societies, who, by smearing their bodies with whitish ash, are transformed into supernatural beings.

"Nyâsa", the rite of touching

The nyâsa rite consists in caressing and worshipping all the parts of the human body, since the whole man is considered the manifestation of the god in his various aspects, and is thus his image. Nyâsa stems from a verb which means "to put, to place". It consists in a process of awakening and summoning the divine energies which are present at certain points and in certain precise organs of the body. "Through nyâsa, various deities, or shaktis, in different parts of the body and particularly in the 'visual points', are placed, aroused, or awakened... If the hand is made alive by a shakti, the part touched becomes alive, divine life flows in it, and, in the material organ, the organ made of vajra (the thunder-bolt) or sattva guna (the ascending tendency) begins to awaken... The hand is passed over the whole body so as to 'coat' its surface with 'divine fluid'." (J. Evola, Le Yoga tantrique, pp. 162–163.)

This practice is found in all magical traditions, including those of the West. In one of the chapters (III, 13) of Agrippa's De occulta philosophia (fifteenth century), it says: "If a man capable of receiving the divine influx keeps one of his limbs or any organ of his body

189

undefiled and purifies it, it becomes the receptacle of the corresponding limb or organ of the god, who hides himself there as it were under a veil. But these are jealous mysteries which should not be spoken of publicly."

"The body is in no way considered an enemy... The characteristic of the Tantric schools is to give the body itself a hyperphysical dimension, thus establishing analogico-magical relationships between macrocosm and microcosm... The body is therefore not despised; its secrets and the powers it contains are assumed and explored." (J. Evola, *Le Yoga tantrique*, pp. 162–164 and p. 105.)

According to the *Kûlârnava Tantra*, "The body is the temple of god. The living being is the image of Sadâshiva, Shiva in his aspect of *being*. The adept pronounces the identification formula. 'I am he'." To worship the body is thus to worship the god whose image it is. We worship the god by worshipping his work, even though we are not conscious of its divine aspect. Love of beauty is, in fact, love of God. Nonnos, in his *Dionysia* (canto III, 274), can easily speak of "ritual touching transformed into a loving caress".

According to the *Linga Purâna* (I, chap. 85), "The *nyâsa* rite leads to all kinds of realization (*siddhi*). It is practised in three ways which may be compared with the growth, duration and decline of the world and of living beings. The apprentice practises the rite in the form likened to growth (*utpatti*), the mature man in the aspect of duration (*sthiti*), and the ascetic in the aspect of decline (*samhriti*).

"Touching (*nyâsa*) may be of three kinds: touching of the limbs (*anganyâsa*); of the hands (*karanyâsa*); or of the body (*dehanyâsa*). The *nyâsa* of the hand should first be performed, then that of the body, and lastly that of the limbs. Contact should begin with the head and end with the feet when practising the *nyâsa* of growth. In the *nyâsa* of decline, it begins with the feet and finishes with the head. The *nyâsa* of the heart, face and neck, is that of duration.

"The *nyâsa* of the hands, which begins with the right thumb and ends with the left and concentrates on each joint of each finger, is the *nyâsa* of growth. In inverse order, it becomes the *nyâsa* of decline. The *nyâsa* of duration begins with the thumb and finishes with the little finger of each hand.

"Following this, the *nyâsa* of the body is performed, then that of the limbs, first over the whole body and then for each part, ending with the fingers while pronouncing the corresponding sacred formula preceded and followed by the syllable AUM.

RITES AND PRACTICES

"The practitioner must face east or north, after having washed his feet, and be clean and attentive. He must concentrate his thought on his ancestors, the rite, the deity, the seed (*bîja*) or magic syllable, the energy (*shakti*), the soul, and on the person of his preceptor. Repeating the sacred formula or *mantra*, he must dry the hands [of the person worshipped] and implant the syllable AUM in his palms and on the first and last joint of each finger. He shall implant the seed (*bîja*) [here a magic syllable] with the 'starting point of life' (*bindu*) [here a nasalization of the syllable] on the five middle joints.

"According to the order of the stages of life, he shall perform the *nyâsa* of growth as well as the other two with both his hands, beginning with the feet and ending with the head. Repeating the *mantra* to which the syllable AUM is added, he shall touch the body:

1. On the head, face, neck, heart, penis, and lastly the feet.
2. On the penis, heart, neck, the middle of the face and head.
3. The heart, penis, feet, head, face and neck.

"Having thus touched the limbs [of the person he is worshipping], the practitioner meditates on the five faces of Shiva, beginning with the one facing east and finishing with the one facing upwards. He shall concentrate on the five syllables of the *mantra*, starting with *Na*, in proper order (*Na, Mo, Shi, Vâ, Ya*). He shall then perform the *nyâsa* of the six limbs in their respective order, taking pleasure in it.

"The *nyâsa* is accompanied by the magic syllables of offering to the gods, which are: Namas (Obedience), Svâhâ, Vasa, Hum, Vausat and Phat. In the Shiva *mantra*:

Aum is the heart, the very nature of the god;

Na corresponds to the head, the colour yellow, the East, to Indra, the King of heaven;

Mo corresponds to the lock of hair, the colour black, the South, and to Rudra, the destructive aspect of Shiva;

Shi corresponds to the mouth, the colour grey, the West, and to Vishnu, the conservative or female principle;

Va corresponds to the eye, the colour of gold, the North, to the Creator Brahmâ;

Ya corresponds to the arrow (penis), the colour red, the Zenith, and to Skanda, the young god.

"The gods of the Four Corners of space, starting from the southeast, are respectively:

"To the southeast, Vighnesha, who removes obstacles;

To the northeast, Durgâ, the unattainable;

191

To the northwest, Kshetrajña, Knowledge of the sphere of action;
To the southwest, Nirriti, Decline and Death.

"The practitioner fixes them with the tip of his thumb pressed against the tip of his index finger, while smiling broadly. Saying, 'Protect us', he worships each of the four deities in succession." (*Linga Purâna*, I, chap. 85.)

"In the *nyâsa* rite, the *Aghora* (favourable) aspects of Shiva are found in eight parts of the body: heart, neck, shoulders, navel, stomach, back and chest. Thirteen parts (*kalâ*) of the body correspond to his magical aspect (*Vâmadeva*). These are the anus, penis, thighs, knees, calves, buttocks, hips, sides, nose, head and arms." (*Shiva Purâna, Vâyavîya Samhitâ*, II, chap. 22.)

"The accomplished *bhakta* performs the *nyâsa* of the hand and fingers, starting with the index, using his own thumb. He also carries out the *nyâsa* of the centre of the neck. The enlightened *bhakta* is purified by the *nyâsa* rite... He will repeat the five-syllable *mantra* which was handed down to him by grace of his preceptor." (*Linga Purâna*, I, chap. 85, 79–82.)

"Pancha-Tattva", the secret ritual of the five elements

The characteristic aspect of the Tantric way, the way of the Left Hand or way of "mysteries", is the transformation of negative into positive; the utilization, as an opening towards the creative principle, of the most elementary physical functions which are the first to reveal themselves and, thus, the prime basis of creation. The "ritual of the five elements" (*pancha-tattva*) involves the utilization of the essential vital functions of the human being as the basis of all development. In Hindu and Shivaite Tantrism, this "secret ritual" is reserved for the *vîra* (hero), meaning the initiated adept who has the power and will to conquer and to vanquish matter as well as those forces which hold man enslaved. Those who try to ignore the essential functions of life, or to leave them undefined, are doomed to failure, since man is an indivisible entity and must remain conscious of the fact that, before thinking, he must live, that is, feed (kill), excrete, and reproduce. This is the basis of all life, and of every possibility of existing, and therefore of all thought, all consciousness, all sprituality and all self-realization. "Without the ritual of *pancha-tattva*, it is impossible to attain fulfilment (*siddhi*) and difficulties will be met with at each step." (*Mehânirvâna Tantra*, V, 13.) "Whatever the *pashu*, the animal-man, accomplishes in an obtuse fashion, according to the amasic world of need and desire, should be lived by the *vîra* (hero, dept)... on a cosmic basis." (J. Evola, *Le Yoga tantrique*, p. 179.)

The hero or *vîra*, the self-realized man, dominates the powers which surround him. He is not subject to decline or sickness and can choose the hour of his death. He is in strong contrast to the materialistic man who is aggressive and ambitious, but who is also the mere plaything of his own passions and the subtle forces which inspire them.

In the *pancha-tattva*, the five essential vital functions are compared with their five corresponding elements: hearing (ether), sight (fire), touch (air), taste (water) and smell (earth). In the ritual, the sexual function (*maîthuna*) is symbolic of ether; wine and other intoxicants (*madya*), of air; meat (*mâmsa*) of fire; urine (*mutra*) of water, and excrement (*mala*) of earth. In some Tantric traditions, the fish (*matsya*) symbolically replaces urine, and certain meals (*mudrâ*) are substituted for excrement. The names of the five substances in Sanskrit all begin with the letter M. Tantric secret ritual is consequently called the ritual of the five M's (*pancha-makara*).

The five substances of the *pancha-tattva* also correspond to the five main *vâyas* (airs) or *prânas* (breaths), which are the basic forms of vital energy. The ether principle, or subtle solar current, is revealed in the breathing wind, ritually controlled with the aid of the sexual act. The principle is manifested in the Apâna, the power of elimination, ritually controlled with the aid of intoxicating substances. The fire principle is manifested in the Samâna, or power of assimilation and digestion, ritually controlled by the consumption of meat. The water principle is shown in the Vyâna, the circulation of blood and other internal fluids, ritually controlled with the help of urine or of the fish. The earth principle is revealed in the Udâna, or muscular and motive energy, ritually controlled with the aid of excrement or other symbolically equivalent substances.

The use of intoxicating drink in the *pancha-tattva* rite has the aim of restoring youth to mature men, in the same way that the consumption of meat increases intelligence and energy.

The magic Aghora rites

Aghora, the "Non-Terrible", is a name given to the destroyer-aspect of Shiva in order to appease him. The Aghora rites serve mainly for black magic, and for ruining or destroying the enemy. They are described in the *Linga Purâna* for the use of court magicians, but are generally used by private individuals even today. In one of the forms of Aghora rites used for the destruction of an enemy, "the officiant furiously bores holes, placing in them effigies of the king's enemies, head downwards, feet uppermost. He then brings a fire-brand from a funeral pyre and silently lights a fire. The officiant then takes a human skull and fills it with human hair and nails, coals, ears of corn, dirty underwear, a piece of bark clothing, sweepings, teeth of poisonous snakes, bulls and cows, tiger claws and teeth, and the teeth of cats, mongoose and wild boar, while repeating the Aghora *mantra* one hundred and eight times. [This list is purely indicative. The essentials in current use are hair, nail-parings, dirty clothes and animals' teeth.] The skull and its contents are then wrapped in a winding sheet taken from a corpse. The whole is then buried in a field, house or cemetery in the enemy's territory. When the sun enters the eighth sign of the zodiac, or when there is an eclipse of the sun, the *mantra* must be repeated and the enemy will be ruined or perish... If this rite is performed against a relative, it rebounds against the officiant". (*Linga Purâna*, II, chap. 50, 33–48.)

The Aghora *mantra* is made up of thirty-two syllables: "*Aghorebhyo-tha, glorebhyo, ghora, ghoratarë-bhyah, sarvë-bhyah, sarva-sharvë-bhyo, namastë-stu, Rudra rupë-bhyah*." (*Linga Purâna*, II, chap. 27, 238.) "I adore Aghora the terrible, more terrible than the terrible. I adore all the divine archers (*sharva*), the form of Shiva the destroyer." In a *mantra* of this kind, the apparent meaning has only a mnemo-technical value. Some of these syllables have a magic and secret meaning. The rhythm of elocution, which plays an essential part, can only be learned orally.

Brahmachârva or wandering

The "journey" is always a symbol of initiatory trials. Brahmachâri ("Wandering in the immensity") is the name given to an apprentice or wandering monk who is seeking to acquire knowledge and under-standing; he must therefore renounce all material cares for a time and beg for his food. In the first stage of his life, every man must dedicate himself mainly to study, after which he must take up wandering and undergo his initiatory trials. Only after this may he take part in social and ritual life and get married.

"In order to be free, a man must satisfy the sages by study, then the gods by sacrifice, and lastly his ancestors by begetting sons." (*Shiva Purâna, Vâyavîya Samhitâ*, II, chap. 12, 32.) In everyday life, the rite of wandering may be purely symbolic. Before the rites of marriage, the husband-to-be takes the raiment and staff of a wanderer, leaves the house by one door and comes back in by another. In the Dionysiac world, the young man, before marriage, also had to leave his father's house, go away into the countryside or mountains where he would to some extent revert to primitive life and receive certain kinds of initiation.

The wandering life is obligatory for monks, and above all for the great Shivaite initiates who have definitively renounced the world and who go teaching from village to village. In Shivaite tradition, there can be no material organization, church, or monastery. The heads of the hierarchy, the Shankarâcharyas, are wandering monks, who possess only a draped cotton robe of an orange colour and a leather pot for their ablutions.

"When he is about to renounce the world, the candidate for the wandering life must invite two priests, wash their feet, offer them food, and give them clothes and money. Taking with him only a loin-cloth, a sacred cord and a staff, as well as the accessories for offertory rites, he must then retire to the seashore, the mountains, or near to a river, where he will accomplish his rites." (*Shiva Purâna, ibid.*, 85–87.)

"The man who seeks to attain knowledge must preferably live in the forest (*vanaprastha*), free from all material cares. He must find a skilled master and do everything to please and serve him." (*Shiva Purâna, ibid.*, 32–33.)

The Shivaite monk is called a Sannyâsi, from *sannyâsa* (total abandonment of goods). If he is not a wandering monk, he may retire to the forest. With the aid of Yoga he learns the language of animals who come to him without fear, obey him and follow his teaching. These naked ascetics are occasionally encountered in the forests of central India. Others retire to live in caves or cells situated in the mountains. They see no one, and feed on fruits and on roots. In some cases, their followers bring them food which is left for them at a certain distance. The inaccessible cells of the hermits on Mount Athos are very probably the ancient hermitages of Dionysian recluses. A few provisions are brought to them from time to time, which they draw up to their cells by means of ropes.

The word *brahmachâra* is nowadays often given the meaning of "chaste", although chastity is an ambiguous notion. No man is chaste, since in one way or another he periodically releases his semen, even if only while sleeping. It is not sexual practices which are forbidden to the Brahmachâri but attachments, and particularly reproductive acts whose consequence is to bind man to society and deprive him of his freedom. The Brahmachâri may have no sexual relationship involving the risk of conception. He must, in all cases, be sparing of his seed, as he has to dedicate his life to study. On the other hand, in certain rites, a Brahmachâri has to couple ritually with a prostitute. The word *brahmachâri* more or less corresponds to bachelor, and the idea of chastity is thus not necessarily implied. Shiva is often represented as a Brahmachâri, a wandering young ascetic, whose appearance troubles the hearts of all and inspires desire.

Funeral rites

The Shivaite world is most clearly distinguished from the Vedic Aryan world by its funeral rites. In Shivaite tradition, dwellings are built for the dead, whereas Aryan tradition requires the building of pyres. The Semites generally bury their dead quite simply without accessories. The fourth way of disposing of corpses is to leave them to be eaten by animals, or even by man. The Parsees expose their dead in enclosures to be eaten by vultures and the "Kafirs" of Pamir leave them out on the mountains. These various practices have occasionally intermingled. It appears, however, that wherever mortuary chambers are found, with the same characteristics and accessories as the dwellings of the living, Shivaite influence has been paramount, whether among the Egyptians, Etruscans, or the people of the dolmens.

"Cremation is not permitted for adepts. They must return to the Earth... At the time of death, other adepts foregather around the dying man. They speak to him of the splendour of Shiva until death intervenes... The body is washed with water and venerated with flowers. The *mantras* of the goddess, of Shiva, and of Enlightenment are recited, as well as passages of the *Rudra Sûkta*. The body is sprinkled with water contained in a conch. A flower is placed on the dead man's head and his body is dried while the syllable AUM is repeated. A new loin-cloth is put on him. The body is smeared with ash, according to the rules. The triple mark (*tripundra*) is traced on his forehead, which is anointed with sandalwood ointment in accordance with the rites. The body is then adorned with garlands of flowers. Rosaries made of Rudraksha seeds are placed on the breast and around the head, neck, arms, wrists and ears of the dead man.

"Incense is burned. The body is then tied with cord into a sitting

196

position, placed on a litter carried by five bearers, and decorated with garlands of perfumed flowers. . . . It is borne in procession around the village to the accompaniment of dancing, music and the singing of *mantras*.

"The adepts dig a grave to the depth of a pilgrim's staff, in an auspicious place near a sacred tree oriented towards the east or north. The bottom of the grave is covered with a bed of *dharba* grass. A piece of material, doeskin, or mat of *dharba* grass is placed on top. The body is again sprinkled with drops of the five products of the cow (milk, curds, butter, dung and urine) and with water contained in a conch, while repeating the *Rudrasûkta mantras* and the syllable AUM. A flower is placed on the dead man's head. . . The corpse is placed in the grave, seated in the Yoga posture and facing east. It is adorned with perfumed flowers. Incense is again burned. A staff is placed in his right hand, a cup full of water in his left. The head and centre of the eyebrows are then touched while repeating the *mantras* of Shiva. The skull is then broken with a coconut and the grave filled in.

"A platform two cubits (*aratni*) long and one cubit high is constructed over the grave. It is plastered with cow-dung. A *yantra* is drawn in the middle and worshipped with perfumed flowers, Bilva and Tulsi leaves and grains of corn. Lamps are swung above the grave and incense is burnt. Offerings of milk and food are then placed on the mound, which is circumambulated by the adepts, after which they prostrate themselves five times." (*Shiva Purâna, Kailasa Samhitâ*, chap. 21.)

Ceremonies at the tomb take place on the eleventh and twelfth day after the death.

In the south of India, these joyful funeral processions are still often to be seen, resembling the train of Dionysus, with musicians, dancers, and expressions of joy. The dead man is seated on a cart in the Yoga position, kept in place by cords. The procession wanders here and there until it meets the "stranger", the messenger of the gods, who is asked, "Where is the magnificent dwelling of Mr. X . . ." The stranger points out the direction of the underground chamber in which the dead man will rest together with the required accessories for his journey to the next world.

Among the Etruscans, Bacchic dances always preceded funeral processions. According to Denys of Halicarnassus, the dancers were disguised as satyrs. In pre-Aryan Minoan practice, as also among the Etruscans, the custom was interment in a circular vaulted chamber, called a *tholos*, similar to the Buddhist *stupas*. The *trulli* of Apulia, in the south of Italy, which are today used as dwellings, were originally *tholoi*. Pre-Celtic funeral rites, using dolmens, seem to have been similar to those described in the Purânas. The ritual breaking of the skull has often been misinterpreted and considered as an accident of war, thus turning the necropoli into a sort of battlefield!

Some modern Shivaite sects today practise cremation, according to Aryan custom. Interment is however still the usual method, above all in southern India. For Yogis who die voluntarily, stopping the beating of their heart of their own accord, a funerary chamber is built around them, without touching the body.

Chapter 10

GOD OF THE DANCE AND THE THEATRE

God of the dance
According to Hindu cosmology, the universe has no substance. Matter, life and thought are merely energetical relations – rhythm, movement and mutual attraction. The Prime Cause which gave birth to all the worlds and to the various forms of beings may thus be conceived as a harmonic and rhythmic principle, symbolized by the beat of drums and the movements of dance. As the creative principle, Shiva does not *utter* the world, he *dances* it. "Whatever the Dance of Shiva may originally have been, it became with time the clearest image of god's activity that any art or any religion may pride itself on having invented." (see Ananda Coomaraswany, *The Dance of Shiva*, p. 67.)

According to the Greek writer Lucian (second century A.D.), "It seems that the dance appeared at the beginning of all things and was revealed at the same time as ancient Eros, since we can see this first dance clearly appear in the ballet of the constellations and in the over-lapping movements of the planets and stars and their relationships, in an ordered harmony".

As the manifestation of primordial rhythmic energy, Shiva is the "Lord of the dance" (*Nata-râja*) and the cosmic universe is his theatre. He is the ithyphallic dancer who is the beginning of all life. That which binds Creator and Created, the divine being and the apparent world, may be expressed in terms of rhythm, movement and dance. The Creator dances the world and, by analogy, the dance of men may be envisaged as a rite, as one of the means by which we are able to go back towards the origin of things, draw near to the divine, and unite with him. Erotic intoxication and ecstatic dancing are the most direct means of establishing contact with the supernatural.

All dancing and theatre spectacles are under the aegis of Dionysus, who is invoked at the start of any performance. In the same way, Shiva is also invoked before dances and plays. Dionysus' greatest claim to glory was the invention of the dithyramb and drama competitions. According to Apollodorus' *Bibliotheke*, it was following his two-year expedition to India that Dionysus first organized musical recitals. Euripides says that he invented the flute and tambourine. Shiva's drum, the *damaru*, shaped like an hour-glass, is formed of two human skulls as a reminder that life is born of death. Several different types of dance should be distinguished: ritual or symbolic dancing, ecstatic dancing, erotic dancing and theatrical dancing. Their forms and aims are different, but they are all connected with the cult of Shiva-Dionysus and are under his patronage.

Ritual dances, which are usually performed by a group, recall by their rhythmic figures the movements of the stars and the rhythms of creation. According to Lucian (*Peri Orcheseos*, XV, 177), "It is impossible to find a single ancient mystery in which dancing had no part". In Cretan and Mycenaean religious ceremonies, processions and dances filled an important rôle and included bull-dances, erotic dances and labyrinth dances. According to Plutarch (*Theseus*, 22), "At Delos, Theseus, together with the young people, performed a dance which, they say, is still in use among the local inhabitants; it imitates the twistings and windings of the labyrinth, and develops in a rhythmic movement formed by continual evolutions and turnings". The labyrinth dance of the Romans is mentioned by Virgil, Pliny, Tacitus, and Suetonius. Similar spiral dances are even nowadays performed among the *Munda* tribes of India. Other similar dances exist among the Dervishes of the Middle East, derived from the astrological dances of the Parsees. In fact, many popular or folk dances have their origin in ritual farandoles and are performed during the rites for religious festivals, weddings, etc.

In the Shivaite temple, the dance area is an essential element. Sacred female dancers form part of the temple personnel and some dances are often associated with ritual prostitution.

"Kîrtana" and Dithyramb

Ecstatic dancing, whether individual or collective, is not usually performed in public: it concerns the performers only. It is a technique utilizing certain movements aimed at inducing a state of intoxication or trance. It was Shiva himself who revealed it to mankind. It forms an essential part of the Dionysiac cult, and is the dance of the maenads and Bacchants, its movements and rhythms also being found in the ecstatic dances of India.

200

GOD OF THE DANCE AND THE THEATRE

The Hindu *kîrtana* (song of glory), which corresponds to the Greek dithyramb, is a rite in which the participants, led by a soloist, sing the god's praises while performing dances with rhythmic movements. A state of trance is induced during which prophetic powers may be manifested among the participants.

In orgiastic intoxication and dancing in India, the participants may be possessed by various spirits (*bhûta*), powers, gods or goddesses, who speak through their mouths. We find the same concept in Euripides: "Are you possessed by Pan or by Hecate, by the terrible Korybantes or by the Mountain Mother?"

Those in ecstasy, inspired or possessed by the god, acquire perceptions of the invisible world, as well as oracular and magical powers. In a semi-unconscious hypnotic state induced by the beat of the drums and the movements of the dance, the make contact with gods, and bewitch wild beasts and even stones. Ancient vases and frescos reproduce their convulsive and spasmodic movements, the backward flexion of the body, the reversal and agitation of the nape of the neck, which nowadays can be observed in the ecstatic dances of India. It is said that the Korybantes were so called because they tossed their heads like bulls, during their dancing.

In the dithyramb as in the *kîrtana*, a circle is formed by the participants, whose number varies according to the importance of the thiasos or congregation. They dance and repeat in chorus the words sung by the leader of the ceremony (the Greek *exarchon*), who chants one of the god's legends. According to Pindar, a liturgy danced at night to the light of torches is called a *telete*, which is not a mystery and thus occasional spectators are not excluded. In the classical dithyramb, male performers originally predominated. "Historians of the Dionysus cult should be greatly interested in the possibility of discovering the primitive form of the ritual action, of which the dithyramb was the accompaniment." (H. Jeanmaire, *Dionysos*, pp. 232 and 442.) This form is found, in every aspect, in the Hindu *kîrtana* as performed nowadays, with its leader who sings the god's legend, accompanied by percussion, flutes or oboes, whilst the participants dance in a circle, swaying their heads in accordance with particular movements. Some of them gradually enter into a state of trance induced by the rhythmic movements of head and body. Various forms of *kîrtana* exist, some of which are more refined and more oriented towards musical accomplishment at an artistic level, and others which are more popular and more violent. It is in these more violent forms that some of the participants go into a trance and sometimes prophesy.

The Phrygian mode, as recommended for the music of the Bacchanal, corresponds to the India Kâfi mode (*râga*), often used today for ecstatic dances. Certain rhythms and their gradual acceleration play an important rôle, as well as the sudden changes in rhythmic formula causing a psychological shock to the dancers. The dithyramb tradition has been preserved in the *zikr*, practised by the Sufi brotherhoods in the Islamic world. The *zikr* is itself a continuation of the Greek rite, and is very close to both dithyramb and *kîrtana* in technique, effect and purpose. It is practised in Iran, Turkey and Syria, as also in Morocco, where the Aissaoua ritual is the continuation of a Dionysiac rite. The Aissaoua of Fez, moreover, practise omophagy and wear the sacred lock of hair of the Dionysiacs and Shivaites.

Mystico-erotic Dionysiac dances continued for a long time in the West. The chroniclers of the Middle Ages have left remarkable descriptions of them, notably of those practised up to the fourteenth century in the Rhine valley and Flanders. The dances of the *Tarantolati*, in Apulia, could be seen until quite recently.

Jeanmaire mentions the Nestenarides ceremonies of the last century in the villages of eastern Thrace (Costi region), as a demonstration of the persistence of the Dionysus cult which had flourished in the Greek towns along the shores of the Black Sea.

The dance and noise of the drums have the effect of creating a safety zone and of driving away ill-omened influences. The description of their use is found in the great Tamil epic poem of the third century, the *Shilappadikaram*. In the same way, according to Oppian (*Cynegetica*, IV, 237–277), "The noise created by the Bacchantes around the cradle of Dionysus had the effect of shielding him from the persecution of his enemies, as did the dance of the Kouretes around the cradle of Zeus". A very high level of sound is useful in inducing states of trance. The god of the dithyramb is called the Noisy One (Bromios), the Great Shouter (Eriboas). Shiva, too, is called the Howler, the Noisy One.

It may be noted that, in the modern world, young people when dancing willingly confine themselves in a closed space where the sound level is very high. They appear to have a feeling of being insulated, isolated from external worries and constraints, and to reach a state of exaltation which, if properly oriented, could easily lead to a form of mystical intoxication.

Apart from dances of an ecstatic kind, there are also erotic dances in which the participants wear phallic emblems and mine the sexual chase and act. These dances are still practised in India and in certain areas of North Africa. It is to these dances and mimes that Aristotle attributes the origin of comedy. The train of Dionysus, like that of Shiva, is preceded by dancers giving themselves over to obscene mime which, like erotic images, plays an important rôle in driving away evil powers. The procreative act, the act of life, is thus opposed to the powers of destruction and death. The rhythm of the sexual act is included among those of the dance.

The *Tandava* dance reveals Shiva in his aspect as Bhairava (the Terrible) or Virabhadra (the Destroying Spirit). The god is represented peforming this dance in burial grounds and places of cremation. Shiva dances savagely, surrounded by a troupe of unrestrained goblins, and is sometimes accompanied by the goddess. This dance which the god taught to man, is very close to ecstatic dancing and is occasionally performed in the theatre. Equally it is a part of the rites connected with sacrifice and orgiasm.

There are many literary descriptions of the dance of Shiva.

"Having installed the Mother of the Three Worlds on a golden throne adorned with precious stones, the bearer of the hunting spear (Shûlapani) dances on the peaks of Mount Kailâsa, surrounded by all the gods. Sarasvatî (goddess of Arts and Science) plays the vînâ, Indra (the King of Heaven) the flute, Brahmâ (the Creator) holds the cymbals which beat out the measure, Lakshmi (Fortune) intones a song, Vishnu plays the drum. All the gods surround them.

"The heavenly musicians (Gandharvas), Gnomes (Patâgas), Snakes (Urâgas), the Blessed (Siddhas), the Realized Ones (Sâdhyas), the Guardians of the World (Vidyâdhara), the immortals, the nymphs of heaven and all the inhabitants of the three worlds, assemble to see the heavenly dance and to hear the music of the divine orchestra at the hour of twilight." (*Shiva Pradosha Stotra.*)

The theatre: the fifth Veda

Aristotle attributes the origin of the theatre to the sung narrative of the dithyramb. "Tragedy as well as comedy derive their origin from a form of sung improvisation. The first stems from the bards who led the dithyramb, the second from those who directed the phallic songs... It was Aeschylus who first brought the number of actors up to two, reduced the part of the chorus and gave pride of place to speech." (Aristotle, *Poetics*, IV, 1449 et seq.)

In India, it is easy to see how the sung narrative of the *Kîrtana* can be developed, first by dividing the narrative between two actors replying to each other and, then to the recited and mimed play. Theatre, music and dance are called the fifth Veda, since they are considered a means of teaching the people, even while amusing them with the legends of the gods and virtues of the heroes. In the same way in Greece, the theatre was considered a means of spreading the gospel of Bacchus.

Diodorus emphasizes the relationship of Dionysus with the theatre, as well as the character of the associations of theatrical professionals as "Dionysiac artists". Dionysus' patronage of actors' companies was not a mere convention. Dionysiac artists often appeared as propagandists of the Dionysus cult, and there is little doubt that they exercised both religious and political activities. Bards, actors, musicians and dancers formed a class apart, of a semi-sacerdotal nature, on the fringe of society.

Theatrical dancing is professional and requires difficult techniques and a long apprenticeship, besides artistic talent. The language of gestures (*mudras*) and mime (*abhinaya*), together with a plasticity of movement and rhythm, are its essential components. It is this kind of dance, known as *lasya*, which is performed by the sacred temple dancers. In the world, the goddess herself teaches it. It is nowadays called *Bhârata Nâtyam*, after the sage Bhârata who codified the rules. Although danced exclusively by women, this kind of dance is traditionally taught by men. Male theatrical dancing is today mainly represented by the Kathâkali, Chhau, and Kuchapuri and the teaching of it is attributed to Shiva. The language of gesture is almost identical to that of the *Bhârata Nâtyam*. The numerous actor-dancers perform plays whose subjects are always connected with mythology and the legends of gods and heroes. The very thick make-up or masks worn by the actors transform them into mysterious characters.

The theatre is connected with magic and the actor, like the poet, is divinely inspired. When he acts the rôle of a god or hero, he becomes the very character himself. He is a sort of medium, and what he expresses may well go beyond his own understanding. In the Kathâkali, the actor, once made-up, is no longer himself. He is addressed, not as himself, but as the character he impersonates and is venerated as such. This constitutes a sort of priesthood, which inevitably affects the actor. The same happens in the Japanese Nô theatre.

In Greece as in India, the theatre became in important spectacle and has left a great number of literary masterpieces. However, after the almost total annihilation of the princely courts in India following the Muslim domination, spoken plays have practically ceased to exist. On the other hand, the more ancient popular forms, such as the *kîrtana* and dancing theatre, have continued down to our own times.

The dance floor

It appears that, in the most ancient form of the rites of Shiva-Dionysus, the cult-centre was a place under the open sky called "the dance floor". This sacred enclosure stood for the temple and was the god's sanctuary, as is still the case among the primitive tribes of India. In the ancient Tamil epic, the *Shilappadikaram*, the dance floor is described as the village sanctuary, where contact can be made with the mysterious world of spirits. In Minoan Crete, dance floors surrounded by tiered rows of seats were religious appurtenances. Homer speaks of the "beautiful dance floor" (kallichoros). "it seems likely that the Labyrinth at Knossos was an arena or *orchestra* of solar pattern for the performance of a mimetic dance, in which a dancer masqueraded as a bull and represented the movement of the sun." (R. F. Willetts, *Cretan Cults and Festivals*, p. 102.)

This concept may be compared with the sacred clearing of the Celts, and also with the Temple of Heaven, a raised terrace from which the Chinese emperors communicated with the celestial powers. The same applies to the Islamic mosque, which was originally a simple enclosure open to the sky. The word *templum* comes from the root *tem* (to cut, cut off, separate), whence *temenos* (sacred enclosure). In India, the temple is a vast enclosure in which the sanctuary proper occupies only a minimal part.

Festivals and processions

As the principle of life, Shiva is the god of Youth, Erotic Activity, and Renewal. His festivals take place at the beginning of Spring, the beginning of the year itself (March-April), when the whole of nature is in flower, casting its seed to the wind, as well as in the Autumn when nature yields its fruit.

This succession of apparent death and renewal is found in all aspects of life. Shiva, like Dionysus, is the god of Nature and Vegetation. Their festivals are those of the Winter solstice and

Spring. Holi, the festival of Shiva, is the Indian carnival and Spring festival. The Great Dionysia were celebrated after the full moon in March, immediately after the Feast of the Dead, because Dionysus brings with him the Spring, and the renewal of life. Vegetation deities were supposed to spend a part of the year underground, in the kingdom of the dead, and such is the case with Dionysus and Osiris. Shiva, too, is the lord of life and death, while Osiris is essentially the king of the dead.

According to Plato (*The Republic*, 475), the Great Dionysia took place in March-April. The Cretan year, on the other hand, began with the Autumnal equinox. The Eleusinian mysteries were celebrated in September (the time of sowing), and the Dionysiac Bacchanalia at the end of October, after the grape-harvest. According to Thucydides, the Anthesteria – the most ancient festival of Dionysus – was celebrated in the Ionian cities on the 11th, 12th and 13th of the month of Anthesterion, immediately before the full moon of March. The three days of the Anthesteria were in reality days of ill omen, on which the spirits of the dead appeared, and the festival thus exercises a sort of counteraction. The 11th of the month, which was the first day of the *triduum*, was called *Pithoigia*, the opening of the *pithoi*, in which the wine of the last harvest was desacralized. The Roman Liberalia took place on March 17th. Calculating the days of the lunar month, it is during this period that new wine is even now tasted and bottled in Italy. The 11th of the lunar month (*Ekadashi*) is a day of vigil for the Hindus, and the orgiastic Spring festival takes place more or less at the same date.

Megasthenes, who lived in India from 302 to 298 B.C., noted the similarity of the Dionysiac processions to those of India. During the Spring festival, nowadays known as Holi in India, a naked man represents Shiva; he is smeared with white plaster or ash and, bearing a trident, is led in procession riding an ass. In the animal world, the ass is "untouchable", the representative of the humble: Jesus, too, entered Jerusalem riding on an ass. Shiva is preceded by a rowdy crowd wearing wooden phalli or bearing images of ithyphallic monkeys. The participants sing and dance, shout obscenities and hurl insults. Many of them have pails full of coloured water and long squirts with which they spray each other, a practice which has been replaced elsewhere by confetti. This is the day on which the oppressed have the right to insult the powerful, which they never fail to do, and no grudges are held against them afterwards.

"The... processions dedicated to Isis, Demeter and Flora, with their phallic emblems... were accompanied by the singing of erotic songs and lecherous horseplay amplified by *Fescennine* (i.e. erotic) joking." (P. Rawson, *Primitive Erotic Art*, p. 74.)

"Aischrology, meaning the lewd and scurrilous language so frequently mentioned in modern cases of possession, and whose rôle in certain religious occasions in Greece is known, can be interpreted as an effect of relaxation... Dionysus' association with festivities in which the phallus was paraded is certainly very ancient... The phallic emblem and the pranks to which its solemn procession gave rise are doubly suited to Dionysus as the god of the joy and licentiousness of the festival." (H. Jeanmaire, *Dionysos*, pp. 170 and 256.)

Masquerades were a constant element in Athenian festivals, in which Dionysus occupied a central place. The divine beings revealed their presence in the procession of masks. The carrying of phallic emblems and the excitement of the god-possessed Bacchants announced the triumphal entry of the spirit of the new year. Eroticism, transvestism and bisexuality also have a symbolic rôle. Apollonius of Tyana mentions the lascivious dances of the ephebes dressed in purple or saffron-coloured robes. In Thrace, the procession included cars drawn by young men dressed as girls. "The licentiousness of the Saturnalia... is a suspension of law and custom, since the behaviour of the sexes is then exactly the opposite of what it should be normally. This reversal of behaviour involves a total confusion of values, which is the specific sign of all orgiastic rituals. Morphologically, intersexual transvestism and symbolical androgyny are homologous to ceremonial orgies." (M. Eliade, *Méphistophélès et l'Androgyne*, p. 141.)

"[At] the Athenian Dionysia, [derived from] the Cretan Thio-daisia... the image of Dionysus Eleuthereus was carried from the city to a shrine on the road to the village of Eleutherai, on the frontier between Attica and Boiotia, reputedly its original home. It was escorted by the armed *epheboi* of Athens... Animals were sacrificed, the most important [of which] was a bull... chosen as 'worthy of the god'. After being sacrificed, the bull was presumably roasted and the meat then shared among the state officials. The procession returned to the city by torchlight in the evening, when the feast was over, and the *epheboi* took the image of Dionysus to the theatre. Here it remained, on an altar in the middle of the orchestra, until the festival concluded... According to Plutarch, [at the Oskhophoria festival]... two young men carried the vine-branches in honour of Dionysus and

Ariadne, the vine-god and his bride... Ten *epheboi* from each of the ten tribes... formed a chorus and this number corresponded to the number of young men chosen as tribute for Minos for ritual reasons... The two who actually led the procession... were dressed as women." (R. F. Willetts, *Cretan Cults and Festivals*, pp. 196 and 205.)

A fifth-century inscription prescribes that the Athenian colonists in Thrace should send a phallus each year to the Athenian Dionysia. According to Demosthenes; a sacristan, waving snakes above his head, danced about at the head of the procession. "Dionysus is portrayed in a car drawn by panthers, tigers, or harts. In other cases, he is drawn by two satyrs. The prow of the car is in the shape of a pig's head, its stern like the neck of a swan. Inside, two naked satyrs play the flute. Dionysus holds a vine-branch. In front of the car, a trumpet-player, flute-player, bearers carrying a perfume altar and others carrying garlands, precede the sacrificial bull, adorned with white fillets." (H. Jeanmaire, *Dionysos*, p. 51.)

On arrival, the procession is welcomed to the sound of flutes and tambourines by a multitude of Bacchants and young people dressed, according to Plutarch, as satyrs and as Pan. Herodotus noted the same processions in Egypt. At Ephesus, the faithful wore masks and phalli. Like the Roman Liberalia, the festivities took place at night and, together with drunkenness, were the occasion for the most licentious behaviour. "As regards the rest of the Dionysian festival, the Egyptians celebrate it just as the Greeks, in everything except the dances." (Herodotus, 2, 48.)

The festivals of Shiva and Dionysus have always been those of the poor and humble. In Greece, it was the custom to invite the household servants, as is also the case in India, where the Holi festival in the Spring is the feast of the *shudras*. The *Shudras* (slaves) are working men and servants who, on that particular day, are accorded every privilege. "According to Ephoros, certain festivals were regularly celebrated for the serfs of the district of Kydonia, during which no free persons entered the city; the serfs were masters of everything and even had the power to flog the free-men. It is tempting to connect this account with the statement of Karystios that festivals of Hermes were celebrated in Crete, and, while the serfs were feasting, their masters assisted in menial duties." (R. F. Willetts, *Cretan Cults and Festivals*, p. 287.) Ganesha, the Indian Hermes, is also the favourite deity of the poor. "With his Silenus, mule, goat-skin bottle and intoxicated retinue, this Dionysus of rustic Priapic rites, satyric drama and the dance, has always had a propensity for having a fling after drinking." (H. Jeanmaire, *Dionysos*, p.156.)

Survivals of the processions of Shiva and Dionysus are to be found wherever there are carnivals or Mid-Lent festivities with floats, masks and fancy dress. Festivities for the first of May, with masked dances and orgies, although nowadays much subdued, still exist in Switzerland, Germany and Spain. At Basle, there is a special law forbidding the punishment of excesses committed during the carnival. The Shrove Tuesday and Mid-Lent festivities in the Christian world, with their libidinous outbursts during the period of fasting and penitence preceding the death of the god, recall the Anthesteria, the vigils of the feasts of the dead.

The festivals of Shiva-Dionysus, in which other aspects of the god are evoked, do not have the same lewd character. This is particularly so in the case of the Winter solstice, the feast of the god's birth, later transferred to the Christian *bambino*, which is also the feast of Skanda's birth, a cult which today is often transferred to the infant Krishna. "In the fixing of the dates for the feasts of the Christian year . . . it is possible to glimpse the memory of many of the ceremonies belonging to a previous era. At Delphi in Winter, the Thyades, the Bacchantes of Parnassus, used to awaken a baby in a cradle, the *liknites*, or infant Dionysus, whose reappearance was celebrated about the time of the Winter solstice . . . The establishing of the feast of the Christian Nativity (starting from the fourth century of our era) on a date close to it in the calendar . . . accounts for the mechanism by virtue of which a new god is inserted at a liturgical period which existed before the spread of his own cult." (H. Jeanmaire, *Dionysos*, pp. 46 and 77.) It should be remembered that the date of the twenty-fifth of December was chosen to celebrate the birth of the infant god. There is no historical or traditional data concerning the date of the birth of Jesus.

Chapter 11

LIFE AND SOCIETY

The life of the "Bhakta"

According to the *Linga Purâna* (I, chap. 89, 24–29), the rules of conduct for the "participant" (Bacchant or *Bhakta*), or "companion" (*kaula*), who desires to dedicate himself to the search for wisdom, are five in number: not to steal (*asteya*); wandering and renunciation of marriage (*brahma-chârya*); absence of ambition (*alobha*); renunciation of wordly goods (*tyâga*) and non-violence (*ahimsâ*). To these may be added for apprentices: absence of anger (*akrodha*); his master's service (*gurusushruta*); cleanliness (*shaucha*); moderation in eating (*ahâralâghava*) and study (*adhyaya*).

In the Christian world, those belonging to religious orders make the three vows of chastity, poverty and obedience, meaning that they renounce the three essential assets of man, pleasure, riches, and freedom, in favour of the superior of the order, who is considered the representation of "God". The difference between the Christian and Shivaite concept is profound. Non-marriage does not necessarily imply chastity, but means remaining outside the social responsibilities which marriage involves; the absence of sexual activity is, in any case, a practical impossibility. The Greek *agela* is somewhat similar. For the *Bhaktas*, poverty and the lack of covetousness and possessions also excludes communal property, i.e., the monastery. The wandering Bhakta is a hermit and wayfarer, who begs for his food and makes no provision for the future.

Obedience is a virtue only for the student and, even in this case, is limited to his master's service. The disciple never surrenders his free judgement or independence, nor does his master ever take the responsibility of imposing a determined way of life or thought. He replies only to those questions which are asked him and his opinion is only advisory.

Cleanliness and personal hygiene are an essential duty. The body is an image of god and must be considered as such. It is the instrument of all self-realization and should be kept in the best possible condition of physical harmony by means of exercise, bathing and massage. All corporal functions must, moreover, be considered as rites.

"A man must rise before dawn and accomplish his natural functions. This must be in a place away from the house, but screened. He must squat facing north. Natural functions should never be performed in front of water, fire, a Brahman, or the image of any god. The penis must be covered with the left hand and the mouth with the right. He must not look at his excrement. He must wash with water contained in a vessel, never directly in a river or pool. The anus must be cleaned with fresh clay, five or three times. In order to wash the penis, a handful of clay, the size of a cucumber, must be used.

"After cleaning himself, the hands and feet must be washed and he must gargle eight times. The teeth must then be cleaned with a stick [of Spanish liquorice or rose-wood, which is chewed to make a sort of brush], but fingers must not be put into the mouth. After this, a bath must be taken, according to the rites." (*Shiva Purâna, Vidyeshvara Samhitâ*, chap. 13.)

Hesiod mentions similar rules among the Greeks: "When dawn breaks, take care not to offer libations to Zeus with hands which you have not washed, any more than to other gods; know that they will not hear you and will despise your prayers. Do not make water standing, turning towards the sun; and, from when it sets to when it rises, remember to urinate neither on the road, nor off the road, nor merely by raising your tunic . . . The pious and prudent man squats or goes to the wall of an enclosed courtyard . . . Never urinate at the mouth of rivers falling into the sea, nor near springs; avoid doing so; do not bathe there either; it is not a good thing". (Hesiod, *Works and Days*, 725–732 and 755–760.)

Ritual bathing is indispensable before eating, after sexual intercourse or after contact with any person or non-purified object. The bath must be taken in a stream or pool, or else with water coming directly from them. Should this prove impossible, there are ritual formulas for turning ordinary water into Ganges' water.

The ritual garments, which are also worn at meals, must be seamless, and must be washed only with saponaceous herbs, without using soap. Soap is also forbidden for use in ritual bathing, clay or oil being used instead. As an initiate, Jesus also wore a seamless robe. At Mecca, the Moslems still observe this rule.

Dietary laws are very strict. Food must be prepared by the person who consumes it, or by a member of his family or other person who will observe all the rules of ritual purity of the caste to which the consumer belongs. Only the flesh of animals sacrificed according to the rites may be eaten, and most particularly so in the case of sacred animals such as bovines. The right hand only is used in touching food, and any cup which has touched one's lips is immediately broken.

Women

Shivaite society was originally matriarchal. Property, houses, land and servants belong to women. Man is only a fecundator, a wanderer, occupying himself with arts, war, or games, or else dedicating himself to an intellectual or spiritual life. In sedentary, agricultural societies, property usually belongs to women, and is handed down from mother to daughter: the dowry is a survival of this custom. In nomadic societies based on stock-raising the male is predominant, and wives are bought. The main problem of societies stemming from the Aryan invasions lies in the fact that they have become sedentary while retaining the patriarchal system of nomadic society. Women represent property, the material world and the slavery of men.

According to the Purânas, the first men were sages, practising meditation and rites, and they reproduced by a projection of the spirit. The power they acquired by their merits became a threat to the gods. Thus the latter created woman and reproduction by means of the sexual act, in order to lead men away from their virtues and destroy their power. According to Hesiod, woman was created by Zeus so as to chastise the human race. "Formerly the human race lived on the earth set aside and sheltered from affliction, hard labour and painful illnesses, which brought death to mankind. But woman... scattered them all over the world and caused sad anxiety for men." (Hesiod, *Works and Days*, 90–95.) "When, instead of good, Zeus created this beautiful calamity, he took her where gods and men were..., and the immortal gods and mortal men marvelled at the sight of this deep and inescapable snare which was destined for mankind, since from her came forth that accursed brood of women, that terrible scourge set in the midst of mortal men." (Hesiod, *The Theogony*, 585–592.)

In the chapters of the Purânas dealing with the way of liberation and detachment, woman – the symbol of society – is considered as the greatest obstacle in the path of spiritual realization.

"Shiva spoke, 'Do not bring that girl near me, with her slim figure, beautiful hips and her moon-face. I have already forbidden it many times. Woman is the source of illusion... a girl is a danger for an ascetic. I am an ascetic, a Yogi, over whom illusions have no hold. Why should I encumber myself with a woman... At the contact of a woman, the material world imprisons you, detachment flees, the virtues acquired by asceticism are destroyed. An ascetic should have nothing to do with women. Woman is the source of all worldly ties. She destroys wisdom and detachment... Marriage is no use to man. Marriage is the bond which most enslaves you. There are many forms of dependance, but associating with women is the worst of bonds. You can free yourself from all ties, save those created by women'." (*Shiva Purâna, Rudra Samhitâ*, chap. 12, 28–33 and chap. 24, 60–61.)

"Women are light-minded. They are the cause of all trouble. Men who seek liberation must avoid attaching themselves to women. Women love only those who run after them, have intimate relations with them and are of service to them. When women cannot find men for their pleasure, they have sexual relations among themselves. Women are never satiated however many lovers they may have." (*Shiva Purâna, Umâ-samhitâ*, chap. 24, 3 and 19–29.)

"Women never adapt themselves to odious poverty, but only to abundance. In like manner, in the recesses of the rocks where swarms are born, the bees support the drones who only follow evil pursuits." (Hesiod, *The Theogony*, 593–595.)

"Woman is like a fire-brand, man like a jar of oil. It is better to avoid all contact." (*Linga Purâna*, I, chap. 8, 21–23.) This, however, in Tantric rites, does not prevent woman from being worshipped as the goddess, or procreative power through which the god is revealed. It is for this reason that women take part in orgiastic rites. The rules for women who choose the *bhakta* life are similar to those for men. For a woman who is drawn to a mystical life and ecstatic experience, all permanent ties with men are an obstacle. Man is an enemy who prevents woman from freeing herself from the bonds of society, property, and the family. Either, like the vestals, she avoids all relations with men, or else sexual relations must be a kind of ritual and sacred prostitution which creates no permanent or sentimental ties with man and avoids procreation. It is the couple who form the social bond, the hearth which is the real hindrance to the *bhakta*'s freedom. Bacchantes shun society and its restrictive laws, but not necessarily occasional sexual relations.

Sacred prostitution

Self-realization on the erotic level is an essential aspect of the human being's development. Prostitution is a beneficient and sacred profession, since it allows erotic ecstasy to be practised by the wanderer, monk, poor man, and even the married man whose relations, having a procreative aim, do not have the same value. In another way, it is comparable to the alms, shelter and food due to wanderers. In India, many girls were dedicated to the temple where they carried out this social and religious duty, which is the gift of love. They received a careful education, including music, dancing and erotic techniques. The same is found in the Greek world, particularly at Corinth, where prostitution was considered a kind of divine service. Male and female sacred prostitution was also known to the Hebrews.

Apart from its religious role, which is to allow all men to experience erotic ecstasy, prostitution also plays an essential social function with regard to the stability of the family. Political treatises such as the *Artha Shastra* give it great importance and lay down regulations for it. When the Nehru government tried to prohibit prostitution in India, a delegation of strict Brahmans went to Delhi to protest and to remind the government that, according to the sacred texts, "In countries without prostitution, every house becomes a brothel". Like the members of other professions, the prostitutes of both sexes form highly organized associations. At the time of India's independence, the corporation of male prostitutes offered its support to the National Congress government.

The institution of temple dancer-prostitutes of whom there were sometimes thousands, was forbidden by the British legislature, thus causing, among other things, a decline in the arts of music and dancing which are closely connected with the institution itself.

Male prostitution, mainly in the form of transvestism, still exists today in many small Indian towns and villages, just as it did at Athens. It also played a ritual rôle in connection with the Hermaphrodite cult, as also found in Shamanism, but today appears to be in decline. However, transvestite prostitutes have their place in society. In popular performances of the *Krishna-lîlâ*, they play the rôle of Krishna's shepherdess-lovers. Transvestite prostitutes generally live on the outskirts of towns, where the sanctuaries of Shiva-Dionysus stood in former times. Female prostitutes, on the other hand, are housed in the temple enclosure itself.

214

Duties towards guests

Shivaism is a nature religion and commends life in the forest for initiates, as well as the wandering life and living apart from the city. All this involves the obligation of assistance from those who continue to lead an active life. Men who dedicate themselves to acquiring material goods have the function and duty to finance temples, priests, monks, artisans and artists and to keep an open table for wayfarers. Hospitality is an essential duty: the wanderer or lost traveller must never find a closed door. Before eating, each householder must see whether there is not a vagrant monk or traveller in need of food, who must be served before anyone else. In theory, duties towards guests have no limit.

"Venerating a guest is the best way of acquiring merits. One day, the sage Sudarshana (Beautiful-to-behold), who wished to vanquish the god of Death by his own virtues, said to his chaste wife, 'Never must you refuse to honour a guest. A traveller is always the image of Shiva and everything belongs to him'. Dharma (moral law) then took the appearance of a wandering monk and approached the sage's dwelling during his absence. The wife of Beautiful-to-behold offered him the customary hospitality. Once satiated, he said, 'I have had enough cooked rice and other food; now you must give yourself to me'. She therefore offered herself to him. At that moment, Beautiful-to-behold returned and called his wife. But it was the guest who replied, 'I am making love with your wife. Simply tell me what I must do now, since I have finished and am satisfied'. Beautiful-to-behold said to him, 'Excellent man! Take your pleasure in peace; I shall go away for a while'. Dharma then revealed himself to him and said, 'By this act of piety, you have vanquished death'. All guests must be honoured in like manner." (*Linga Purâna*, I, chap. 29, 45–64.)

Race, caste and social function

Shivaism recognizes a difference in the rôle and aptitudes of the various human races and animal species. Man has no single origin: there are four races of men, each of a distinct family. This notion, which was for long denied by Westerners for mainly Biblical reasons (the Adam and Eve myth), is nowadays contemplated by certain anthropologists. Diversity of species and race is an essential aspect of the harmony of creation. Restrictions regarding interracial marriage seek to avoid the degeneration of the various species, so as to preserve the nobility and beauty of each. The purpose of the caste system is to facilitate the coexistence of different races within the same society by giving to each social group its own profession and distinct privileges. It was part of the social organization of ancient Shivaism.

According to Hesiod, man's evolution passes through four stages, which correspond to the four races of the Hindus. These four stages are symbolized by four colours: white, red, yellow and black. The four corresponding races of men successively play a predominant rôle in the various ages of humanity. The sage, belonging to the colour white, was the man of the Golden Age, the Krita Yuga. Then the warrior-man, of a brown or red colour, appeared in the Age of Rites or Silver Age, the Treta Yuga. The yellow man, agriculturist and merchant, is the man of the Age of Indecision, the Age of Bronze or Dvâpara Yuga. Lastly comes the black man, the artisan and worker, who dominates in the Age of Conflicts, the Iron Age or Kali Yuga.

Even in non-multiracial societies, castes tend to re-establish themselves on the basis of aptitudes, since these are an essential aspect of every society.

The social system of the Egyptians and Cretans is little known. According to Herodotus (chap. 2, 164–168), the Egyptians recognized seven professional castes: priests, warriors, cowherds, swineherds, merchants, interpreters and boatmen. Aristotle remarks that the Cretan caste-system was similar to the Egyptian one and he attributes its origin to Sesastris in Egypt and Minos in Crete.

This division of mankind according to functions and capacities is found in all traditions. Among the Celts, the Druids were priests and jurists; the military aristocracy, the *flaith*, were the representatives of power; the *bo-airig* (owners of cows) formed the agricultural class. The attribution of a particular social rôle to races of different origins does not appear to be peculiar to India and is, in any case, a latent tendency in all societies.

Mankind can only find its equilibrium and happiness when the four human groups forming the basis of the four castes are themselves in harmony. This alone can avoid the four tyrannies of which Manu, the great law-giver, speaks: the tyranny of priests, of warriors, of merchants, and of the working classes, which are all equally distastrous and succeed each other indefinitely until a social balance is restored.

It is not necessary to go as far as India to observe this ineluctable cycle. In the recent past, Europe itself has experienced the seizing of power by the Church, then by the nobles, followed by the capitalist bourgeoisie, and lastly by the dictatorship of the proletariat. None of these formulas is stable or effective and they inevitably lead to tyranny and injustice. Only the recognition of the four groups essential to any society and the allocation of their respective rights and privileges will allow a stable and just social organization to be established. An organization of this kind – the caste system – has allowed India to maintain a civilization uninterrupted since Antiquity, despite many invasions and wars. The European Middle Ages attempted to establish an organization of this type, but it was the Church at the time of the Inquisition, which destroyed the balance.

A man, born in a given category corresponding to particular aptitudes, must exert himself to reach full self-realization within the framework of his family's profession. The ambitious man, who wishes to occupy a position for which he is not fitted, leads to social disorder. Whether in the animal or human world, the mixture of races produces degenerate individuals who distort the harmony and beauty of creation, since they no longer possess the characteristic virtues of either race. We know this full well as regards animals, but try to ignore it in the case of men. Pure-bred animals have definite characteristics which cross-breeds do not have. A sheep dog is not a hunting dog. You cannot make a knight out of a shopkeeper.

It is at the level of spiritual realization, of the progress of the human being, as well as in rites and religious and magical practices, that Shivaism recognizes no difference between one man and another. Its teaching is open to all, which is why it is so severely censured by the Aryan Vedic texts. The highest spiritual realization is in fact considered easier for the humble than for the powerful. In the Kali Yuga, the most favoured are working men, and women, since their social duties and responsibilities are more limited than those of priests and princes. Detachment and the abandonment of daily tasks does not involve any omission of important duties. It is easier for the poor man than for the rich to lead the life of a Bacchant, draw near to the divine, identify himself with Shiva the wandering god, and enter the god's kingdom.

The differences and inequality between men are the source of all progress and civilization. The association of certain aptitudes with certain races is fallacious. However, each race, collectively, may possess aptitudes which some others do not have, and the same is true of individuals within each group. The real social problem is to give each person the maximum possibility of developing according to his tendencies, capacities and needs.

Certain ideas are only true on one level and are not applicable on another. It is at this point that simplistic slogans become absurdities. The Indian grammarians' classic example is the following: "Before the gods all beings are equal; therefore my mother, my wife and my daughter are equal and thus I can sleep with any one of them". The so-called egalitarian and democratic theories of our times inevitably lead to a levelling out which is a frustration and slavery for all alike. Freedom is the right to be different. The fact that power and privilege are badly shared out is something that can be remedied; an egalitarianism which is a mere abstraction is something quite different. It can only lead to the elimination of the weak, and often of the most talented as well, those who create the values and *raison d'être* of a society. The repression of "intellectuals", as also of men who, by their talents, have obtained success and fortune, is a characteristic of so-called "socialist" countries.

All electrical or dynamic energy is based on potential difference, and this is also true of all activity and life. "Levelling is death", say the Tantras. Water, the female principle which always tends to become level and cease to move, is the image of the negative principle. Fire, on the other hand, which tends to rise up and destroy, is a symbol of life and energy.

Chapter 12

THE MODERN AGE

The Kala Yuga

World evolution is subject to cycles. Many times, mankind together with the animal and vegetable species have known the cycle of their infancy, golden age, decline, and destruction. Each of these cycles is divided into four periods known as *Yugas*. This division of the ages of the world was known to the Egyptians, the Greeks, and all the ancients. The first age is the Golden Age or Age of Truth, the Satya Yuga, in which man is a sage, still close to the divine. The second is the Silver Age, the Treta Yuga, the age of the three fires or age of rites. The third is the Age of Bronze, the Dvâpara Yuga or Age of Indecision. The last is the Age of Iron, the Kali Yuga, the Age of Conflicts. It is in this last age, in which we are now living, that mankind engineers its own destruction. The word *kali* means "conflict, quarrel", and has nothing to do with the goddess Kâlî, the "Power of Time" and of death.

During the Kali Yuga, the disruption of the balance of nature, as well as of society and its basic values, occurs at an ever-increasing pace. These disruptions announce the end of the cycle and the near destruction of mankind, an end which can no longer be far away. Man's supremacy over the terrestrial world and his gradual destruction of other living species provokes the god's vengeance which is revealed in the folly he inspires in those who oppose him. This folly is very evident in the behaviour of mankind today, formed of ignorant masses led by irresponsible and evil leaders.

"Plunged into the depths of ignorance, and thinking, 'We are wise and educated people', these fools, exposed to a thousand evils, stray about aimlessly like the blind led by a blind man." (*Mundaka Upanishad*, I, chap. 2, 8.)

"Now is [the age of men] of the race of iron. During the day they shall not cease to suffer hardship and misery, nor during the night to be consumed by the deep anguish which the gods shall send them. They may at least still find some good mixed together with their ills.

219

But the hour will come when Zeus, in his own time, shall annihilate this race of mortal men: that will be the time when they shall be born with white temples. The father shall then no longer resemble his sons, nor the sons their father; the guest shall no longer be dear to his host, nor friend to friend, or brother to brother, as in the past. To their parents, as soon as they grow old, they shall show only contempt; in complaining of them, they shall use harsh words, these evil ones, and shall not even know the fear of heaven. To the old people who have fed them, they will refuse food. No value shall any more be given to the keeping of an oath, to what is just and good; the organizer of crime, the completely immoderate man, will receive respect; the only right shall be force; conscience shall no longer exist. The coward shall attack the brave with tortuous words which he shall support with false oaths. Jealousy shall dog the steps of the whole miserable race of man, with bitter language and a countenance full of hate, delighting in evil. Then, leaving the wide roads of earth for Olympos, hiding their beautiful bodies under white veils, Conscience (Aidos) and Shame (Nemesis) shall abandon man and rise to the Eternal Ones. Only unhappy sufferings shall remain to mortal men: against evil, there shall be no recourse." (Hesiod, *Works and Days*, pp. 175–200.)

The *Linga Purâna* describes the men of the Kali Yuga as "tormented with envy, irritable, sectarian, indifferent to the consequences of their actions. They are threatened with sickness, hunger, fear, and terrible natural calamities. Their desires are misdirected, their knowledge utilized for malignant ends. They are dishonest. Many shall perish. The castes of nobles and farmers will decline. During the Age of Kali, the working classes will claim the right to govern and will share knowledge, meals, offices and beds with the scholars. Heads of State will be mostly of low origins and will be dictators and tyrants.

"They kill the foetus and the hero. The workmen wish to fill intellectual rôles, and the intellectuals those of the workers. Thieves become kings and kings become thieves. Virtuous women are rare. Promiscuity is widespread. The stability and balance between castes and the ages of man disappear on all sides. The earth produces almost nothing in some places, and a great deal in others. The powerful appropriate the public weal and cease to protect the people. Wise men of low origin are honoured like Brahmans and deliver the dangerous secrets of knowledge to unworthy people. Masters demean themselves by selling knowledge. Many take refuge in a wandering life. Towards the end of the Yuga, the number of women will increase, and the number of men diminish.

"During the Age of Kali, the Great God, Shiva, the peacemaker, dark-blue and red, will reveal himself in a disguised form in order to restore justice. Those who come to him shall be saved.

"Towards the end of the Yuga, animals will become violent, and the number of cows will decline. Upright men shall withdraw from public life. Pre-cooked food is sold in the public squares. Sacraments and religion are also for sale.

"The rainfall will be erratic. Merchants will be dishonest. Those who beg or seek employment will become more and more numerous. There is no one who does not use coarse language, who keeps his word, who is not envious... Men without morals preach virtue to others. Censorship reigns... Criminal associations are formed in towns and villages. Water will be scarce as well as fruit. Men will lose all sense of values. They will have stomach trouble and will leave their hair in disorder. Towards the end of the Yuga, some will be born whose life expectancy will be only sixteen years. People will be envious of others' clothes. Thief shall steal from thief. Many will become lethargic and inactive; contagious illnesses, rats and snakes shall torment mankind. Men suffering from hunger and fear shall be found near the river Kaushiki (Bengal).

"No more shall anyone live out his normal life-span, which is one hundred years. Rites shall decay in the hands of men without virtue. People practising corrupt rites will be widespread. Unqualified people shall study the sacred texts and shall become so-called experts. Men shall kill each other and shall also slay children, women and cows. Sages will be condemned to death.

"Some, however, shall attain perfection in a very short time. Excellent Brahmans shall continue to perform the rites." (*Linga Purâna*, II, chap. 39, 42–45.)

In a sense, the Kali Yuga is a privileged era. The first men, those of the Satya Yuga, were sages still close to the divine. But the last men, those of the Kali Yuga, in drawing near to death, also draw near to the principle to which all things return at the end. In the middle of the moral decadence, injustice, wars and social conflicts which are characteristic of the end of the Kali Yuga, contact with the divine by means of the descending, Tamasic way is more and more easily accomplished.

"The merits acquired in one year during the Treta Yuga may be obtained in a month in the Dvâpara, and in one day during the kali Yuga.

"At the end of the Kali Yuga, the Lord of Justice shall be born of the dynasty of the Moon. His name is Pramiti (Proof). He shall begin his campaign in his thirty-third year and shall continue for forty years. He shall massacre men in their millions. Men shall slay each other and anarchy will be complete. Fear shall reign everywhere and each shall mistrust his neighbour. Men shall feed on wine, meat, roots and fruit. The few who survive at the end of the Age of Kali shall be in a piteous state. In their despair, they will begin to reflect. It is then that the new golden age shall suddenly appear. The survivors of the four castes shall be the seed of a new humanity." (*Linga Purâna*, II, chap. 39, 46–47.) Very similar descriptions of the end of the world are found in the Judeo-Christian Apocalypses, including that of St. John, which are clearly inspired by the same sources. "The end of the present world will be caused by a fire under the sea (*kâlâgni*), born of an explosion like that of a volcano called the 'Mule's Head' (*Vadavâmukha*), which will consume all the water that the rivers have brought to the Ocean. The water shall overflow from the Ocean and shall drown the Earth. The whole world shall be submerged." (Commentary on the *Shiva Purâna, Rudra Samhitâ*, chap. 24, 38.)

According to certain experts in atomic energy, a nuclear explosion at a certain depth in the Ocean could provoke a chain reaction which would decompose the water of the sea. Nevertheless, it concerns only the end of the present cycle of life on earth. Destruction will not be total: after the flood, a new golden age will be born. The end of the universe is not yet here. Mankind must be born and die another seven times. At the end of time, matter will be reabsorbed by an inverse process to the one through which it appeared following the primordial explosion. Nothing is immortal, neither matter, gods, nor souls.

"When the universe reaches its end, everything which exists, whether movable or immovable, will dissolve. Everything will be plunged into darkness. There will be no more sun, stars, or planets. There will be no more moon, nor anything to separate night from day. There will be no fire, nor wind, neither water, nor earth. The principle of manifestation itself will exist no longer. Space will be empty of any energetic principle. Good and evil will no more exist, neither sound, touch, smell, colour, nor taste. The directions of space will no longer be marked. The darkness will be so dense that it cannot be pierced by a needle... This state, which is incomprehensible to the soul, cannot be expressed in words. It can have no name, nor colour; it is neither thin, nor dense, great nor small, light nor heavy; growth exists no more, nor decline, beginning or end." (*Shiva Purâna, Rudra Samhitâ*, chap. 6.)

The religions of the age of conflicts

Among the characteristic phenomena of the Kali Yuga is the appearance of false religions which lead man away from his rôle in creation and serve as an excuse for his depredations and genocides, finally driving him to collective suicide. The religions of the city take precedence over the religion of nature.

According to the Purânas, the struggle of the city religions against the god of nature took an evil form by creating illusory religions which corrupted the true interior religion.

In the *Shiva Purâna*, the creation of new religions mainly refers to Jainism, a puritan, moralistic and atheistic religon (mostly practised nowadays by the merchant caste), which is the basis of modern religions, since it deeply influenced Buddhism and, later on, both Orphism and Christianity.

According to the *Shiva Purâna*:

"The god Vishnu, in order to be able to destroy the Asuras, the Titans who were votaries of the Phallus-cult, tried to interfere with their rites, saying, 'As long as they worship Shiva and follow the Shivaite rules of conduct, it will be impossible to destroy them. It is thus necessary to destroy their religion and make them renounce their worship of Shiva's phallus'. Vishnu therefore began to ridicule the rites, so as to put a stop to the Asuras' virtuous practices... He created a sort of prophet who, with shaven head, preached a new religion. This prophet made four disciples who taught heretical rites. They carried a pitcher in their hand. They covered their mouth with a piece of cloth. They spoke little, saying only a few words, such as, 'virtue is the greatest good, the true essence of things', and other such banalities. They walked slowly so as not to harm living creatures. They established themselves in a garden on the outskirts of the town. [1]But their magic was powerless so long as Shiva was worshipped there.

[1] In the *Bacchae*, we see Dionysus halt in front of Pentheus' palace and order his retinue to play the flute and drum to attract attention. This practice is imitated from the Jainas who use it in order to draw a crowd and preach their religion whenever they arrive in a new town.

"The treacherous Brahman Nârada went to visit the king of the Asuras and said to him, 'An extraordinary man has come who possesses all wisdom. I have known many cults, but I have never seen anything like this one. Great King of the Asuras, you should be initiated into this cult'. The King was initiated together with his kin and the inhabitants of the three cities. The town was filled with disciples of the prophet, that great expert in the arts of illusion . . .

"The prophet taught them non-violence: 'There is no virtue other than charity towards living things . . . Our duty is to abstain from killing. Non-violence is the greatest of virtues . . . Those texts encouraging animal sacrifice are not acceptable to an upright man. How can a man expect to reach heaven by cutting trees, killing animals, spreading blood and burning grains of ginger and butter. Our forefathers believed that the different races of men came out of the mouth, the arm, the thigh and the feet of Brahmâ. How could the children of the same body have different natures. No consideration should be given to the idea that there are differences between one man and another'. He then criticised the women's lack of virtue, extolled continence amongst the men, and spoke with contempt of the rites and phallus-cult. The citizens became enemies of the rites, and the evil spread. Thus, the gods were able to destroy the city." (*Shiva Purâna*, *Rudra Samhitâ*, V, chap. 3-4-5.)

This discourse, with few changes, could have been addressed by a Christian to a Roman emperor. It also recalls the teachings of Gandhi. "After the downfall of the three cities of the Asuras, the tonsured heretics presented themselves before the gods, saying, 'O gods, what must we do? We have destroyed the Asuras' faith in Shiva. It was according to your desire that we accomplished this abominable act. What will become of us?' The gods said, 'Until the coming of the Age of Kali, stay hidden in the desert. When the Kali Yuga comes, you shall propagate your religion. The mad fools of the Age of Conflicts shall be your followers'." (*Shiva Purâna*, *Rudra Samhitâ*, V, chap. 12.)

Relying on these concepts which replaced respect for the gods and the divine work with alleged human virtues, kings and cities opposed Shivaism with violence. The ancient gods were devalued and dispossessed. The new religions, Jainism and Buddhism, spread in India; Judaism, Orphism, Christianity and Islam, in the West. These religions, whatever the character and original intentions of their founders, have become essentially State religions of a moralistic kind. They have allowed a centralized power to impose an element of unification on peoples who have very different beliefs, customs and rites. These religions, although speaking of love, equality and charity, have everywhere served as an excuse and as an instrument for cultural and material conquests, and more. Buddhism, born in the royal caste of the Kshatriyas, allowed the Indian emperors to free themselves from the domination of the sacerdotal class, and was a prodigious instrument of colonial expansion. The massacre of the Shivaite populations of Orissa left traces still are to be seen today. The Maurya emperor Ashoka and his successors imposed Buddhism on India. Through this religion, Indian influence gradually spread over central Asia, to Tibet, Mongolia, China and Burma, over Southeast Asia and as far as Japan on one side, and, to a lesser degree, in the Middle East and Mediterranean region on the other.

In the West, Orphism inserted itself into Dionysism and modified it. Orphism was an adaptation of Dionysism to suit Greek tastes, and corresponds to the forms of Shivaism which were incorporated into Aryan Hinduism. The sources of Orphism are considered obscure. For the ancient poets, such as Pindar, Simonides, Aeschylus and Euripides, Orpheus is only a wonderful singer. In the texts referring to the Dionysiac mysteries, there are no references either to Orphism or to the sacrifice of the young god Zagreus, torn to pieces by the Titans. Orphism appears as a sort of reformation within Dionysism itself, and the influence of Jainist thought can be felt. It would be an error to consider it as being representative of original Dionysism. Orphism gives to Dionysus an exceptional rôle in the new age of the world, but it is a Dionysus who has been adapted to another tradition and who in many ways leaves behind the main principles connected with the older Dionysus cult. Dionysiac society was, in fact, hostile to the Orphic movement.

Numerous Indian monks propagated the Jaina philosophy in Classical Greece and their theories held a great attraction for the Greeks. It was, moreover, a Jaina sage whom Alexander brought back with him from India, but who committed suicide on the way according to the Jaina rite, predicting the coming death of Alexander. Like Jainism, Orphism puts great emphasis on abstinence. Orpheus taught men to abstain from murder (*phonos*) and, like the Jainas, applied the notion of murder to include all living creatures. His followers were strictly vegetarian and, again like the Jainas, wore white clothes, when they did not go about naked. The use of wool was forbidden, as being of animal origin. Later on, the Sufis reacted to this by requiring their followers to wear wool. Orphism was a powerful element in emasculating Dionysism and in preparing for the coming of Christianity, which it also profoundly influenced.

The cult of Mithras, which developed in the Roman Empire during the same period as Christianity, was an attempt to return to ancient Shivaism. It also played a part in the development of Christian myths and rites.

According to Plutarch, this cult was introduced into Italy in 67 B.C. by Cilician pirates captured by Pompey, and became widespread all over Europe. It was a secret society with occult rites, reserved for men only, and one of its original aims was armed resistance to Roman imperialism. Mithras is the Aryan god of Friendship and Contracts. He is the personification of comradeship and was ideally suited to a secret organization of sworn soldiers. All its symbols and rites of initiation, however, are derived from Shivaism, with a central position given to the cult and sacrifice of the bull. As in Shivaism, the crescent moon symbolizes a cup of bull's sperm, which is the source of life. In the sanctuaries, the image of Time is represented by a lion-headed monster covered with snakes. This is a transposition of Kâlî, the "Power of Time", who is also covered with snakes and is personified by the lion in the animal kingdom. The Mithraite sanctuary is a cave, in which the bull-sacrifice takes place. Riding the bull, Mithras, the invincible, takes the place of Nike (Victory), who was worshipped by the Roman legions. The rites were preceded by banquets at which bread and wine were consumed, as well as the flesh of the divine victim, who was the sacrificed bull. The birth of Mithras was celebrated on December 25th. He was born from a "fire-stone", which evokes the stone axe, the symbol of the labyrinth. This warrior-cult which failed to become the religion of the Empire and which was so opposed to Christianity, gradually died out during the fifth century. Mithraism was an attempt to recreate a Shivaite-inspired initiatory society in the Western world, and its experience may one day serve as an example.

Monotheism

The monotheistic illusion is one of the characteristics of the religions of the Kali Yuga. The techniques and rites which make us aware of the presence of subtle beings must take into account the whole human being and his place in the cosmos. The principle of the world is indefinable, but all existence involved multiplicity. The Prime

Cause is beyond all manifestation, beyond number, beyond unity, and beyond the created world. "It cannot be distinguished by the eye, or by speech, by the other senses, or by ascesis or ritual practices." (*Mundaka Upanishad*, III, 1, 8.)

In Shivaite philosophy, the divine is defined as "that in which contraries co-exist". The same definition is found in Heraclitus. For Nicolas de Cusa, "The Union of opposites" (*coincidentia oppositorum*) was the least imperfect definition of God.

Since man is part of the created world, he can conceive or know only the multiple aspects of divinity. Hence, monotheism is an aberration from the point of view of spiritual experience. Deriving from a cosmological concept leading to the idea of a prime cause, or even of a prime dualism, monotheism can never apply to the reality of religious experience. It was not feasible to communicate with the Prime Cause of the universe, beyond the galaxies, in order to receive personal instructions of a practical order. Such simplification is part of what the Hindus call "the metaphysics of fools" (*anadhikâri vedânta*).

Metaphysically, the number "1" does not exist, if not to represent a partial or a sum, since things only exist in relation to something else. The origin of the world can only be attributed to the opposition of two contrary principles and to the relation which unites them. The first number is thus the number "3", which is represented in Hindu cosmology by a trinity whose mark is found in every aspect of the created world, but whose component principles can only be perceived or conceived in their multiple manifestations. The subtle powers which we may call gods or spirits, whose presence we can perceive and who concern themselves with the world of the living, are as innumerable as the very forms of matter and life over which they preside.

The Prime Cause itself cannot be personified. "Only the adept (*dhîrah*), through his superior knowledge, can begin to perceive in all things the presence of that which cannot be perceived or apprehended, which is without attachments or characteristics, which has neither ears, nor eyes, nor hands, nor feet, which is eternal, multiform, omnipresent, infinitely subtle and inimitable, the matrix of all beings." (*Mundaka Upanishad*, I, 1, 6.)

The monotheistic simplification appears to derive from the religious concepts of the nomads, a people who wish to assert themselves and justify their occupation of territories and their conquests. God is imagined in the image of man. He is reduced to the rôle of a guide, accompanying the tribe during its migrations, and giving personal instructions to its chief. He is only interested in man and, among mankind, only in the group of the "chosen". He becomes an easy excuse for conquests and genocide, and for the destruction of the natural order, as can be seen throughout history. To begin with, he does not exclude the gods of other tribes, or "false" gods, but this is only in order to oppose and destroy them and to impose his own domination and that of his "chosen people". The passage from polytheism to exclusivism, and then to monotheism, can be followed in the religious evolution of the Hebrews.

Through ecstatic practices, all men are able to contact the mysterious world of spirits, a world whose nature is always indefinable and uncertain. It is the so-called "prophets" who are the principal artisans of the deviations of the modern world. They claim to communicate directly with a personal and only god, issuing rules of conduct which are in reality nothing but social conventions and which have nothing to do with religion or the spiritual domain. Monotheism is contrary to men's religious experience: it is not a natural development, but an imposed simplification. The notion of a god who, having created the world, would wait several million years – a delay which is difficult to excuse – before teaching man the way of salvation, is a patent absurdity.

The starting point for all monotheistic religions is always the thought or teaching of one man who, whether he claims to be so or not, considers himself the messenger and interpreter of a transcendental power which he calls "god". Such religions express themselves in dogmas, and in regulations concerning the life of man. They inevitably become political and form an ideal basis for the expansionist ambitions of the city. Among these religions, Judaism, Buddhism, Christianity and Islam are theistic, whilst Jainism and Marxism are atheistic.

Adopted by Judaism, which was not originally monotheistic, the concept of an "only god" in human form is largely responsible for the disastrous rôle of later religions. Moses, probably influenced by the ideas of the Pharaoh Akhnaton, made the Jewish people believe in the existence of a tribal chief, whom he called the "one god" and from whom he claimed to receive instructions. Later on, Mohammed behaved in much the same way. These impostors are the source of religious perversion in the Semitic and Judeo-Christian world. This "god", whose intentions so many others after them have claimed to interpret, even in the most relative fields of life, has served as a pretext and excuse for the domination of the world by various groups of "chosen people", and for the arrogant isolation of man in relation to the rest of the divine work.

The impertinence and arrogance with which "believers" attribute to "god" their own social, alimentary, and sexual prejudices, which moreover vary from one region to another, would be comical if they did not inevitably lead to forms of tyranny of a purely temporal nature. The obligation to conform to arbitrary beliefs and modes of behaviour is a means of degrading and enslaving the personality of the individual which all tyrannies, whether religious or political, right- or left-wing, know only too well how to use.

The problem of Christianity

It is necessary to distinguish Christianity from other monotheistic religions. Even though it has become a typical example of city religions, it is not at all certain that it represents the real teaching of Christ as it claims to. The message of Jesus is opposed to that of Moses and, later on, to that of Mohammed. It seems to have been a message of liberation and of revolt against a Judaism which had become monotheistic, dry, ritualist, puritan, pharisaeic and inhuman. In its Roman form, Christianity was at first in opposition to the official religion of the Empire, in the same way in which it was opposed to official Judaism as a State religion. We know very little of the sources of Jesus' teaching, or of his initiation, his sojourn "in the desert" towards the East. The Christian myths appear to be closely linked to those of Dionysus. Jesus, like Skanda or Dionysus, is the son of the Father, of Zeus. He has no wife. The goddess-mother alone finds her place next to him. He is surrounded by his faithful, his *bhaktas*, who are of the people, fishermen. His teaching is addressed to the humble and the outcast. He welcomes prostitutes and those who are persecuted. His rite is a sacrifice. It is in the Orphic tradition that the passion and resurrection of Dionysus occupy a central position. It is through Orphism that many of Dionysus' "miracles" were attributed to Jesus. Several aspects of the Orphic legend of Dionysus are to be found in the life of Jesus. The parallel between the death and resurrection of the god and of Christ is self-evident.

The myths and symbols tied to the birth of Christ, to his baptism, his following, his entry into Jerusalem on an ass, the Last Supper (banquet and sacrificial rite), his Passion, death and resurrection, the dates and nature of the various feast days, his power of healing and of changing water into wine, inevitably evoke Dionysiac precedents.

It would therefore seem that Jesus' initiation was Orphic or Dionysiac and not Essenian as sometimes suggested. His message, which is an attempt to return to tolerance and to a respect for the work of the Father-Creator, was totally perverted after his death. Later Christianity is, in fact, diametrically opposed to it, with its religious imperialism, political rôle, wars, massacres, tortures, stakes, persecutions of heretics, and its denial of pleasure, sexuality and of all the forms of experiencing the divine joy. This was not apparent at its beginnings, when the Christians were accused of bloody sacrifices, and erotic and orgiastic rites. It is difficult to know what these accusations were founded on. They were often repeated later on against organizations of a mystical and initiatory nature, all more or less secretive, which tried to perpetuate original Christianity. Such sects have a tendency to reappear in the Christian world, even though separated from their original tradition, they are usually naive attempts which are easily exploited and perverted.

Hindu trinitarian symbolism is found at the basis of the Christian Trinity. The Father, by the very fact that he has a Son, represents the generative principle, or Shiva, the Phallus. The son is the protector who is incarnate in the world in order to save it, like Vishnu and his *avatâras*. The Holy Ghost, "who proceeds from the Father and the Son", is the spark which unites the two poles. He is called Brahmâ, the Immensity. The Son, like Vishnu, is the equivalent of Shakti, the female principle or the Goddess, and thus is androgynous. His cult is intermingled with that of the Virgin Mother. The Church's efforts to disguise her sources have led to the significance of the Christian myth being forgotten and to materialistic pseudo-historical interpretations, devoid of any universal meaning.

However, polytheism remained in the background of the Christian world, the names of ancient deities simply being substituted by those of saints. Like Mahâyâna Buddhism, Christianity has assimilated many of the rites, symbols and practices of the older cults which it has replaced. There are practically no Christian sanctuaries dedicated to "God". They are all under the aegis of the Virgin Mother or of innumerable deities called saints. In polytheistic surroundings, Christianity easily melts into traditional religion, as may be observed for example in popular India, where the Virgin is invoked as much as the goddess Kâlî, where the cults of Skanda or of the infant-Krishna

230

have been mixed with that of the child Jesus, and the spirit (*bhûta*) which possesses the participants during the ecstatic dance ceremonies, is given the name of one Christian saint or another.

Christianity only became an important religion from the time when it served as an instrument for the imperial power of Rome. Dionysism and its variants disputed pride of place for a long time. It should not be forgotten that Nonnos' *Dionysia* dates from the fifth century of our era. In the fourth century, Constantine decided to utilize the Church as a means of imperial unification: the religious history of the world and the evolution of Christianity itself would have been quite different if his political choice had not fallen on this new faith.

Christianity thus became an instrument of conquest and world domination, just as Buddhism had been for the Indian emperors. This kind of activity has lasted down to our own times, causing the elimination of autochthonos cults and gods in Europe and the Middle East. Later on, this same activity spread over the whole world, depriving the various peoples of their gods and therefore of their power and personality. It reduced them to a state of moral and ritual dependence, thus becoming the prelude to their complete annexation and assimilation. "Latin" America is a recent example. Islam and Marxism have taken over the job nowadays.

Christian missionaries, who were often sent out by atheist governments, as was the case in France – where, moreover, religious communities were outlawed under the Third Republic –, were often the most powerful tool in depersonalizing the conquered peoples and subjecting them to the conqueror. Religion was the excuse for exterminating refractory elements who remained attached to their own culture, traditions and gods. Later Christianity, "a typical religion of the Kali Yuga" (J. Evola, *Le Yoga tantrique*, p. 19), is almost the antithesis of what we know of the teachings of Christ. It is in essence a city religion, with moralistic and social characteristics. "If we separate the Gospel from the Church, it becomes madness", wrote Jean Daniélou in his last book, thus demonstrating to what point the Church has strayed from the message of Jesus, which, to all intents, she ignores and rejects.

Islam has likewise utilized the same sort of primary monotheism and aggressive puritanism as a means to conquest and domination. In India, subjected first to Islamic and then to Christian domination, such cults as Muslim-inspired Sikhism, the Arya Samâj of Dayânanda Sarasvati, the Brahmo Samâj of Devendranâth Tagore (father of the poet), and lastly Gandhism with its monotheistic tendencies, puritanism and sentimentality inspired by Christian missionaries, are recent manifestations of the same attempts to adapt traditional religion by conforming to the social prejudices of the conquerors, so as to (allegedly) combat them more effectively. In all cases, this can only lead to cultural and human tragedy. The Marxist cult, which nowadays tends to replace Christianity, is only interested in the social man and impedes his individual realization. It is the last outcome of this tendency, and is the absolute antithesis of Shivaism and Dionysism.

Can the message of Jesus be recovered? It is not impossible. It requires a less selective return to the Gospel and the rediscovery of everything which the Church has so carefully hidden away and destroyed of its sources and history, including the texts of the so-called apocryphal gospels, certain of which are older than those recognized by the Church. This would allow us to go back to what Christ's teaching could have been in reality, i.e., the adaptation, for a particular world and period, of that great human and spiritual tradition of which Shivaism and Dionysism are the heritage. Original Christianity was not separated from its sources until quite a late period, and it long sheltered initiatory and mystical sects which continued Dionysiac practices. The rediscovery of its primitive meaning is not absolutely precluded. Stripped of the false values which, since St. Paul, have surrounded his teaching, the person of Christ may eventually be incorporated into the Shivaite-Dionysiac tradition. It is evident that this can only be done outside of those who dare to claim to be the representatives of "God" on earth and the exclusive interpreters of "His" will. A true religion can only be based on a humble respect for the divine work and its mystery. It is strange indeed that nowadays it is atheistic science, in an unprejudiced effort to comprehend the nature of the world and man, which is closer to true religion than the aberrant dogmatism of the Christians.

"It is said that the modern West is Christian, but that is a mistake. The modern spirit is anti-Christian because it is essentially anti-religious... The West was Christian during the Middle Ages, but is so no longer." (René Guénon, *La Crise du monde moderne*, pp. 111–112). It was effectively around the year 1000 A.D. when the idea appeared that man is capable of dominating the world, of rectifying creation and of giving some sort of a hand to God. This represents a profound transformation of the attitude of the Christian world. Hence, it is outside the churches that Christianity, by going back to its source, could once more become a true, or universal, religion. A religion for the whole man, for man who thus recovers his place in the natural world and re-establishes relations with the world of spirits, of nature, and of the gods. The last to understand this in the Christian world was St. Francis of Assisi. As a principle, religion is a method or way of drawing nearer to the divine. A true religion cannot be exclusive, cannot claim to hold the only truth, because divine reality has many aspects and the ways which lead to the divine are innumerable.

The return of Dionysus

Shivaism is a heritage of religious and human experience, accumulated since the origins of mankind. Its codification as we know it only became necessary with the development of important urban civilizations which threatened the equilibrium of the natural order.

According to the doctrine of the Tantras, the cult of Shiva-Dionysus and the practices of Tantrism are the only ways open to mankind in the Age of Conflicts – in which we are at present – to approach the divine. Without a return to the respect of nature and to the practice of erotico-magic rites allowing the self-realization of man in harmony with all the other forms of being, the overall destruction of the human species cannot be long delayed. Only the followers of the god will survive to give birth to a new human race.

All religions which oppose Shivaism, Dionysism and the mystical sects, have accentuated those tendencies which lead to the destruction of world harmony. Each return to Shivaite concepts, even if only a trend in that direction, is equivalent to a new era of equilibrium and creativity. The great periods of art and culture are always connected with an erotic-mystical renewal.

Throughout the history of India, Shivaism has been the religion of the people. Due to Tantrism, it gradually won back a very important place in the religious life of the higher castes. It also infiltrated the Buddhist world in the form of the Mahâyâna. About the same period, it appears in a revitalized form in Egypt, the Middle East, Greece and Italy. The cult of Dionysus, like the god himself, is always reborn from its own ashes.

Many times through the ages, the eternal tradition linked with the cult of Shiva-Dionysus has been vanquished by new religions deriving from the ambition and illusions of men. Nevertheless, it has always reappeared, as it is bound to do once more in the modern age.

233

Conditions nowadays seem favourable for a return to the traditional concepts of Shivaism. Even in the Western world, where Dionysiac survivals have been savagely persecuted, an instructive return to Shivaite values is apparent. The instinct of survival in a threatened world can be seen in spontaneous trends such as ecology, the rehabilitation of sexuality, certain Yoga practices, and the search for ecstasy through drugs. These impulses, though generally corrupt and perverted, are however indicative of a deep need to find an approach to the world, man and life, which is founded on real values and which conforms to the real nature of man and to his rôle in creation. These forms of experience can only find their logical accomplishment in a return to Dionysism. Such a return requires the recognition of certain basic principles, since it is with their help that it may be possible to rediscover the bases for a true civilization and thus contribute to limiting the disasters caused by an aberrant anthropocentrism. These principles, as summarized on the basis of Shivaite data, are as follows:

1. Creation is one. The divers aspects of the world, being, life, thought and sensation are all inextricably bound together and interdependent. Science, art, and social and religious systems are only valid as different applications of common principles.

2. The human being is one. He can in no wise be divided into body, soul and spirit. The vital functions of the intellectual and emotive elements cannot be separated from the activities of the physical body and of the mind. Our beliefs, which often have the nature of irrational passions, and our trends of thought, are directed by the hidden forces present within us, of which we must become aware in order to be able to control them.

3. Life is one. There is no boundary between the vegetable, animal and human worlds. They are interdependent, and their common survival depends on respect of their harmony, whereby none assumes the rôle of predator, or the right to alter the balance of nature.

4. The gods, subtle spirits and living beings, all come from the same principles and are indissolubly bound together. The gods and subtle energies are present everywhere in the world and within ourselves. It is not possible for a living being to attain or to conceive the Prime Cause except in its multiple manifestations in the world. For man, there is no one God, but many gods.

5. Truth is one. There is no Oriental and Occidental wisdom, or knowledge which opposes religion. There can only be various forms

of the same research. Religions are only valid when they represent man's efforts to apprehend the divine and to understand the nature of the world, so as to be able to play more effectively the part assigned to him in the framework of creation. Such research must always be open-minded and cannot be expressed by intangible dogmas.

According to Orphic and Pythagorean texts, the supremacy of Dionysus will reappear during the second part of the Age of Iron, or Kali Yuga, and his cult will be the only valid form of religion. This is also the affirmation of Shivaism. Only Tantric Yoga methods are efficacious in this age in which values are lost; the rites, asceticism and virtues of other ages are ineffective. It may be observed that the recent discoveries of psychology, ecology and natural science, suggest the same approaches to universal and human problems as those which Shivaism has always recommended. "It is not impossible that our epoch will be known to posterity as the first to rediscover the 'manifold religious experiences' which were abolished by the triumph of Christianity... It appears that all these elements are preparing for the rise of a new humanism, which will not be a replica of the old, since above all it is the researches of orientalists, ethnologists, psychologists, and religious historians, which must now be integrated in order to reach a total knowledge of man." (M. Eliade, *Méphistophélès et l'Androgyne*, pp. 10–11.) Such a knowledge of man involves the place he occupies in creation, a recognition of his limitations and of his rôle in the hierarchy of living beings. A return to Shivaite wisdom would appear to be the only way to ensure a respite to a human race which is running towards destruction at an ever-increasing pace.

According to René Guénon, "It is thus only a question, in short, of reconstituting that which existed before the modern deviation, with those adaptations necessary for the conditions of a different era. The East may well be able to come to the rescue of the West, if the latter really wants it, not in order to impose strange concepts, as some people seem to fear, but to help the West rediscover its own tradition whose meaning has been lost". (René Guénon, *La Crise du monde moderne*, pp. 46 and 129.)

CHRONOLOGICAL TABLE

PALAEOLITHIC

– 15000   MAGDALENIAN

Europe:
Lascaux,
Altamira,
Cave paintings

– 10000   END OF ICE AGE, REWARMING OF CLIMATE

MESOLITHIC

Cave paintings

– 8000   NEOLITHIC

– 7000

– 6500

Anatolia: Çatal   *Cyprus*:
Höyük. Stone   Mother Goddess
idols, frescos

– 6000   *India*:
Codification of
Shivaism

GREAT MIGRATION FROM INDIA TO PORTUGAL

– 5600

Cyprus: End of Lascaux
Stone idols;   and Altamira
Khirokidia
civilization

– 5000

Egypt:
predynastic;
Bull-cult

– 4500   CHALCOLITHIC

Anatolia:
Copper industry

Crete: Beginning
of Minoan era
Egypt:
ithyphallic Min

236

– 4000	*China*: Beginning of Neolithic		
– 3800	*India*: Develop ment of the Indus cities	*Malta*: beginning of megalithic monuments	

SPREAD OF MEGALITHIC MONUMENTS IN ASIA AND EUROPE

	Sumer: Arrival of Sumerians from the Indus. Antediluvian dynasties	*Egyptians* occupy the Nile valley. Written documents	New Mediter- ranean people in Northern Europe
– 3300		*Malta*: Temple of Skorba. Bull and phallus cults. Atlanto-mediter- ranean race	

– 3200	OLD BRONZE AGE

	Foundation of *Troy*	*Egypt*: Old Old Empire. *Cyprus*: Goddess statues *Crete*: Copper industry

– 3000	*Sumer*: historical Flood	ARRIVAL OF ATLANTO- MEDITERRANEANS IN ARMORICA

		Malta: Tumulus temples of Ggantija	*Carnac*
	Anatolia: Beyce Sultan		
– 2800	*Sumer*: Post- diluvian dynasties		
– 2700	*Troy*: sumptuous palaces	*Egypt*: the Great Pyramids, Gizeh *Cyprus*: Bull-cult	

– 2600			*Crete*: City development	
– 2500	Height of *Mohenjo Daro*	*Syria*: Height of Ebla (Semites)	*Malta*: total destruction of the Ggantija civilization	Stonehenge
– 2370		*Sumer*: reign of Sargon at Arkad		
– 2300		Sack of Troy and Anatolian cities by Aryans	*Malta*: Tarxien civilization. Bull and phallus cults. New race	
– 2200			*Egypt*: End of old Empire. Relations between Crete and Egypt	
– 2052			*Egypt*: Middle Empire	
– 2016		*Sumer*: End of Sumerian dynasties		
– 2000	*Africa*: Drying-up of the Sahara *India*: Rig-Veda hymns		*Greece*: Arrival of the Achaeans *Crete*: Palace of Knossos *Malta*: End of the Tarxien era. Total destruction	*Carnac*: "Alignments"
– 1894		*Babylon*: First Semitic King: Suabum		
– 1800			GREEK ARYANS ESTAB-LISHED IN THE BALKANS	
			Corsica: Phallic menhirs with faces	*Italy*: Valcarmonica; labyrinths

– 1778		*Egypt*: End of Middle Empire
– 1770	Abraham of Ur leaves Sumer for Canaan	
– 1700	*India*: Destruction of Mohenjo Daro by the Aryans	Explosion of Santorini volcano. Knossos burnt
– 1650	*Syria*: Destruction of Ebla by Hittites (Aryans)	*Greece*: Development of Achaean culture *Egypt*: Invasion of the Asian Hyksos
– 1600	LATE BRONZE AGE	
		Hebrews leave for Egypt
– 1595	*Babylon*: Sacked by the Hittites (Aryans). End of Semitic dynasty	
– 1567		*Egypt*: New Empire
– 1530	*Babylon*: Kassite domination	*Malta*: New peoples
– 1500	IRON AGE	
	The pharaoh Thutmosis III conquers the Middle-East up to the Euphrates	*Greece*: The Achaeans occupy the Peloponnese. Beginning of the Mycenaean civilization
– 1400	*India*: Aryan conquest of Northern India *Mahâbhârata* war near Delhi	*Crete*: End of the kingdom of Minos: destruction of Knossos by the Achaeans.

239

	Atharva Veda: Shivaite doctrines incorporated into Aryan religion	Minoan doctrines incorporated into Mycenaean (Aryan) religion and Mycenaean influence in Crete
– 1372		*Egypt*: Height of the Empire
– 1350	*India*: Shatapatha Brâhmana	*Egypt*: Akhenaton attempts monotheism
– 1312	*India*: Chhandogya Upanishad	*Egypt*: Death of Tut-Ankh-Amon
– 1300	*Babylon* taken by the Assyrians (Semites). *Trojan* War	*Egypt*: Death of Ramses I *Cyprus*: Mycenaean colonization. New gods *Malta*: Mycenaean influence
– 1280	*Troy* destroyed by earthquake	*Italy*: Arrival of the Etruscans from Lydia, according to Herodotus
– 1250	*Hebrews* banished from Egypt; Moses.	
– 1200	DORIAN INVASION	
	Disappearance of writing in Greece	
	North India aryanized	*Iran* aryanized	*Greece*: Dorians descend to Southern Greece

240

− 1190		*Troy*: Final destruction. Non-Aryan *Phrygians* from Thrace arrive in Anatolia	*Italy*: Aeneas, fleeing from Troy, establishes himself on the Palatine
− 1150			*Cyprus*: Destruction by the Dorians
− 1129		*Babylon*: Nabuchodonosor I (Semite)	*Mycenae*: Destroyed by the Dorians *Crete*: Totally destroyed by the Dorians
− 1025			*Egypt*: End of the New Empire
− 1020		*Israel*: Samuel establishes the royal house. Beginning of the Kingdom of Judah	*Italy*: Occupation of Latium by Latin (Aryan) tribes
− 1000	*India*: Aryans penetrate to the Gujerat	Reign of David	
− 960		Death of David	*Egypt*: Beginning of the Period of Decline
− 930		End of Solomon's reign	
− 900	*India*: Adoption of Brahmi (Phoenician) writing	*Anatolia*: Kingdom of Urarthu (Aryan)	*Greece*: Homer. Reappearance of writing. *Malta*: Phoenician influence
− 817	*India*: Birth of Parshvadeva, 23rd Jaina prophet		*Cyprus*: Assyrian followed by Egyptian conquest

–	800	*India*: Aryan domination of Ganges valley		Foundation of *Carthage*	
–	753			Foundation of *Rome*	
–	750				Arrival of the Celts
				Greece: Hesiod	
–	700		The Phrygian King Midas	*Italy*: Beginning of Etruscan art	
–	627		*Babylon*: Chaldean dynasty		
–	616			*Rome*: Etruscan kings	
–	612		Niniveh taken by Babylonians and Scythes		
–	600	*India*: Adoption of Kharoshthi (Aramaean) writing		*Cyprus*: pre-Hellenic kings	
–	605		*Babylon*: Reign of Nabuchodonosor II		
–	586	*India*: Passage from Vedism to Hinduism	Jerusalen taken by the Babylonians. End of the Kingdom of Judah. Jews in Babylonian captivity.		
–	562	*India*: Birth of Gautama Buddha	*Babylon*: Death of Nabuchodonosor II		
–	559	*India*: Birth of Mahâvira, 24th Jaina prophet			

– 558		Destruction of Uarthu by the Aryan Medes and Scythes. Cyrus, Aryan King of Persia
– 539		*Babylon* taken by the Persians
– 525		*Egypt* invaded by the Persians
	Reign of Darius I	
– 522	The Achaemenid Empire extends from India to Greece. The Indus annexed by the Persians	Etruscan development in northern *Italy*
– 500	Panini's Sanskrit grammar	*Rome* becomes an important city. Etruscan zenith
– 487	Death of Mahâvira	
– 483	Death of Buddha	
– 480		*Athens* destroyed by the Persians
– 429		Death of Pericles *Greece*: Plato, Herodotus
– 396		Etruscan Veii destroyed by the Aryan Romans
– 356		Alexander
– 350		End of the Etruscan Empire
– 347		Death of Plato

–	330		*Egypt*: End of the Period of Decline
–	326	*India*: Alexander's expedition	
–	323		Death of Alexander
–	300	Megasthenes at the court of Chandragupta	
–	274	Ashoka imposes Buddhism	*Italy*: End of the Etruscans. Taranto taken by the Romans
–	237	Death of Ashoka	
–	218		*Malta*: Roman occupation
–	206	Anthiochus' (of Syria) expedition to India	
–	146	Ajanta	*Carthage* and *Corinth* destroyed by the Romans
–	135	Bactria invaded by the Scythes	*Greece* submits to Rome
–	64	Syria annexed by Pompey	
–	50		Alesia taken by Caesar
–	26	Indian embassy to Augustus	
–	4	Birth of Josuah (Jesus), called Christos (anointed or initiated one). Reign of Herod Antipas in Judaea	

244

+ 1	Stupa de Sanchi		
29		Crucifixion of Jesus	
60			*Malta*: Shipwreck of St. Paul
67			Death of Saul (Paul) and Cephas (Peter) at Rome
68			Death of Nero
70		Destruction of the Temple at Jerusalem	
79			Destruction of Pompei
80			Building of the Colosseum
100	Indian embassy to Trajan		*Rome*: Cult of Cybele and Attis
160	*China*: Arrival of Buddhism		
212			Baths of Caracalla
323		Christianity becomes the State religion	Reign of Constantine
330		Constantinople, capital of the Roman Empire	
340	Indian embassy to Constantine		
400	The Huns take Gandhara		

430			Death of St. Augustine
451			Defeat of Attila
460	The Huns invade Rajputana, the Punjab and Kashmir		
481			Clovis
590			Gregory the Great
622		Beginning of the Hegira	
711			Arab conquest of Spain
778	*Java*: Burubudur		
788	*India*: Shankarâchârya. Monist interpretation of Shivaism		
962			Foundation of the Germanic Holy Roman Empire
1000	*India*: Khajuraho. Arab conquest of India and Afghanistan. Dispersion of the Indian tzigane tribes towards the West		
1030	Death of Mahmoud of Ghazni		
1037			Death of Avicenna
1055	*India*: Ramanuja. Non-dualist philosophy		Beginning of the Cathars
1085			St. Mark's, Venice

1100	Angkor Vat		
1119			Creation of the Order of the Templars
1162		Gengis Khan	
1163			Notre-Dame, Paris
1126			Death of St. Francis of Assisi
1227		Death of Gengis Khan	
1244			End of the Cathar Stake of Monségu
1327			End of the Templars

BIBLIOGRAPHY

1 – GREEK AND LATIN TEXTS

AESCHYLUS, *Plays*.
APOLLODORUS, *Bibliotheke*.
ARISTOTLE, *Poetics*.
ATHENAGORAS, *Apologia*.
DIODORUS SICULUS, *Bibliotheke Historike*.
EURIPEDES, *The Bacchantes*; *The Cretans*.
HERODOTUS, *History*.
HESIOD, *The Theogony*; *Works and Days*
HOMER, *Hymns*.
LIVY, *History*.
LUCIAN, *Dialogues of the Gods*.
NONNOS OF PANOPOLIS, *Dionysia*.
OPPIAN, *Cynegetica*.
PLATO, *The Republic*.
PLINY, *Natural History*.
PLUTARCH, *Parallel Lives*
STRABO, *Geographica*.

2 – SANSKRIT TEXTS

Skanda Purâna.
Shiva Purâna.
Linga Purâna.
Bhagavata Purâna.
Agni Purâna.
Kandapuranam (Tamil).
Mahâbhârata.
Atharva Veda Samhitâ.
Rig Veda Samhitâ.
Gopatha Brâhmana.
Shatapatha Brâhmana.
Shvetâshvatara Upanishad.
Taittiriya Upanishad.
Mundaka Upanishad.
Shiva Samhitâ.
Gheranda Samhitâ.
Shiva Svarodaya.
Kulârnava Tantra.
Mahânîrvana Tantra.
Tantra Râja.
Manu Smriti.
Hatha Yoga Pradîpika.
Ashvalayana Grihyasutra.
Rudrasukta.
Shiva pradosha stotra.

BIBLIOGRAPHY

II – CONTEMPORARY STUDIES

AYYAR Narayana, *Origin and Early History of Saivism in South India*, Madras, 1974.

BANERJEE P., *Early Indian Religions*, Delhi, 1973.

BECHERT Heinz, *The Cult of Skandakumara in the Religious History of South India and Ceylon*, Third Conference of Tamil Studies, Paris, 1970.

BORD Janet and LAMBERT Jean-Clarence, *Labyrinthes et dédales du monde*, Paris, 1977.

BURLAND Cottie, *Africa South of the Sahara* (in *Primitive Erotic Art*).

COGNI Giulio, in *Indologica Taurinensia*, vol. III–IV, Turin.

COLLI Giorgio, *La Sapienza greca*, Milan, 1977.

COOMARASWAMY Ananda, *The Dance of Shiva*, Bombay, 1948.

COTRELL Leonard, *The Bull of Minos*, London, 1971.

CUMONT Franz, *Les Religions orientales et le Paganisme romain*, Paris, 1929.

DANIEL Glyn, *The Megalith Builders of Western Europe*, London, 1961.

DANIÉLOU Alain, *Hindu Polytheism*, Princeton, 1964; *Yoga, Method of Reintegration*, London, 1964, reprint 1973; *Les Quatre Sens de la vie*, Paris, 1976; *La Sculpture érotique hindoue*, Paris 1973; *The Ankle Bracelet*, New York, 1965; *Le Temple hindou*, Paris, 1977. *Le Roman de l'Anneau*, Paris, 1961; *Le Temple hindou*, Paris, 1977.

DE SANCTIS Gaetano, *Storia dei Greci*, Florence, 1961.

DESSIGANE R. and PATTABIRAMIN P. Z., *La Légende de Skanda*, Pondichery, 1967.

DETIENNE Marcel, *Dionysus mis à mort*, Paris, 1977.

DUMEZIL Georges, *Fêtes romaines d'été et d'automne*, Paris, 1975.

ELIADE Mircéa, *Histoire des croyances et des idées religieuses*, Paris, 1976: *Méphistophélès et l'Androgyne*, Paris, 1962; *L'Univers fantastique des mythes*, Paris, 1976.

EVANS Sir A. J., *The Palace of Minos*, London, 1936.

EVOLA Julius, *Le Yoga tantrique*, Paris, 1971.

FAURE Paul, *La Vie quotidienne en Crète au temps de Minos*, Paris, 1973.

FESTUGIÈRE A. J., *Études de religion grecque et hellénistique*, Paris, 1972.

FRAZER Sir James, *The Golden Bough*, London, 1923–1927.

GAVOT Jean, *Le Folklore vivant du comté de Nice*, Nyons, 1971.

GUÉNON René, *Symboles fondamentaux de la science sacrée*, Paris, 1936; *La Crise du monde moderne*, Paris, 1946.

HAWKES F. C., *The Prehistoric Foundations of Europe*, London, 1940.

HERAS Rev. H., *Studies in Proto-Indo-Mediterranean Culture*, Bombay, 1953.

HEURGON Jacques, *La Vie quotidienne chez les Étrusques*, Paris, 1976.

JEANMAIRE H., *Dionysos, histoire du culte de Bacchus*, Paris, 1951.

KALYANA, *Shakti-anka*, Gorakhpur, 1938; *Shiva-anka*, Gorakhpur, 1937.

KARPÂTRI Svâmî, *Ganapati rahasya*, Benares, 1938; *Lingopâsanâ Rahasya*, Benares, 1939; *Shiva aur Shivarchana Tattva*, Benares, 1939.

LE SCOUËZEC Gwenc'hlan, *Guide de la Bretagne mystérieuse*, Paris, 1966.

MACALISTER R. A., *Ireland in Pre-Celtic Times. Proceedings of the Royal Irish Society*, XXIV, 1921.

MARSHAK Alexander, *The Roots of Civilization*, New York, 1972.

MARTIN-DUBOST Paul, *Commentaire sur la Mundaka Upanishad*, Paris, 1978.

MCGRINDLE J. W., *Ancient India as described by Megasthenes and Arrian*, London, 1877; Calcutta, 1960.

NANDIMATH S. C., *A Handbook of Virasaivism*, Dharwar, 1942.

NILAKANTA SASTRI K. A., *Murugan, Transactions of the Archaeological Society of South India*, Madras, 1969.

Les Religions de la préhistoire, Valcamonica Symposium, 1977.

Symposium d'art préhistorique, Valcamonica Symposium, 1968; *Evolution and Style in Camunian Rock Art*, Valcamonica Symposium, 1976.

PARGITER F. E., *The Purâna Text of the Dynasties of the Kati Age*, Benares, 1913 (new ed. 1962); *The Markandeya Purâna*, Calcutta, 1904.

PATIL D. R., *Cultural History from the Vayu Purâna*, Poona, 1946.

PAYNE KNIGHT Richard, *Le Culte de Priape*, London, 1786.

PICARD Charles, *Les Religions préhelléniques*, Paris, 1948.

RADHAKRISHNAN S., *History of Indian Philosophy*, London, 1923.

RAWSON Philip, *Primitive Erotic Art*, London, 1973; *The Art of Tantra*, London, 1973.

ROUX Georges, *Delphe, son oracle et ses dieux*, Paris, 1976.

SANTARCANGELI Paolo, *Le Livre des labyrinthes*, Florence, 1967; Paris, 1974.

SARKAR S. S., *Aboriginal Races of India*.

SIDDHÂNTA, *Benares*, 1941–1945.

TRUMP D. H., *Malta*, London, 1972.

VARAGNAC André, *Civilisation traditionelle*, Paris, 1934.

VIEYRA Maurice, *Les Religions de l'Anatolie antique, Histoire des religions*, Paris, 1953.

WHEELER Sir Mortimer, *The Indus Civilization*, Cambridge, 1968.

WILLETTS R. F., *Cretan Cults and Festivals*, New York, 1962.

WOODROFFE Sir John, *Shakti and Shakta*, Madras, 1929; *The Serpent Power*, Madras, 1931.

The Myths and Gods of India

The Classic Work on Hindu Polytheism
From the Princeton Bollingen Series
Alain Daniélou
ISBN 0-89281-354-7 • $19.95 illustrated paperback

This study of Hindu mythology explores the significance of the most prominent Hindu deities and reveals the message of tolerance and adaptability that is at the heart of this ancient religion.

"The style is lucid; the lack of polemic is particularly attractive. The total result is a volume that is a pleasure to behold and an invigorating experience to read." —**American Anthropologist**

While the Gods Play

Shaiva Oracles and Predictions on the
Cycles of History and the Destiny of the Universe
Alain Daniélou
ISBN 0-89281-115-3 • $12.95 paperback

According to the early writings of the Shaiva tradition—still alive in India and dating back at least 6,000 years—the arbitrary ideologies and moralistic religions of modern society signal the last days of humanity. This prediction is only a fragment of the vast knowledge of Shaivism, the religion of the ancient Dravidians. An initiate of this wisdom, Daniélou here revives the essential concepts of the Shaiva philosophy and its predictions, and reflects on what action can be taken to consciously and creatively influence our own destiny.

"These revelatory books are remarkable for their clarity, scholarship, and uninhibited celebration of mystical ecstasy."—**Interview Magazine**

Kundalini

The Arousal of the Inner Energy
Ajit Mookerjee
ISBN 0-89281-020-3 • $12.95 paperback
16 color plates, black and white illustrations throughout

The tantric practice of Kundalini–yoga is a means to awaken the dormant cosmic energy that exists in each of us, harnessing its power for spiritual growth. In *Kundalini: The Arousal of the Inner Energy*, Ajit Mookerjee writes of the core experience of Tantra, the process by which the energy is awakened and rises through the energy centers (chakras) of the body to unite with Pure Consciousness at the crown of the head.

This well-known scholar draws on the ancient texts of India as well as on modern accounts of the Kundalini experience, both Eastern and Western, and describes the findings of clinical studies and research undertaken in the West. An acknowledged expert on Eastern art, Ajit Mookerjee has included illustrations from a wide range of original manuscript sources, which illuminate and enhance the text.

Kali

The Feminine Force
Ajit Mookerjee
ISBN 0-89281-212-5 • $12.95 paperback
18 color plates, black and white illustrations throughout

In India, worship of the goddess in her multiple forms and the vision of the sacred as woman has never ceased. Kali, although seen most often in her warrior aspect as cruel and horrific, is also the creator and nurturer—the essence of Mother-love and feminine energy. In the West, the image of Kali has recently begun to appear as men and women look beyond the outworn stereotypes of a patriarchal society. With the powerful imagery of paintings, sculpture, and writings, this celebration of Kali explores and illumines the rich meanings of feminine divinity.

"*...a splendid achievement of a book.*"—**The Book Reader**

"*Mookerjee's commentary is, as always, illuminating and brings out the universal content of the Kali image to which, if we will allow it, we are likely to find archetypal resonances within us.*"—**Spectrum Review**

Yoga

Mastering the Secrets of Matter and the Universe
Alain Daniélou
ISBN 0-89281-301-6 • $10.95 paperback

In this book, Daniélou gives an account of the principles and practices
of yoga, compiled from the teachings of many of its living exponents
and from published and unpublished Sanskrit sources. It is fully
authentic in its presentation of the aims, methods, and different forms
of yoga, explaining the technical processes by which, according to the
doctrines of yoga, the subconscious may be brought under control, the
senses overpassed, and modes of perception obtained, which can lead
to remarkable achievements, both spiritual and intellectual.

The Yoga–Sutra of Patañjali

A New Translation and Commentary
Georg Feuerstein
ISBN 0-89281-262-1 • $12.95 paperback

Approximately two thousand years old, *The Yoga-Sutra of Patañjali* is the
landmark scripture on classical yoga. The translation and commentary
provided here are outstanding for their accessibility and their insight into
the essential meaning of this ancient and complex text.

A scholar of international renown who has studied and practiced yoga
since the age of fourteen, Feuerstein also brings to this text his experience
as a professional indologist, with his faithful and informed rendering of the
aphorisms (sutras) based on the original Sanskrit sources.

*"...in Georg Feuerstein we have a scholar of the first magnitude, an
extremely important and valuable voice for the perennial philosophy, and
arguably the foremost authority on yoga today."*

—**Ken Wilber**
Author of *The Spectrum of Consciousness*

The Divine Library

A Comprehensive Reference Guide to the
Sacred Texts and Spiritual Literature of the World
Rufus C. Camphausen
ISBN 0-89281-351-2 • $9.95 illustrated paperback

From the Angas to the Zend Avesta, from Apocryphal writings to the Yogini Tantra, from the Bible to the Zohar, this quick reference is the first to offer a concise directory to the primary religious literature of past and present cultures. More than 120 entries are defined and explained, with bibliographical references to available editions, translations, and commentaries. In addition, the author traces many sacred texts back to their origins in the oral tradition of pre-literate cultures. An extended glossary and index make this a comprehensive and accessible guidebook to the diverse streams of spiritual wisdom.

The Encyclopedia of Erotic Wisdom

A Reference Guide to the Symbolism, Techniques, Rituals,
Sacred Texts, Anatomy, and History of Sexuality
Rufus C. Camphausen
ISBN 0-89281-321-0 • $19.95 illustrated paperback

Explore the avenues of sacred sexuality with this comprehensive reference book. Medical, psychological, historical, and anthropological information is included along with material on the inner and outer Tantric and Taoist teachings and the secrets of the Western alchemists and qabbalists. Extensive cross-references guide you from any point of departure into further discovery of the myth and meaning of sexuality.

These and other Inner Traditions titles are available at many fine bookstores or, to order directly from the publisher, send a check or money order for the total amount, payable to Inner Traditions, plus $2.50 shipping and handling for the first book and $1.00 for each additional book to:

Inner Traditions
One Park Street
Rochester, VT 05767

Be sure to request a free catalog.